TO BE
DISPOSED
BY
AUTHORITY

SWEDISH ECONOMIC POLICY

SWEDISH ECONOMIC POLICY

Assar Lindbeck

Professor of International Economics, University of Stockholm
Director of the Institute for International Economic Studies

© Assar Lindbeck 1975

First published 1975 by
THE MACMILLAN PRESS LTD
London and Basingstoke
Associated companies in New York
Dublin Melbourne Johannesburg and Madras

SBN 333 13542 3

Printed in Great Britain by
R. AND R. CLARK LTD
EDINBURGH

Contents

List of Charts and Tables		vii
Introduction		xi
1	The Swedish Economy – A Long-Term View	1
	Development without Planning	1
	Fluctuations	10
	Economic Policy	22
2	The Regulated Economy – 1945–50	25
	The Record	25
	The Criticism	31
3	Full Employment and Price Stability: The Early Debate	37
4	Stabilisation Policy after 1950 – a General Outline	50
	A Verbal Business Cycle Model	50
	Assessments and Forecasts	69
	Trends in Stabilisation Policy	70
5	General Fiscal Policy	82
	Principles	82
	The Record	88
6	Innovations in Fiscal Policy	94
	Theoretical Developments	94
	Investment Taxes, Investment Subsidies and Investment Funds	97
	Public Investment and Housebuilding	102
	Labour Mobility Policy and Public Works	104
7	Experiences of Short-Term Monetary Policy	108
	The Record	108
	The Criticism	121
	Lessons of Swedish Monetary Experience	124
	Monetary Theory	127

Comparison between Interest Rate Policy, Investment Taxes and Investment Funds Policy   130

8   Contemporary Problems in Stabilisation Policy   139

Cost Components behind Changes in Consumer Goods Prices   140

Problems in Demand Management   142

Neglect of Cost Side?   143

Full Employment versus Price Stability Revisited   151

Labour Market Policy and Demand Management   156

The EFO–Effect   157

International Complications   161

To Reduce the Disadvantages of Inflation and Unemployment   163

9   Long-Term Planning   165

The Long-Term Reports   165

The Optimum Savings Ratio   169

Criteria for Allocation Policy   172

The Future of Long-Term Planning   182

10   Allocation Policy   184

11   Income Distribution Policy and Structural Changes   195

Personal Income   196

Income Distribution between Private and Public Sectors   207

Ownership of Capital and Supply of Credit   214

Profits, the Financing of Capital Formation and Structural Change   219

12   Summary and Concluding Remarks   228

Shifts in Economic Policy   228

Successes and Failures   233

Lessons for Economic Theory and Policy   238

Capitalism or Socialism?   245

Appendixes   249

References   253

Index   265

List of Charts and Tables

CHARTS

1:1 Real GNP *per capita* and implicit GNP-deflator
1861–1972   11

1:2 Unemployment, 1911–1971   12

1:3 Real GNP and implicit GNP-deflator:
GNP OECD (five-year averages): yearly rates
of change   13

1:4 Consumer prices and labour costs:
yearly rates of change   14

1:5 Total investment and private consumption:
yearly rates of change   15

1:6 Fixed investment in manufacturing
(*tillverkningsindustri*)   16

1:7 Unemployment rate   17

1:8 Real GNP, actual and full capacity level   18
(potential GNP)

1:9 Current foreign balance and exchange reserves   21

4:1 Schematic picture of typical business cycle
in Sweden   51

4:2 Fluctuations of exports and inventory investment:
yearly changes   55

4:3 Fluctuations in private investment, public
investment and dwellings: yearly changes   56

4:4 Fluctuations in private consumption and total
investment: yearly changes   57

4:5A Balance of payments; components (million
Sw.kr.)   60

4:5B Balance of payments: components (per cent of
GNP)   61

4:6 Some business indicators for Swedish
manufacturing   67

4:7 Official forecast and outcome of GNP: yearly
changes   69

4:8A Stabilisation policy actions 1945–59
        – schematic picture   72
4:8B Stabilisation policy actions 1960–71
        – schematic picture   73
5:1   Impact effect on aggregate demand of fiscal
        policy: yearly data   90–91
6:1   Effects of investment fund releases in
        manufacturing industry   101
6:2   Labour force taken care of by Labour Market
        Board   106
7:1   Discount rates and interest rates on
        manufacturing bonds   109
7:2   Money–GNP ratio   114
7:3   Fluctuations in money stock and nominal
        GNP   117
7:4   Fluctuations in the credit stock to the
        business sector: yearly rates of change of
        credit stock from commercial banks and
        from 'organised' credit market (credit
        institutes)   118
8:1   Labour market situation and wage increase,
        industrial workers (all labour costs included)   154
8:2   Phillips curve for Sweden: workers in
        manufacturing (based on data 1955–70)   155
9:1   Development of private and public investment,
        and GNP   174
9:2   Development of private and public consumption,
        and GNP   175
9:3   Development of housing and exports, relative
        to GNP   176
11:1 Lorenz curves for vertical income distribution
        before tax in Sweden   198
11:2 Direct impact of taxes on income
        distribution of households, 1966   200
11:3 Distribution of household income before tax –
        Lorenz curves   205
11:4 Distribution of national income between
        households, firms and the public sector: factor
        income (i.e. incomes before taxes and
        transfer payments)   209

11:5 Disposable income and taxes   210
11:6 Household savings ratio   213
11:7 Wage costs per unit of output, relative   222
      to other countries
11:8 Number of merged firms and their share
      in total employment   223

Appendix A   Real GNP *per capita* 1862–1970:
             yearly rates of change   249
Appendix B   Implicit GNP-deflator 1862–1970:
             yearly rates of change   250
Appendix C   Relative wage levels in different
             industries, 1939–68   251
Appendix D   Unemployment (U), vacancies (V), and
             shortage of labour (VS), 1949–70.
             Second and fourth quarter   252

TABLES
1:A   Growth rate 1950–71   2
1:B   The role of exports in the growth process   4
1:C   Importance of the public sector in the Swedish
      economy   9
6:A   Yearly releases from investment funds   100
6:B   Number of persons in public works, in
      protected works and retraining (yearly
      averages)   105
7:A   Effects on investment in manufacturing of
      investment tax and interest rate policy – as
      estimated by questionnaire studies   119
8:A   Changes in consumer goods prices 1960–71,
      broken down by cost components   141
8:B   Internationalisation of the Swedish economy   162
9:A   *Ex post* 'elasticities' for public expenditures
      with respect to GNP   178
11:A Taxable income and disposable income for
      various groups in 1967; average incomes
      and measure of inequality within groups   202
11:B Distribution of disposable income   208

11:C   Origin of saving   212
11:D   Supply of funds from organised credit market
       (net flows)   216
11:E   Sources of credit to private industry
       (flow)   217

Introduction

Economic and social policies in Sweden have for a long time raised considerable interest abroad, an interest, in fact, quite out of proportion to the size of the country. There are several reasons for this. One is presumably the high standard of living in Sweden in the postwar period as compared with most other countries in the Western world. This means, in fact, that many trends and problems have occurred earlier in Sweden than in other countries, except possibly for the US. It is also probably fair to say that economic and social policies in Sweden have been rather pragmatic and experimental. For these reasons, Sweden might to some extent be regarded as a 'laboratory' for economic and social experiments, which may be of interest for other countries as well.

Information about Sweden abroad has often been provided in 'apologetic' reports by Swedish public officials, which probably means that it has often been the intention and rhetoric, rather than the factual reality, which have been communicated to foreign audiences. Also, foreign writers about the Swedish scene have often relied heavily on official documents and statements, though some foreign books and articles no doubt have given fresh and interesting insights into particular aspects of the Swedish society and its economic policy. All this means, in my opinion, that the picture of Swedish economic and social policy abroad has been less interesting than it really is.

The purpose of this book is to survey *economic policy* in Sweden, though the 'borderlines' to social policies are occasionally trespassed. The analysis is mainly confined to the period after the Second World War. However, earlier developments are briefly sketched.

The analysis of the policy is made against the background of major trends in the Swedish economy and the problems connected with these trends, as well as against the background of the theoretical discussions by Swedish economists. The emphasis is placed on questions that are characteristic for the Swedish scene. However, most of the problems discussed here are probably relevant to every industrialised market economy, particularly if it is closely tied to the international market system and if the policy debate in the country is influenced by the international discussions on economic and social problems.

Four phenomena, in particular, are analysed in the book: (1) the economic trends during the postwar period; (2) the economic policy pursued; (3) the problems confronting this policy; and (4) some suggestions that have been discussed for solving these problems.

Concerning the last point, it is mainly the contribution by professional economists that will be considered. No attempt is made to analyse the debate between the political parties.

The study begins by presenting a bird's-eye view of the economic system in Sweden and its long-term development, as well as of economic fluctuations and economic policy in Sweden. The time perspective is the last one hundred years, though with the emphasis on the period after the Second World War.

Chapters 2 and 3 deal with the policy of 'repressed inflation', by way of direct controls, in the period immediately after the war, and the associated controversy over the problem of reconciling full employment and price stability; this has in a sense been the dominant theme in Swedish economic policy discussions throughout the postwar period. Chapter 4 presents a general outline of stabilisation policy from the early fifties to the present, against the background of the cyclical pattern of the Swedish economy. The following chapters (5–7) deal with some main policy issues and innovations in this period: the debate of the general principles of fiscal policy (such as those of balancing the budget), new methods for influencing private and public investment for stabilisation purposes, the experiments with labour market policy, the experiences of monetary policy, etc. Chapter 8 attempts a summary analysis of contemporary problems in stabilisation policy.

Chapter 9 deals with long-term planning, or (maybe) rather the *absence* of systematic long-term planning. Problems of resource allocation, including public interventions in the allocation of resources in the private sector, are analysed in Chapter

10, and questions concerning the distribution of income and related problems on structural changes are considered in chapter 11. The last chapter is an attempt to summarise and characterise the main trends in economic policy during the postwar period, and to judge where the economic system in Sweden is heading.

It has, of course, not been possible to discuss all main problems of postwar economic policy in Sweden. Examples of questions that are hardly discussed at all here are the Common Market issue and questions related to Swedish aid to underdeveloped countries.

Thus, we may say that the book deals with four main targets of postwar economic policy in Sweden: stability, growth, the allocation of resources and the distribution of income. Though all these aspects are in fact interwoven in a complicated way, it is probably fair to say that stabilisation policy has dominated both the factual policy and the qualified discussion. This emphasis on stabilisation policy is also reflected in the present book.

I have consistently tried to keep the paper 'non-technical'. The main ambition has been to transmit 'ideas' rather than technical-analytical points.[1]

[1] The book has grown out of a survey which was originally published in the *American Economic Review* (June 1968) Supplement, 'Theories and Problems in Swedish Economic Policy in the Post-War Period', and a somewhat extended Swedish edition, *Svensk ekonomisk politik* (Stockholm, 1968). The present study is a thoroughgoing revision and extension of those publications. Richard Murray, Torkel Backelin, Gustav Adlercreutz and Christer Öhman have helped me as research assistants. Marianne Biljer has drawn the diagrams and has helped check the text.

I am grateful to a number of colleagues for comments to earlier drafts of various chapters, in particular to Harry G. Johnsson, Peter Kenen, Erik Lundberg, Lars Matthiessen, Gösta Rehn and Ernst Söderlund.

1 The Swedish Economy – a Long-Term View

DEVELOPMENT WITHOUT PLANNING

Sweden was a latecomer to the process of modern economic growth. About 1870, when the modern growth process in Sweden may be said to have started, *per capita* income was substantially below that of most other West European countries (Kuznets [107], ch. 1). However, from that period on Sweden experienced a rapid and sustained rate of economic growth, resulting in a relatively high *per capita* income at the present time. In fact, the growth rate in Sweden during the last one hundred years is second only to that of Japan, and the *per capita* income, converted at current (1972–4) exchange rate, is now approximately at the US level.[1]

For the period 1870–1970 the growth rate in Sweden may be estimated at 2·1 per cent per year on a *per capita* basis, as compared with 1·5–2·0 per cent for most other countries in Western Europe and North America and 3·1 per cent for Japan. The general level of *per capita* income in Sweden at the present time (1972) is estimated at about US $5100 as compared with about US $3600 for the (weighted) average of West European countries and about US $5600 for the United

[1] A description of growth and fluctuations in Sweden during the early phase of modern economic growth is given in Lennart Jörberg ([89], [90]). Standard works on the Swedish economy from the First World War to the present time are Erik Lundberg's studies, particularly [130], [131], [136], [138] and [141]. Other important documents, for the period after the Second World War, are the official long-term reports ([268]–[273]) and the yearly national budgets [267], as well as the periodical reports on the economic situation by the 'Konjunkturinstitut' (The National Institute of Economic Research) [267]. (The national budgets, which should not be confused with the state budgets, are analyses and forecasts of the short-term macroeconomic development, mainly in terms of national accounts.)

States.[2] Thus *per capita* income in Sweden was in 1972 about 40 per cent higher than in the rest of Western Europe and about 10 per cent lower than in the US; it was somewhat *higher* than in the US at exchange rates prevailing in 1973–4.

As in most other countries, the growth rate has been higher during the period after the Second World War than earlier. While (real) *per capita* GNP increased on the average by about 2·5 per cent during the period between the world wars, the corresponding figure for the postwar period (until 1971) is about 3·3 per cent. However, as the acceleration was even greater in most other countries, the growth rate in Sweden during the postwar period may be characterised as somewhat below the average for Western Europe, though higher than North America (on a *per capita* basis).[3]

There is probably no generally agreed-upon explanation for the very successful process of economic growth in Sweden during the last one hundred years. However, a number of favourable circumstances may be mentioned.

When a rapid process of industrialisation started in Sweden,

[2] Western Europe is defined here, and in the rest of the book, as European OECD countries except the 'developing countries', Yugoslavia, Portugal, Spain, Greece and Turkey.

According to Angus Maddison ([148], p. 30), the growth rate per head of population was 2·3 per cent per year in Sweden and Japan during the period 1870–1913, as compared with 1·6 per cent for the (unweighted) average of a number of industrial OECD countries, excluding Japan. During the period 1913–50 the growth rate was, according to the same source, 1·6 per cent in Sweden as compared with 1·1 per cent for the same OECD countries. For similar figures see Simon Kuznets ([106], [107], ch. 1).

[3] The statistics for GNP *per capita* in US $ (in 1972) are based on OECD statistics, and computed at exchange rates at the end of 1972. The *per capita* growth rate of real GNP during the postwar period (1950–71) in Sweden and certain groups of countries is presented in the following table. All figures refer to GNP per head in constant prices.

Table 1 :A

Growth rate 1950–71 (at constant prices)

	GNP total	GNP/capita
Sweden	3·7	3·3
Western Europe	4·5	3·7
Western Europe and North America	3·9	2·5

a substantial productivity increase had already taken place in agriculture. The structure of farmholdings had changed substantially, mainly owing to the consolidation of geographically fragmented landholdings for individual peasants, through land consolidation reforms (*laga skifte*) starting during the second half of the eighteenth century culminating in 1827. Moreover, output in agriculture had increased considerably, in particular from the middle of the nineteenth century, when Sweden in fact had substantial exports of agricultural products (mainly oats), together with exports of timber and iron.

Industrial growth in Sweden was to start with basically an export-led, or export-biased, process, closely connected with the expansion of international demand for Swedish exports, mainly forest products – to begin with timber, but later on also more refined forest products, such as pulp and paper. The export impulses contributed to generating a sustained and regionally rather dispersed growth process in Sweden. One reason for this response of the Swedish economy to the export stimulus was presumably that forestry work, as well as the production of oats, at that time was a very labour-intensive activity, and that it was also spread out over large areas of the country. Thus, the character of the products themselves, as well as the existing, economically profitable production technology, prevented the growth impulse from being isolated to a small geographical enclave of the country, as was experienced in the twentieth century by several presently underdeveloped countries, with heavy exports of raw materials such as minerals and oil. Of importance for the Swedish success story is also that the terms of trade improved by about one per cent annually during the period 1870–1914 (L. Ohlsson [188], pp. 126–8).[4]

The expansion of the export sector started before an elaborate infrastructure, such as in transportation, had been created. However, such an infrastructure was developed later, particularly from the 1870s, largely on government initiative. It is also interesting to note the emergence of a fairly well paid, competent and honest class of civil servants during the nineteenth century. The smallness of the government responsibilities

---

[4] The role of exports in the growth process during different periods may be illustrated by figures over the change in exports as a fraction of the change in GNP. (cont. next page.)

during the 'ultra-liberal' period over most of the nineteenth century probably helped this emergence of an honest public administration; the temptations for dishonesty were small (as compared, for instance, to the administration in the under-developed countries of today).

Moreover, it is quite likely that the fairly advanced education reforms in the middle of the nineteenth century, both at the elementary level (compulsory schooling from 1842) and at the more advanced levels, helped the economy to respond to the growth impulses from abroad. Mainly owing to private initiatives, a rather advanced banking system was also developed as early as in the middle of the nineteenth century.

Another favourable factor was presumably that Sweden had a very big capital import during the early industrialisation process, during the period 1870–1910 usually amounting to about 5 per cent of GNP ([188], ch. 1). The import of capital took the form mainly of government borrowing, for the purpose of railroad building; consequently, the domestic capital market was to a large extent reserved for private long-term borrowing.

International factor mobility was important for Sweden in the case of labour too. The severe underemployment problem, linked to a surplus (excess supply) of labour in agriculture, was relieved by a substantial emigration, mainly to the United States. During the period 1870–1910 about one million people emigrated, which should be related to a total population in 1910 of 5·5 million.

Thus, early Swedish economic growth was closely connected with imports of capital and with exports of commodities and labour.

Table 1:B

The role of exports in the growth process

	Per cent	
	Current price	Constant price
1871–90	27	
1890–1913	20	
1921–30	113	39
1930–9	9	18
1946–66	20	33
1966–71	27	43

Source: [188], p. 51, and national accounts.

A remarkable aspect of the Swedish growth process during the last one hundred years is how this poor and 'overpopulated' country, relying to begin with on exports of raw materials, during the last decades of the nineteenth century and the first half of the twentieth rapidly developed into a producer and exporter of more and more sophisticated manufacturing products — for example, quality steel, sophisticated machines, transport equipment (ships, aircraft, cars, trains, etc.) and to some extent durable consumer-goods. Whereas manufacturing (mainly engineering products) in 1890 accounted for about 2 per cent of exports, and in 1913 7 per cent, it had reached 25 per cent in 1946 and 40 per cent in 1970 ([188], ch. 1 and national accounts). To a very large extent this expansion of manufacturing during the first decades of the nineteenth century was based on Swedish innovations — steam turbines, centrifugal separators, ball bearings, the adjustable spanner, the safety match, air compressors, automatic lighthouse technique, various types of precision instruments, techniques for precision measurements, etc.[5] This first period of the development of a sophisticated sector of manufacturing — about 1890–1930 — is presumably one of the most impressive periods of modern Swedish economic history. It is also of interest to notice that the income distribution turned in the favour of profits during the dynamic period 1890–1915; the wage-income share of national income seems to have fallen continuously from about 65 per cent to about 50 per cent during this period (Jungenfelt [88] ch. 1).

It is possible that this impressive technological development had something to do with the establishment, as early as the eighteenth century, of a number of technical schools, some of which during the last three decades of the nineteenth century were developed into technical colleges. Another important factor was probably that there existed (or rather *emerged*) a class of able private entrepreneurs in trade, industry and banking and that they were given a wide scope for 'uninhibited' entrepreneurial initiatives in production, investment,

---

[5] Erik Dahmén has analysed the relative roles of what he calls 'demand-pull-processes' (such as international demand) and 'supply-push-processes' (such as changes in the production structure, partly by domestic innovations) (Dahmén [34], part 1).

distribution and finance. The guild system (*skråväsendet*) was removed in 1846, and freedom of business and trade (*näringsfrihet*) was formally guaranteed by a law in 1864. These reforms presumably helped to boost entrepreneurship – how much is open to debate. It is possible that the regulations then abolished had not been very effective obstacles, in practice, to the *new* forms of business and industry that emerged during the early course of the industrial revolution. The most important aspect on Swedish legislation on entreprenurial activity at this time was probably that no *new* legislation was introduced to regulate the new industrial and business activities.

It has sometimes also been suggested, somewhat speculatively, that a favourable factor for the economically and socially 'favourable' development in Sweden has been that the labour force was ethnically and perhaps also culturally fairly homogeneous as compared with several other countries. This factor might have helped to create an atmosphere of co-operation between different groups of employees, and possibly also between employees and employers, as was manifest for instance in the agreement at the end of the 1930s between the workers and employers to settle labor disputes in a peaceful way – the so-called '*Saltsjöbads*-agreement' in 1939 between the Confederation of Trade Unions (LO) and the Employers Confederation (SAF). It is also possible that the establishment of a labour (Social Democratic) government in 1932 – still in power in 1974 – was another favourable factor for the peaceful labour–management relations, and for the integration of workers in society in general.

A typical feature of the development was that it was promoted mainly on private initiative, without much government intervention or support, and in a highly competitive setting. The manufacturing industry, particularly on the export side, had from the beginning to compete on the world market. Typical for the development was also that Swedish manufacturing firms very early established a system of 'worldwide' subsidiaries, rather than selling patent-rights. Swedish firms became multinational in their operations very early; the 1920s was a particularly dynamic period from this point of view. Even on the import side a rather free trade policy was pursued, except for the introduction of some tariffs for agricultural products, and also some modest tariffs for manufacturing from about 1890. (Agricultural protection was much further built up in the 1930s and after the Second World War.) Thus, there were very few, if any, 'mercantilist' policies to promote exports, and the importance of import-substitution policy (industry protection) was also quite limited.

For the period after 1913 an important factor behind the success of the Swedish economy is, of course, that the country was spared the two world wars; another is that the depression of the thirties came rather late to Sweden, and that the Swedish economy recovered relatively rapidly from it, mainly because of an early recovery for exports in the thirties.

As a generalisation, we might say that growth and industrialisation in Sweden during the last one hundred years is an example of successful export-led, or 'export-biased' growth, in the context of a private enterprise economy, with a remarkable innovative capacity of private entrepreneurs and with a rather 'liberal', market-oriented economic policy – combined with an elaborate, publicly operated infrastructure in transportation, education, health, etc., and later on a rather comprehensive social security system ([42], [43]).

It is interesting to notice the coincidence of a great number of favourable factors for economic and social developments in Sweden: the 'pre-take-off' developments in agriculture, education and public administration; the development of international demand and technology which suddenly made Swedish raw materials (forests and iron ore) highly valuable; the regionally rather dispersed generation of incomes by way of the production of certain export products (oats and timber); the high capital imports combined with heavy emigration of labour; the favourable development of the terms of trade; the freedom of action for able individuals in the private sector and the emergence of a class of private entrepreneurs, i.e. the absence of government restrictions on entrepreneurship; 150 years of peace; the 'calm' labour market, manifested by agreements between employers and employees about peaceful solutions of labour disputes; etc. It is probably difficult to find many countries with an equally great number of favourable circumstances for economic and social development.

Also, the postwar growth and development took place in the

context mainly of a private enterprise economy. The private domination *on the production side* in the Swedish economy during the postwar period is illustrated by the fact that no more than about 15 per cent of output was produced in the public sector in 1950, though the figure rose continuously to 20–25 per cent in the early 1970s. The public sector is more important on the *demand side*; public consumption and investment accounted for about 20 per cent of GNP in 1950 and the figure had increased to 30 per cent in the early 1970s. In manufacturing the public sector accounts for as little as 5 per cent of output and in agriculture the corresponding figure is close to zero.

Consumers' co-operatives have about the same size as the public sector in manufacturing, about 4 per cent of value added; the production is concentrated on consumer goods, particularly food. The co-operative movement is much stronger in retailing, where it is responsible for about 23 per cent of the sales. Moreover, about 25 per cent of the apartments in apartment houses are co-operative. It is also of interest to note that farmers' *producer* co-operatives play a dominating role in the collection and processing of agricultural products – dairy products, meat, flour, etc.

The *incomes* – in the form of taxes, social security fees, etc. – of the public sector are considerably larger than the aforementioned figures. In fact, total public sector incomes account (in 1971) for about 51 per cent of GNP, which is a comparatively high figure for market economies.[6] Thus, while the degree of nationalisation of *production* in Sweden is 20–25 per cent, and the degree of nationalisation of *the resource use* is 30 per cent, the degree of nationalisation of *income directing* in Sweden in 51 per cent. Therefore, whereas nationalisation of the means of production is rather small, there is a considerable nationalisation of income formation.

The difference between the 51 per cent that public authorities take in – as taxes, fees, etc. – and the 30 per cent that they use for public consumption and investment is largely repaid to the private sector in the form of income transfers, which in 1970 amounted to about 18 per cent of GNP. A smaller fraction –

[6] The figure refers to public incomes as a percentage of GNP at market prices. As a percentage of GNP at factor costs (excluding indirect taxes in the denominator) it is 55 per cent.

2–5 per cent of GNP – consists of public financial saving (mainly credit supply from the semi-public pension fund). Thus, public disposable income – public consumption, public investment and public financial saving – accounts for about 33 per cent of GNP.

The increased importance of the public sector in income formation also implies an increased public role for saving and credit supply. This development has been particularly pronounced during the sixties. The public sector – including the semi-public pension fund (the 'AP'-System) – in the early seventies accounts for about 43 per cent of gross saving[7] and 40 per cent of the supply of credit (mainly from the pension fund) in the organised credit market. However, in commercial banking the public sector accounts for no more than about 10 per cent of the stock of assets, and in the total banking sector (including the postal bank and savings banks), about 22 per cent.

The overall importance of the public sector in the Swedish economy is schematically illustrated by the figures in Table 1 : c.

Table 1:c
Importance of the public sector in the Swedish economy

	1950	1970
		(approximate figures)
	% of GNP*	
Public production	15	20–25
Public production in manufacturing	5	5
Total public incomes	25	51
Public resource use (public consumption + public investment)	20 ⎫	30 ⎫
Transfer payments	8 ⎬ 25	18 ⎬ 51
Financial saving	−3 ⎭	2–5 ⎭
	% of total gross saving	
Public saving	30	43
	% of 'organised' credit supply	
Public credit supply in organised credit market (mainly from the semi-public pension fund)	1	40

* GNP measured at market prices.

[7] About 60 per cent of net saving.

Along with the increased importance of the public sector for income directing, saving and credit supply, a rather liberal economic policy has been followed towards the private sector during the period after the Second World War – low tariffs and relatively little government intervention in the decision-making in production, investment, pricing and wage formation. Economic planning in Sweden has been confined mainly to social policies, to institutional reform and to the establishment of a publicly operated infrastructure, rather than to experiments with government managerial initiatives or detailed regulation of private enterprise; hence, the authorities have always abstained from an aggregated type of input–output planning.

This type of pluralistic and innovative economic development could probably not have taken place in the context of a centralised input–output-type planning – with direct controls and protectionism – such as has been characteristic of the economic policy of many underdeveloped countries in the period following the Second World War.

FLUCTUATIONS

Let us leave the question of growth and development and instead look at the instability of growth, i.e. business fluctuations, and the price trend. Business fluctuations in Sweden during the last century have followed the same general pattern and timing as in most other industrialised countries, though the amplitude of the fluctuations has usually been smaller than in most other countries. Consequently, the development of GNP shows a relatively smooth and steady development.

The behaviour of the Swedish economy over long periods is illustrated in Charts 1:1 and 1:2, showing the development of *per capita* GNP (in 1959 prices) and GNP prices since 1860, and the unemployment rate since 1911. A short-run cycle, with a span of about four or five years, may be discerned throughout the last century with particularly deep depressions on four occasions – 1866–8, 1875–8, 1921 and 1931–3 (the setbacks in 1917/18 and 1940/41 being the result of specific historical incidents – the two world wars. (See also charts A and B in the Appendix.)

The short-run behaviour of prices has usually followed the

CHART 1:1   Real GNP *per capita* and implicit GNP-deflator 1861–1972

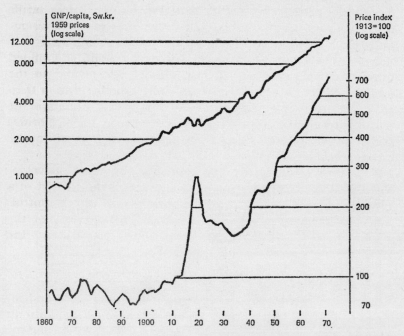

Source: Ö. Johansson [87] and Central Bureau of Statistics: National
Accounts.

cyclical pattern of the volume components, possibly with a
time lag. No long-term price trend seems to have existed for
prices in the period 1860–1913, probably because of a calm
long-term price development on international markets during
the gold-standard era, a high domestic unemployment rate
and weak labour unions. The price trend from 1913 is dominated by the inflation during the First World War, the deflation
in the early twenties and the steady price trend (of about 4 per
cent per year) starting at the beginning of the Second World
War, and probably accelerating.

Between the two world wars the unemployment rate (according to labour union statistics) was seldom below 10 per cent,
even in boom periods (average for the year; unemployment

CHART 1:2 Unemployment 1911–71

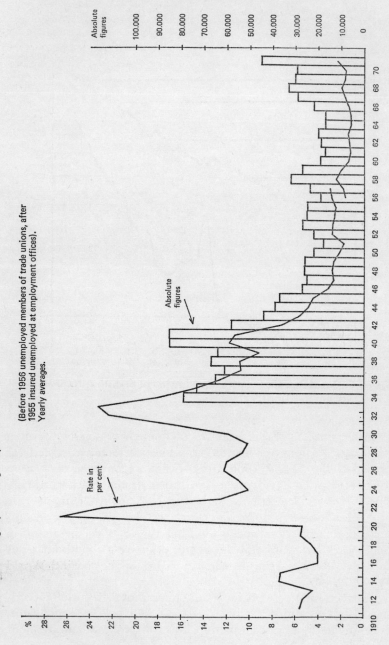

(Before 1955 unemployed members of trade unions, after 1955 insured unemployed at employment offices). Yearly averages.

Source: P. Silenstam [208] and Labour Market Board: Labour Market Statistics.

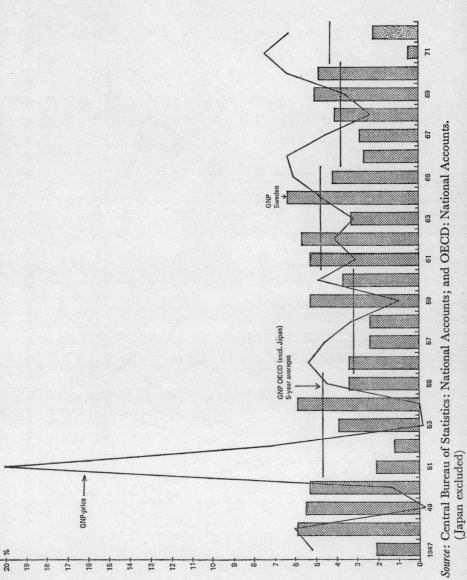

Source: Central Bureau of Statistics: National Accounts; and OECD: National Accounts. (Japan excluded)

CHART I:4 Consumer prices, and labour costs per man-hour: yearly rates of change

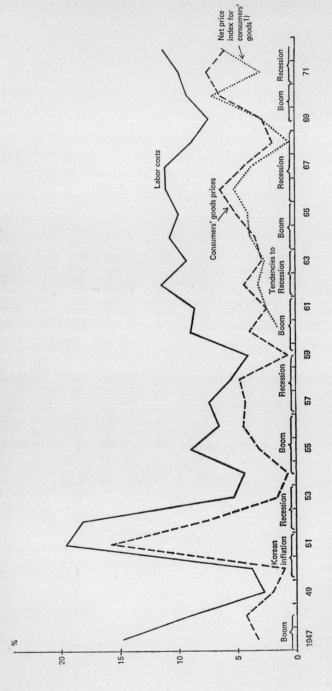

(1) Prices at "factor costs"

Source: Central Bureau of Statistics: Statistical Abstract of Sweden (Prices), and National Accounts (Labour Costs).

CHART 1:5   Total investment and private consumption: real terms (1959 prices): yearly rates of change

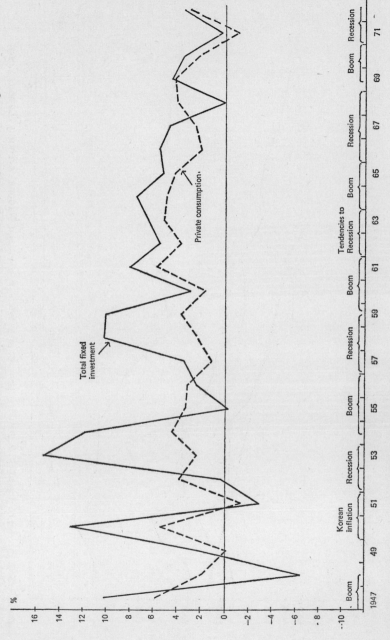

Source: Central Bureau of Statistics: National Accounts.

CHART 1 : 6   Fixed investment in manufacturing ('tillverkningsindustri'): Sw.kr in real terms (1959 prices)

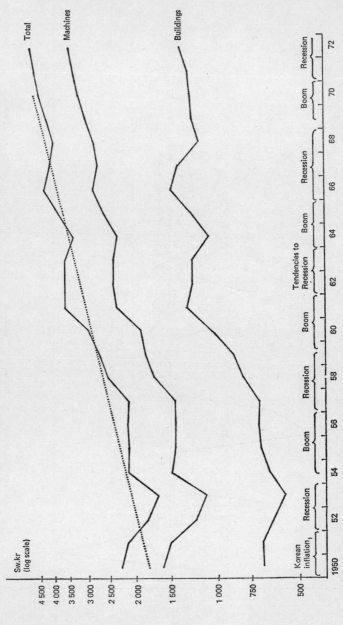

Source: Central Bureau of Statistics: National Accounts.

CHART 1:7 Unemployment rate

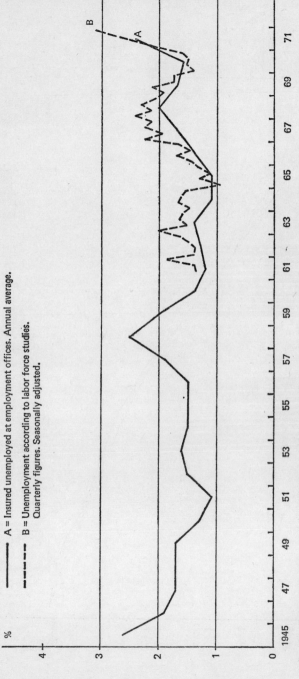

%

A = Insured unemployed at employment offices. Annual average.

B = Unemployment according to labor force studies.
Quarterly figures. Seasonally adjusted.

Source: Central Bureau of Statistics: Statistical Abstract of Sweden; and Labour Market Board: Labour Force Studies. Figures before 1956 based on the trade unions' statistics.

CHART 1:8   Real GNP, actual and full-capacity level (potential GNP)

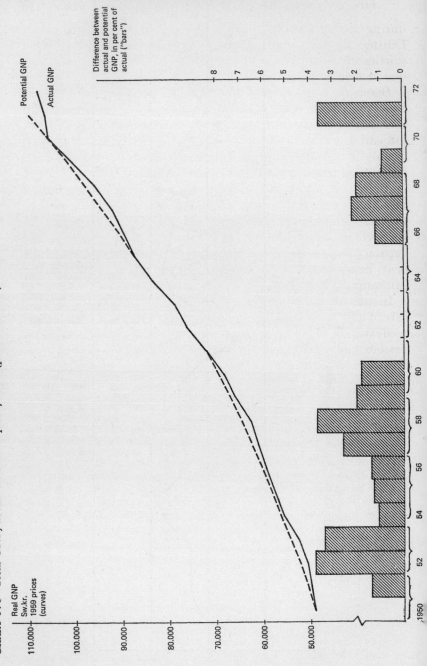

during the summer was often 3–4 per cent during booms). During the deep depressions in the early twenties and early thirties the unemployment rate among labour union members was as high as 25 per cent (Chart 1:2).

During the postwar period the instability problem has changed character, in Sweden as elsewhere. Instead of fluctuations up and down in the *level* of aggregate production (GNP and industrial output) and prices, the instability has consisted mainly of variations in the rate of growth, in the rate of inflation and in the degree of full 'employment' (Charts 1:1–1:5 and charts A and B in the Appendix). Registered unemployment has been rather low, measured by historical as well as international standards (Charts 1:2 and 1:7). Consequently, the level of output has most of the time been fairly close to full capacity utilisation; it has seldom been more than about 2 per cent below what is *conventionally* regarded as full capacity utilisation (Chart 1:8).

In the recession periods the (seasonally adjusted) monthly rate of registered unemployment seems as a rule to have reached a maximum of about 2·5–3·0 per cent, whereas in the boom periods the unemployment rate was about 1·5 per cent, *as measured by labour force studies*. According to unemployment

---

Source (to Chart 1:8): Central Bureau of Statistics: National Accounts.

Note: Potential GNP estimated by exponential functions between years of 'full' capacity utilisation (1950, 1961, 1965, 1970).

In years when the reduction in the number of working hours (due to legislation or bargaining agreements) has been particularly large, the 'losses' in GNP indicated by the bars in the chart probably imply an overestimation as compared to other years. Available studies suggest the following *percentage* reductions in working hours during various years

1951 +52	58 +59 +60	64	65	67	68	69	71	72	73
1·1	4	0·8	0·8	1·0	1·0	1·0	0·4	3·5	0·3

(Figures compiled by Lars Matthiessen from various studies.)

Considering the large reduction in minimum working hours in 1972 the 'loss' in GNP is probably of about the same magnitude as in 1971, possibly somewhat higher.

insurance and labour market exchange statistics, the unemployment figures are on the average about 0·5 percentage point
lower (Chart 1:7).

Even considering the expansion of protected activities (including conventional public works) and retraining of the
otherwise unemployed – each involving about one per cent of
the labour force (see pp. 104–7) in recent years – the improvement in the employment situation from the prewar period,
dramatically illustrated in Chart 1:2, is obviously one of the
most fundamental features of the post-Second World War
economy.

However there is not much evidence that the amplitudes of
the fluctuations of GNP and prices have become gradually
smaller over time during the course of the postwar period,
although the yearly rate of change of total gross fixed investment seems to have fallen off over time, owing mainly to
slower expansions during boom periods (Charts 1:3–1:5).

Another characteristic feature of the Swedish economy has
been that exports and imports have usually developed quite
parallel, although the trade balance, and the balance of payments, usually tend to deteriorate somewhat during the
second year of each boom (Chart 1:9). This parallel development is probably one of the reasons why Sweden has been able
to go along with rather small exchange reserves, relative to the
size of foreign trade. (There has been more instability since
1970.)

On the price side, the economy has been dominated by the
substantial price and wage increases, particularly during and
immediately after boom periods. In the period after the Korean
inflation, 1953–1970, the yearly rate of inflation in Sweden,
measured by changes in consumer goods prices, was about 3·7
per cent, as compared to 3·8 per cent for the (weighted)
average of Western Europe – 2·7 per cent for Western Europe
plus North America. Charts 1:3–1:4 suggest a possible tendency for the yearly rate of inflation to rise, even neglecting the
world-wide 'price-explosion' in 1973–4 which doubled inflation.

The rate of wage cost increase (including social fees and
taxes on labour use) seems to have shifted to a higher level
from the fifties to the sixties – from about 5–7 per cent per year
in the fifties to about 9–11 per cent during the sixties.

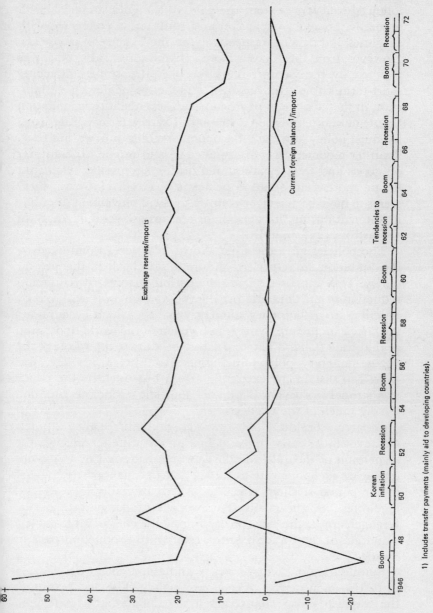

1) Includes transfer payments (mainly aid to developing countries).

Source: Central Bureau of Statistics: Foreign Trade; and Central Bank of Sweden: Sveriges Riksbank, Yearbook.

ECONOMIC POLICY

Before the First World War stabilisation policy in Sweden followed to a large extent the rules of the gold standard, with domestic monetary expansion and contraction connected with surpluses and deficits, respectively, in the balance of payments. However, from the 1890s a more active interest rate policy was pursued by the Central Bank for the purpose of influencing short-term capital movements, and hence achieving equilibrium in the balance of payments with less deflation or inflation than would otherwise be necessary. There was very little scope for fiscal policy as a tool of economic stabilisation at that time. Transfer payments were insignificant, and public expenditures on goods and services accounted during the period 1862–1914 for no more than about 6 per cent of GNP. However, there seems to have been a clear counter-cyclical movement in public investment during this period, for reasons not yet fully analysed (Bergström [23], p. 27).

The policies after the First World War were dominated by the ambition to return to the gold standard at the prewar parity. This was done during the period 1920/21; it required a reduction in the domestic price level, and this was achieved by a deliberate deflationary monetary policy, which accentuated the effects on unemployment in Sweden of the world depression at that time (Charts 1:1–1:2). In fact, during the whole of the 1920s monetary policy, including discount rate policy, was geared to sustain the exchange rate. Consequently, the policy was strongly procyclical on the domestic economic situation during much of the twenties.

Greater consideration towards domestic policy targets emerged in the early 1930s. A first prerequisite for this was the suspension of the gold standard, which occurred in 1931 with a floating exchange rate until 1933 when a new parity, related to the pound sterling, was established. Probably by accident, including the effects on the Swedish exchange rate of the Kreuger crash, the new parity implied a considerable undervaluation of the Swedish krona relative to production costs in Sweden.

Stabilisation of domestic prices and employment now started to be the main targets of economic policy. The devaluation of the Swedish krona counteracted the deflationary tendencies, and the undervaluation of the currency was favourable for Swedish exports, which started to expand as early as 1933. This helped to move Sweden up from the deep depression much more rapidly than other countries. The government in 1933 also started a deliberate expansionary fiscal policy, by loan-financed public expenditures, for the purpose of moving the economy out of the depression. However, these policies were mainly of interest from the point of view of *principle*, rather than for their practical importance, which must have been very small in view of the fact that the increase in government spending hardly amounted to more than about one per cent of GNP in the period 1932–4.

In fact, the fiscal actions during the period 1930–2 – *before* the 'new' policy started – seem to have been no less expansionary than the fiscal actions in 1933–4 [23, ch. 1]. Thus, the revival of the Swedish economy from the depression in the thirties was the result of external factors, and hence luck, rather than of any 'new' principles of economic policy.

During the postwar period one characteristic feature of economic policy was the increase in the *number* of policy targets. It is probably correct to say that full employment has been the main policy target. However, during some periods, such as immediately after the war and in connection with several boom periods, considerations regarding the price level have also much influenced the factual policy. The balance of payments target, connected of course with the ambition to defend a fixed exchange rate, achieved emphasis in situations of (factual or conceived) balance of payments problems, above all in 1947 and 1971, and to some extent also in 1958 and 1968.

The growth rate became a target for economic policy in the late fifties, at the same time as increased consideration was given to economic growth in other countries. Problems of regional balance aroused greater interest during the early sixties, and environmental considerations and a concern about the distribution of income and wealth became more pronounced during the late sixties. Moreover, the full employment target has continuously changed character: increasingly it has been applied not only to the labour market as a whole, but to various submarkets, such as married women; the handicapped; employees in individual branches and specific regions, etc.

Employment policy has also, more and more, been concerned with retraining, aid for mobility and specific job-creating activities for people with various types of handicaps and difficulties to compete in the labour market with the rest of the labour force (at negotiated or conventionally established wages).

All this means that economic policy has become increasingly multidimensional, and hence complex, with substantial risks for conflicts of goals and lack of instruments to reach established targets. It is the problems connected with reconciling these various, and more and more ambitious, policy targets during the postwar period that is the main theme of the analysis in this book.

To summarise, economic policy in Sweden during the post-Second World War period has been pursued in the context of a rather decentralised market economy, dominated by private enterprise but with a rather ambitious government policy in the fields of public consumption and public saving, income redistribution, infrastructure and stabilisation policy – a 'liberal–social democratic welfare state' in the context of a 'mixed economy', with a high 'capacity to innovate' [238] both by private enterprise (on the production and financing side) and by the political process (on the side of economic and social policy). The Swedish economy may also be characterised as an inflationary high-employment economy.

In comparison with other countries in Western Europe, the Swedish economy *during the postwar period* might be characterised as (1) an economic system dominated by private enterprise on the *production side*; (2) rather strong and rapidly expanding public activities on the *demand side*, owing to high public consumption and public investment in infrastructure; (3) a high and rapidly rising redirection of the income stream, by public income redistributions and social security systems – and as a consequence high taxes on households and consumption; (4) a rapid rise in public and semi-public savings and the supply of credit since the early sixties (owing to the semi-public pension fund); (5) a somewhat less than medium rate of growth of GNP; (6) usually a rather high level of employment and capacity utilisation; (7) about an average rate of inflation, possibly with a rising trend; (8) a rather parallel development of imports and exports most of the time.

2 The Regulated Economy – 1945-50

THE RECORD

The first five years after the Second World War, 1945-50, represent a distinct period for economic policy in Sweden. The experience of this period has also been of great importance for the subsequent economic policy debate. It is therefore worth while to discuss this period by itself. The experience also has general interest as a case study of problems connected with introducing 'direct controls' in a market system.

Except for the war years, when a coalition government was in office, Sweden has had a Social Democratic government since 1932 (apart from the summer of 1936). When a purely Social Democratic government succeeded the coalition government at the end of the Second World War, two important documents concerning postwar economic policy were published. One was issued by a special government committee, the Commission for Postwar Economic Planning [266], under the chairmanship of Gunnar Myrdal – 'The Myrdal Commission'. The other document, the Labour Movement's Postwar Programme [3], was issued jointly by the Social Democratic Party and the Confederation of Trade Unions (LO).[1]

Both programmes focussed mainly on the problem of keeping up aggregate demand in the face of an expected postwar depression. The expectation of a worldwide depression, a common fear in many countries at that time, was of course based

[1] Among the economists in the secretariat of the Myrdal Commission were Karin Kock, Richard Sterner and Ingvar Svennilson. Ernst Wigforss, Secretary of the Treasury, 1932-49, was the chairman of the Labour Movement Committee. Gunnar Myrdal was an expert consultant to this committee and Gösta Rehn and Richard Sterner formed the secretariat.

on the belief that the postwar world would be more peaceful than it turned out to be, and that the lesson of how to guarantee full employment had not yet been learned by most governments.[2]

Both programmes favoured a successive removal of many direct controls introduced during the wartime blockade; in particular the removal of rationing of consumer goods, but also, at a later stage, the removal of import control, the licensing of building activity and government control of wages. However, both programmes argued that the government should play a much more important role in the economy than it had done before the war. This broadening of the government's role should be achieved by some expansion of the public sector, but above all by some energetic measures to influence the private sector. Thus it was argued in the labour programme that the bulk of investment activity should be planned and conducted by public authorities and that foreign trade in the postwar period should be controlled by the State ([3], pp. 22, 60). However, it was not specified to what extent this conduct and control should be implemented by general economic policies and incentives – such as general monetary and fiscal policy – and to what extent direct administrative controls – i.e. licences from the authorities – would be necessary.

Even though the programmes were characterised by a more interventionistic attitude than was policy in the interwar period, they can hardly be characterised as socialist in the orthodox sense. Very little nationalisation was proposed – only oil distribution and insurance. It is true that there was a general statement in the labour programme that the aim of the programme was to 'give the economy a new organisation and to reshape society in a socialist direction'. However, elsewhere in the programme it was argued that, 'to the extent that private enterprise succeeds . . . in giving the masses as much of the good in life as is technically possible at full and efficient use of labour and material factors of production, it can in the future be allowed to function in about the same way as was usual before the war' ([3], p. 45). In practice, nationalisations of private

---

[2] Gunnar Myrdal [171] in particular was pessimistic about the ability of the American government to prevent a major depression, with repercussions all over the world.

firms have been almost absent from Swedish postwar policy.[3]

In line with the conclusions in the postwar programmes that many wartime regulations should be removed, rationing and import controls were to a large extent abolished immediately after the war (in 1945/46). At the same time, building restrictions were liberalised considerably. Only price control and the control of capital movements were substantially retained. However, even this conformed to the recommendations of the Myrdal Commission and the Labour Movement Programme, which had argued that it was not possible, in the 'disorganised' world after the war, to rely on market forces to guarantee a desirable development of prices and capital movements.

The official policy pursued by the authorities, the government as well as the Central Bank, was first to bring about a reduction in prices in response to rising productivity and greater supply of inexpensive imported commodities (such as fuel). It was believed that part of the fall in the value of money during the war would thereby be recouped, and this was regarded as 'fair' to savers (creditors). (Interest rate was pegged at a low level at this time.)

The opinion that prices should be reduced in step with increases in productivity was a direct heritage from Professor Davidson's well-known norm for economic policy, according to which prices should change in inverse proportion to productivity.[4] However, whereas Davidson's idea was designed

[3] One of the few exceptions is that in the mid-fifties the state took over the 50 per cent of the shares of the Lapland iron ore fields (LKAB) not yet state-owned. And from 1971 a new corporation, dominated by the government, took over the pharmacies. At the end of the sixties and early seventies the government bought a few private firms and participated in some joint ventures with private firms. Moreover, a number of municipalities have bought rather substantial land holdings for housebuilding, which during the postwar period has been dominated by co-operatives and municipalities (about 60 per cent of housebuilding during the sixties).

[4] Adherents to the Davidson norm included Erik Lindahl, Johan Åkerman, Dag Hammarskjöld and the Myrdal Commission. It was mainly Hammarskjöld, Undersecretary in the Treasury 1936–46, who incorporated the Davidson norm into economic policy documents. Davidson's norm was based on considerations of distribution as well as allocation. For an analysis of the theoretical discussion between Davidson, Wicksell and Lindahl see Bentzel [18]. The influence of this norm in policy in the early postwar years is discussed in Lundberg [130, pp. 127–31].

primarily as a norm for monetary policy, the authorities believed that prices had to be brought down by administrative means (price control).

This belief was largely based on the assumption that prices, at least during a period of direct regulations and price control, were determined from the cost side, whereas demand was regarded as being less important For this reason it was believed that inflation could and should be fought – and in fact that prices could be reduced – by policy measures that reduced production costs, including costs of import and retailing. This hypothesis seems to have underlain a number of policy measures in the immediate postwar period, such as the reduction of interest rates in February 1945, the appreciation of the Swedish krona (by 17 per cent) in July 1946, the abolition of the general sales tax from January 1947 and the use of export duties and subsidies on imports, and food subsidies during much of the late forties. (For a schematic picture of economic policy actions in the postwar period, see Chart 4:8 in chapter 4.)

All these measures were introduced *inter alia* as means of reducing prices, or preventing price increases, from the cost side. This was particularly so for the appreciation of the Swedish krona, which was motivated to prevent international price increases, stimulated by the removal of price control in the US, from raising the Swedish price level. However, in the case of the abolition of the sales tax, political pressure from the opposition – led by Bertil Ohlin, head of the Liberal Party – was also an important explanation for the policy. The Confederation of Trade Unions (LO) seems to have pressed in the same direction.[5]

In principle, it is without doubt possible to fight price increases, or even to achieve price reductions, by measures that reduce production costs, such as interest rate reductions, appreciation and the reduction of indirect taxes. However, in a system with market-determined prices (equilibrium pricing), this requires that aggregate demand be sufficiently restrained, for example by higher taxation. Such actions were not undertaken to any significant extent, however, until in 1948 – except for the introduction of a pay-as-you-earn tax collection system

---

[5] This information has been supplied by Gunnar Myrdal in private conversation; he was at that time a member of the Swedish government.

in 1947 (though this reform was not motivated by stabilisation considerations).[6] Instead, an ambitious demand-stimulating social reform programme was initiated with *inter alia* children's allowances and greatly increased old-age pensions.

Another possibility might be to force down prices in conformity with the cost reductions by price control, direct controls over aggregate demand and public intervention in the income formation process, so-called incomes policy. However, the direct controls had to a great extent been removed immediately after the war, and price control was not very effective after the general price freeze had been abolished; (as we shall see later, some controls were reintroduced in the second part of 1947 and in 1948). Moreover, incomes policy at that time consisted mainly of general recommendations by the government to labour unions to show 'restraint' in wage demands; this did not prevent considerable wage increases - 8 per cent in 1946 and 14 per cent in 1947 for industrial workers (Chart 1:4).

In the absence of both a constrictive general economic policy and restrictive direct controls, economic policy did not succeed very well in its objectives. In combination with price control, the expansive monetary–fiscal policy resulted in a high excess demand for commodities and labour. The building market in particular was booming in 1946 and 1947, and encountered shortages of various factors of production, labour as well as building materials, with the result that construction times lengthened. Owing to the decontrol of imports, the excess demand situation in the commodity market caused a huge deficit in the balance of trade. In contrast to a surplus on current account of about 1300 million kronor in 1945, a deficit of 118 million appeared in 1946 and a deficit of close to 1500 million in 1947, resulting in a balance of payments crisis in 1947 (Chart 1:9). The deficit was no less than 23 per cent of imports and 6 per cent of GNP.

Obviously, the trade balance could not withstand all the strains that were simultaneously put on it: the appreciation of the krona (which stimulated import and reduced the incentives for exports), the expansionary monetary and fiscal policies, the removal of a number of direct controls and the large wage increase. The strains on the balance of payments were

[6] See Lars Matthiessen ([150], p. 179).

accentuated by the grant of substantial government credits to a number of foreign countries, mainly the Scandinavian countries and the Soviet Union – partly as a contribution to rebuilding Europe after the war, partly to get new and possibly stable export markets in view of an expected postwar slump in the markets in the West; the latter was a main argument for the credit to USSR. It is also of interest to note that, in spite of price control, consumer goods prices rose by 8 per cent between mid-1945 and mid-1948. Thus, the direct controls were too weak to make the expansionary (or passive) monetary-fiscal policy on the demand side harmless to the economy; the policy did not succeed very well with respect to prices and to the balance of payments. It is difficult to evaluate the relative importance of the different factors behind this expansionary (or passive) policy: incorrect forecasts about business conditions (the expectation of an international postwar slump), poor economic theory (an exaggerated belief in the importance for prices of the cost side) or difficulties of a politico-tactical nature (for instance the demand from the political opposition that the sales tax be removed). In any case, it took the authorities a very long time to adjust their policy to the fact that the main problem was inflation and balance of payments difficulties rather than unemployment.[7]

That inflation was the main problem many economists, businessmen and members of the political opposition had already been arguing in 1945/46. During the first postwar years the National Institute of Economic Research, headed by Erik Lundberg, to a large extent built its analysis of the economic situation on calculations of (*ex ante*) excess demand gaps in the commodity markets – 'inflationary gap calculations' – particularly after late 1946. These calculations were used both for an analysis of actual tendencies in the economy and for a discussion of alternative economic policy actions to restore macroeconomic equilibrium. Such gap calculations later became the main tool of analysis also in the National Budgets, published biannually by the government in connection with the state budget. This approach probably helped to focus the economic policy debate on the demand side more than was earlier the case. There

[7] The pure politico-tactical factors have been stressed by Torsten Gårdlund in particular [51].

seem to be two main theoretical roots to the analytical techniques employed in these studies – Keynes's *How to Pay for the War* [92] and the *ex ante* analysis of expectations and plans developed by 'the Stockholm School' in the thirties (Erik Lindahl, Gunnar Myrdal, Bertil Ohlin, Erik Lundberg, Ingvar Svennilson, Tord Palander, etc.).[8]

In response to increasing prices and a worsening of the balance of payments, economic policy in 1947/48 retreated into direct controls, such as import regulations, stiffer control of building activity and to some extent rationing. In the implementation of building regulations, investment in the export sector, and to some extent in the import-competing sector, was favoured, whereas housing, the service sector and the public sector were cut back. In particular, housebuilding (houses under construction) was reduced by 22 per cent between 1947 and 1948.

Hence, during the three-year period 1947–9 Swedish economic policy became dominated by price controls and regulation of building and of imports, in combination with a still rather passive monetary and fiscal policy. This means that direct controls were retained in Sweden for a rather long time after the war, after the temporary liberalisation in 1945/46. As a consequence, the economy was characterised by a policy of 'repressed inflation' during most of the forties – i.e. tendencies to permanent excess demand for commodities and labour, held back by direct (physical) regulation.

THE CRITICISM

Considerable criticism was directed against the policy of repressed inflation – from the non-socialist opposition and the business world, as well as from a number of economists. Bertil Ohlin stated quite early in the postwar debate that the two policy goals of price stability and full employment in the Beveridge sense of 'more jobs than men' (what Ohlin called 'overemployment'), were more or less incompatible in a free

[8] The first gap calculation was made in 1943 by the National Institute of Economic Research [267]. The analytical technique was later developed during the forties and fifties. Some of the most important contributions were made by Bent Hansen [57]. Börje Kragh [98], Erik Lundberg ([127], [128], [130]) and Ingvar Ohlsson [187].

market economy. Ohlin argued that attempts to reconcile them would easily lead to more and more detailed government regulations.

Among academic economists outside politics, the policy of repressed inflation was criticised mainly on two grounds:

(1) its alleged inefficiency as a means to stabilise the economy;

(2) its alleged unfavourable effects on the allocation of resources.

Some of the most noted critics among economists were Erik Lundberg and the labour union economists Gösta Rehn and Rudolf Meidner.

The criticism by Rehn and Meidner dealt mainly with *stabilisation* ([152], [153], [197], [198], [235], [236]). In particular, they argued that a policy of repressed inflation was doomed to fail in its attempt to stabilise labour cost. Unions could not resist pressure from their members for considerable wage increases in a situation where there was excess demand for labour and when profits were high owing to abundant demand for commodities; the bargaining position of the union was too strong, from the point of view of economic stability. At the same time, market-induced wage drift occurred in response to excess demand for labour. According to Meidner and Rehn the advice of Beveridge and other economists that labour unions should 'exercise restraint and modesty' in their wage claims was self-defeating in a labour market with permanent excess demand (more jobs than men). As an instance, Rehn and Meidner pointed to the experiences in 1949–50 when the labour unions accepted a two-year prolongation of the earlier wage agreement. This wage freeze was secured by a direct appeal from the government, which in its turn promised to keep down price increases by price control and subsidies.

However, the wage-freeze did not prevent wage drift for certain groups later on. According to Meidner and Rehn, dissatisfaction created during such periods of wage restraint tends to result in 'wage explosions' sooner or later; in fact, such an explosion seemed to have happened in 1951 and 1952 in connection with the Korean inflation (see Chart 1:4). A similar, though smaller, wage explosion had already occurred in 1947 after a period of wage restraints. Working as they were inside the labour unions, Meidner and Rehn had also been impressed by the difficult situation that union leaders and functionaries are faced with when the traditional role of the unions to press for wage rises is replaced by the objective of attempting to put a damper on wage increases.

Thus, the attempts in the late forties to pursue a 'delegated incomes policy' via voluntary agreements between labour and employer organisations did not work very well. An explanation might be that incomes policy at this time was implemented in an economy of repressed inflation. Incomes policy became a *substitute* for, rather than a complement to, a general restrictive economic policy. Hence, the experiences of this period may not indicate much about the possibilities for success of an incomes policy supported by a restrictive general economic policy.

Erik Lundberg, too, stressed the difficulties of preventing 'excessive' wage increases in an economy with permanent excess demand for commodities and labour ([130], chs. X–XII). Lundberg argued in addition that direct controls often work with very long time lags and with rather uncertain quantitative impact. (The same could of course be said about many monetary and fiscal measures, in particular measures designed to influence private investment.) Thus it took over one year before the import controls of 1947 became effective. He also pointed out that the system of building licences implied a control only of building starts but not of building activity. The effects on the latter depend also on how rapidly the projects are completed. Moreover, there was, according to Lundberg, a tendency for business firms to 'underestimate' the costs of building when they applied for licences, with the result that the expenditure tended to be higher than expected by the authorities. According to a study of Lars Lindberger, the volume of gross investment in industrial building and other construction over a series of years amounted to more than twice the value of the building permits granted to the enterprises involved ([124], pp. 120–4).

Meidner and Rehn criticised the policy also on allocation grounds. The same is true for Bertil Ohlin, who argued that the continued effects of repressed and open inflation, in combination with direct controls, would in the long run impair the allocation of resources in the economy ([184], [185]). The notion, was, of course, that the authorities lacked criteria for their decisions when the market was not functioning properly; the price relations would be distorted, in the sense that prices would no longer reflect production costs and consumer preferences.

However, the most penetrating analysis and criticism on this score were undoubtedly those delivered by Lundberg, whose discussion of these issues is still one of the most thorough analyses available in the international literature ([130], chs. XI–XII). His basic line of argument was to show how various types of inefficiency and misallocation of resources developed as a result of direct controls in an economy with repressed inflation. In particular, Lundberg analysed the effects of import control, building control and price control. He supported his theoretical analysis by a questionnaire study, which gave numerous examples of the effects he was discussing. The statistical representativeness of the study is somewhat uncertain, however, because of a rather small frequency of answers to the questions ([130], appendix).

In the case of import control, Lundberg stressed the risk of a reduction in competition among importers and therefore also among domestic producers. One reason was that new initiatives were jeopardised by the fact that quotas were usually determined on an historical basis. To find other, more rational, criteria for the distribution of licences is very difficult, in practice probably impossible. The system of building licences was criticised also, mainly on the ground that it was extremely difficult for the authorities to find economically rational criteria for the allocation of permits between sectors and firms. In 1947–9 the controls were geared to promote export industries, and to some extent import-competing industries, for the purpose of solving the acute balance of payments problem. However, the administrators also seemed to be caught by 'physiocratic' and 'mercantilistic' ideas that production of commodities, mainly exports, was more 'productive' than distribution and other services in the home market.

The concentration on export industries and import-competing industries was also due to the fact that the administrators tended to look only at the *direct* effect on the allocation of resources, neglecting the more complicated indirect effects. This meant, Lundberg argued, that no consideration was given to the fact that high profitability investments in the service sector might release resources that could be used in other parts of the economy and in that way promote exports. According to Lundberg, increases in the production of exports brought about in this indirect way could in many cases be several times larger than the effects of direct discrimination in favour of certain export industries. As Lundberg pointed out, such indirect effects via the price system are more or less automatically taken into account via the market mechanism in a system without price controls and direct regulations.

Another typical thesis of Lundberg's was that criteria for direct intervention were destroyed by the interventions themselves, mainly by the price control. One of Lundberg's characteristic formulations was: 'the dilemma of the regulated economy lies in the very fact that although prices have been to a large extent divorced from their function of regulating economic activity, the evidence of prices is nevertheless used as the basis for the evaluation of the effects of the regulations' ([130], p. 312).

Lundberg also emphasised the dynamic role of prices and profits in the economy, reallocating resources in response to changes in technology, taste and foreign demand. Thus, he was critical of attempts to keep prices at some assumed long-term equilibrium level by price control, thereby eliminating the price and profit fluctuations which in a market economy are necessary as incentives to reallocate resources:

> . . . if the dynamics of economic expansion are examined from this point of view, a highly effective price control appears dangerous. If price controls really succeed in bringing about an immediate or very rapid adjustment of prices to the changed cost conditions, with the result that abnormally high profits – or even profit expectations – at various points never appear, certainly one criterion of equilibrium in the price system would eventually be fulfilled [prices being equal to average costs], but the corresponding adjustment of production and investment would fail to come about in due course of time ([130], pp. 317–18).

In the general discussion of price control other well-known effects of such controls were of course also pointed out, such as the difficulties in finding criteria for the distribution of the commodities among households, the development of black markets and the tendency of producers to shift over from standard articles, where price control is simple, to more differentiated products where price control is difficult.

Another noticed complication of price control was that firms that are not allowed to increase prices in view of higher costs may instead reduce, or at least abstain from improving, the quality of products. In the long run, price control can hardly be effective if product qualities, and hence the production process itself, are not also centrally determined and controlled. Thus, in order for the centralisation of price determination to be effective, there must also be a central control of product qualities and production processes, and hence a strongly centralised economic system.

3 Full Employment and Price Stability: the Early Debate

The Swedish economy had by the 1940s already reached a rather low level of unemployment, both by historical and international standards (Chart 1:2) – what is conventionally called full, or overfull, employment. The difficulties which thereupon emerged – in particular of combining full employment with stable prices – resulted in an animated debate among economists, some of the leading participants being Gösta Rehn, Rudolf Meidner, Bent Hansen, Erik Lundberg, Gunnar Myrdal and Bertil Ohlin. This early discussion is in fact highly relevant for the ensuing development of economic policies in Sweden. It is therefore well worth while to recall the discussion in some detail. In fact, practically every argument could as well be repeated today – not only for Sweden but for most high-employment market economies.

Bertil Ohlin argued, from the early postwar period on, for more reliance on general economic policy methods instead of direct controls. However, Ohlin appears to have seen no other solution to the conflict between full employment and stable prices than to reduce aspirations somewhat with respect to the employment level.[1] He believed that such a reduction would not necessarily be detrimental from a welfare point of view, since a lower employment level in his opinion might result in a

[1] Compare the following passage by Ohlin: 'It is true that immediately after the war nobody quite understood how large the disadvantages of overfull employment would be and how important it was to try instead to achieve a high and stable employment of the type of good years in the prewar period' [184]. In another publication Ohlin talked about 94–7 per cent employment as a reasonable degree of full employment, compatible with price stability ([185], p. 5).

higher national income owing to the elimination of distorting tendencies in the labour market.[2]

Ohlin also argued that the 'necessary' reduction in the employment level could be rather limited if labour mobility were increased and if a 'skilful adaptation of public works to local surpluses of labour' was achieved ([185], pp. 5–6). This idea, later developed by Gösta Rehn, had in fact been suggested by Ohlin as early as 1936 ([179], pp. 119–95, 203–6), and by the Myrdal Commission in 1944 [266]. The tradition in Sweden of emphasising labour mobility is even older than that; Gösta Bagge in his thorough analysis in 1917 of the causes and consequences of immobility of labour stressed the possibility of reducing unemployment via greater mobility of labour ([15], chs. V–VI, particularly pp. 357–85). In fact, the idea had even earlier been developed by the British economist and social reformer Lord Beveridge [25].

Ohlin believed that if ambitions concerning the level of employment were modified somewhat, a more liberal economic policy could be pursued. In particular, he argued energetically for a liberalisation of international trade in order to utilise more the advantages of international division of labour and of international competition. However, he also suggested 'round-table conferences' between government, opposition, industry, agriculture and labour to try to reach agreements about stabilisation policy and about moderation in the struggle over income shares – what was later on baptised 'incomes policy'.

Myrdal too asserted, in a couple of articles published at the beginning of the fifties, that direct controls and repressed inflation would not be successful in the long run in combating price increases. Instead of a 'guerrilla war' against price movements in a situation of excess demand, Myrdal argued for more reliance on general economic policy methods, mainly fiscal policy, designed to restore macroeconomic equilibrium. Myrdal on this occasion also stressed the inconveniences

[2] It is also of interest to note that Ohlin wanted to define 'full employment' as a situation without excess demand for domestically produced *commodities*, rather than as a particular situation in the labour market ([185], p. 5). This definition might formally imply less of a conflict between full employment and price stability, since the ambition to reach full employment in this sense would never imply domestic excess demand for commodities.

created for individuals by detailed regulation of their economic life [172]. Instead he argued for economic planning by *general* methods and incentives.

However, the theories and proposals presented by Gösta Rehn in 1947–9 came to play a particularly important role in the debate about full employment and price stability ([197], [198], [236]). The starting point for Rehn's analysis was that full employment can be achieved in two different ways. One way, criticised by Rehn, is to keep a very high level of aggregate demand, so high that full employment will exist even in the weakest sectors of the economy. As a result, excess demand for labour would prevail in several sectors of the economy – 'more jobs than men' à la Beveridge – as firms in such areas would be anxious to expand output and hence employ additional labour. An alternative road to full employment, advocated by Rehn, was a general, restrictive economic policy combined with 'positive', i.e. expansionary, selective job-creating measures to remove tendencies to unemployment in the weakest sectors of the economy, *without increasing the general level of aggregate demand in the economy very much.*

Thus, according to Rehn, a general restrictive economic policy was necessary, but not sufficient, to guarantee both price stability and full employment. Rehn wanted in fact to push restrictive fiscal policy hard enough to create some depressive tendencies in the economy. But to prevent this from resulting in considerable unemployment, he proposed a vigorous labour market policy, with retraining programmes and compensation to labour for moving from one job to another. Thus, the tendencies to unemployment should be fought directly on the spots where unemployment arose, instead of keeping up the employment level by an expansive general policy on the demand side. Rehn's policy proposals to fight unemployment 'on the spot' also included policy measures to stimulate the establishment and expansion of firms in areas with unemployment. According to Rehn, 'some subsidization of marginal firms may also be necessary' ([236], p. 50).

Rehn argued that with his policy the total level of unemployment would in fact be lower than with a policy of repressed inflation ([197], p. 62; [236], pp. 72–3). Thus, Rehn's proposals – partly anticipated by Ohlin and the Myrdal Commission –

may be characterised as an early discussion of problems that have later been formalised by the Phillips curve concept, and as an attempt to outline a number of labour market policy reforms designed to shift the Phillips curve downwards. (For an empirical analysis of Phillips curve problems in Sweden see chapter 8.)

A basic concept of Rehn's programme was that profits should be squeezed between rising wages and a restrictive demand for commodities, achieved by a demand-reducing fiscal policy, preferably by indirect taxes on private consumption. One of the main purposes was to remove excess demand for labour in most sectors of the labour market, whereby market-induced wage drift could be avoided. Low (average) profits were, in Rehn's opinion, also necessary, if the labour unions were not to be provoked into demanding high wage increases in the bargaining process.

Another characteristic feature of Rehn's proposals was that the labour unions should rely on a wage policy based on 'the solidarity principle', implying that the labour unions in sectors with low wages and profits should not hesitate to push for as high wages as those prevailing in other sectors, at the same time as employees in the latter sectors should accept somewhat lower wage increases. As Rehn recognised, a policy of that kind requires rather centralised decision-making on the union side. Such centralisation was advocated also by Meidner. Rehn and Meidner thought that rivalry among unions about their 'fair shares' could be dampened by this centralisation. (Later experiences indicate that this type of policy would be difficult to achieve also *with* centralised bargaining.)

In their view, labour unions should not accept a differentiation of wages between industries in accordance with the profit situation. They argued that general wage inflation could easily occur if wage differentials were accepted as a means of reallocating labour, as a result of claims to restore the initial wage relationships to groups with smaller wage increases than the average. (However, Rehn and Meidner accepted wage differentials *within* industries due to differences in skill.) Instead of reallocating the labour force by pulling it by promises of higher wages, the labour force should be pushed out of weak sectors by contraction of production and by business failures and helped over to other sectors by the labour mobility policy. Rehn argued that this policy would not only reconcile full employment and price stability, but also speed up reallocations of resources, and hence would be desirable for economic growth.

Thus Rehn proposed a system in which the unions should follow a 'solidaric wage policy', and in which the *government* should pay people to move to new jobs. The payments to unemployed labour for moving would have a double function: to stimulate people to move and to compensate them for the welfare losses they suffered in the interest of the economy as a whole. The latter function recalls the compensation payments in connection with reallocation of resources à la Kaldor and Scitovsky, proposed in theoretical welfare economics to extend the applicability of the Pareto criteria for changes in welfare.

Rehn's proposals were to a large extent incorporated in the economic policy programme of the Swedish Confederation of Trade Unions (LO) in 1951 [235] and later (in 1961) in the report by a public committee on stabilisation policy [264].

The main criticism of Rehn's proposals by economists came from Erik Lundberg and Bent Hansen. However, two of Rehn's basic ideas, which nowadays look more self-evident than at the time they were presented, have been generally accepted:

(1) that price stability is difficult to achieve if general excess demand for commodities and labour is not avoided; and
(2) that the possibility of reconciling full employment and price stability is enhanced if the mobility of the factors of production is increased by a vigorous labour mobility policy.

Lundberg criticised Rehn on both theoretical and political grounds. With respect to theory, Lundberg was sceptical about Rehn's belief that wage increases would necessarily be dampened by keeping average profits low if at the same time the unemployment level was as low as in Rehn's proposals and the profits of marginal firms in some cases were maintained by subsidies. Instead of Rehn's hypothesis that wage increases depended mainly on the average profit level in a sector, Lundberg argued that the size of wage increases depends mainly on the relation between aggregate demand and supply for labour (i.e. basically the same idea as implied in the Phillips curve), and hence (at given supply of labour) on the profits of *marginal* firms, in line with traditional marginalist price theory. Thus Lundberg was inclined to deny that a situation with high average profits and great profit differentials would result in greater wage increases than would occur in Rehn's system where the average profit level for firms was lower but where unemployment was as small or smaller and marginal firms in some cases would be subsidised.

The influence of average profits on wage increases is still an open question. In an econometric study during the fifties, Hansen and Rehn found a strong positive relationship between excess demand for labour and wage increases, but no relationship between profits and wage increases. (However, they used a rather unsatisfactory statistical representation of profits [67].) Thus, this empirical study seems to have given some support for Lundberg's position rather than Rehn's. This holds also for empirical studies on later experiences, according to which the labour market situation, but not profits, would seem to have a significant influence on wage formation. (See the analysis in chapter 8, pp. 151–6.)

Lundberg also argued that the levelling of wages, and to some extent also profits, implied in Rehn's programme would be detrimental to an efficient allocation of resources. Selective job-creating actions by the government, particularly subsidies to marginal firms (which did *not*, however, play a major role in Rehn's programme) may hamper a rapid reallocation of resources in conformity with efficiency criteria. In Lundberg's opinion Rehn had misjudged the *dynamic* aspects of allocation of resources, for instance the importance of profit differentials for such reallocations. Lundberg also believed, contrary to Rehn, that some wage differentials were important as incentives for labour to move to expanding sectors.

Looking at this controversy in retrospect, it seems obvious that there is risk of a conflict between stabilisation and allocation aspects in Rehn's programme. Whereas labour mobility policy à la Rehn presumably is favourable both from the point of view of stabilisation and allocation, selective measures to stimulate economic activity in unemployment areas may, in the long run, easily be detrimental to an efficient allocation of resources for the economy as a whole.[3] However, it has to be added that the wage policy proposed by Rehn, based on 'the solidarity principle', would push up wages in particular for low-profit firms; thus the proposed wage policy would force many low-profit firms to close down. The net effects of these opposing tendencies on the rate of structural change and the allocation of resources cannot be determined on theoretical grounds. The outcome depends largely on how aggressive the solidaric wage policy is pushed and how extensive the system with selective subsidies in practice would be. Moreover, Rehn's proposal should be seen in its historical context of an economy with direct controls and repressed inflation, with the 'allocation distortions' connected with such a system. One of Rehn's main ambitions seems to have been to create a system that would at least be 'better' than an economy with excess demand which was 'held back' by physical controls.

Another difference of opinion about policy was that Lundberg argued for monetary policy, whereas Rehn mainly argued for fiscal actions. It should be noted that Lundberg's plea for a larger share for monetary policy was made against the background of the very passive monetary policy, with pegged interest rates, in the previous period. One of Lundberg's arguments was that monetary policy was a much more flexible tool than fiscal policy, as it could be reversed practically 'overnight'. Against this argument could, of course, be said that it is not enough to consider how long it takes for the authorities to undertake policy actions ('the reaction lag'). It is also necessary to consider how long it takes until the effects emerge ('the effect lag'). For certain fiscal policy actions, such as government purchases of goods and services, the effect lag might be considerably shorter than for many types of monetary policy measures.

There was also an ideological difference of opinion between Rehn and Lundberg. One of the reasons why Rehn favoured fiscal policy was that he wanted to transform a substantial part of business saving into government saving, in order to alter the

[3] It would seem that Rehn, in his early proposals, was hardly aware of this problem: 'The way in which new jobs are created is a secondary question' ([236], p. 49).

distribution of wealth between the private and public sector, in favour of the latter. Rehn also saw fiscal and labour market policies as methods by which the government could achieve a closer control over the economy and push the economic system in a 'socialist direction', in spite of removals of direct controls. In fact, the difficulties created for firms by a very contractive fiscal policy would, in Rehn's opinion, open the way for powerful positive employment-creating intervention in the economy by the government. Lundberg, on the other hand, argued instead that government intervention should be kept at the minimum required to guarantee price stability and a high employment level. One reason for his recommendation of monetary policy obviously was that he regarded this method as more 'general', and hence less 'interventionistic', than fiscal actions. Moreover, he argued that large-scale redistribution of wealth and selective government intervention to create new jobs, as suggested by Rehn, would lead to an 'undesirable' concentration of power in the hands of the public sector.

Lundberg's alternative to Rehn's proposal was a flexible general economic policy, mainly implemented by monetary measures, and a 'lower level of full employment' than in the forties, somewhat similar to Ohlin's proposals. One basic difference between Rehn's and Lundberg's proposals was that whereas Lundberg argued for a *flexible* general economic policy, Rehn argued for a *permanently* restrictive general economic (fiscal) policy; finer, short-run adjustment – what has later been called 'fine tuning' – should in Rehn's system be made through labour market policy and the stimulation economic of activity in particular sectors hit by unemployment.

Another critic of Rehn's proposals was Bent Hansen. He mainly criticised Rehn's proposal of a wage policy based on the 'solidarity principle', which according to Hansen would result in unnecessarily great unemployment in the weak industries [62]. For instance, this kind of wage policy might make it impossible for many firms to survive periods of temporarily low profitability. Rehn's policy could also, according to Hansen, lead to rather inefficient movements of labour from one industry to another and back again (for instance back and forth between manufacturing and public works), which in some cases would be unnecessary if a more flexible and differentiated wage structure were allowed to develop. Furthermore, Hansen could not understand why the labour force should not be allowed to choose for itself whether to stay in the present industry or region at low wages rather than to move to other industries or regions in order to get higher wages. Thus, Rehn and Hansen obviously used different social preference functions. Rehn seemed to have in mind a preference function in which GNP should be maximised, whereas Hansen's social preference function seemed to include also the valuation by employees of different kinds of jobs. In Hansen's view it was obviously regarded as advantageous to economic welfare to allow a wage earner to abstain from a given increase of money income in order to remain in his old profession, industry or region.

One obvious difficulty for a solidarity-orientated wage policy is that attempts to raise the wages of low income groups in a full employment society may easily be accompanied by wage drift for groups with higher wages, so that the attempt to change the wage structure would fail. The result would instead be that the wage policy on 'solidaric principles' would be part of a general process of cost inflation, with unemployment tendencies as a result (in an economy with fixed exchange rates). The empirical evidence of the last fifteen years indicates that something like this has in fact happened (Chart C in Appendix). However, this does not necessarily mean that Hansen's criticism would be illfounded; for in the *process* many firms might go broke, even if in a long-run perspective the effects on wage differentials would be rather slight.

Hansen also outlined positive suggestions for resolving the conflict between full employment and price stability. First of all, he argued for institutional rearrangements in the labour market designed to make the bargaining process less inflationary – for instance by changing the *timing* of wage negotiations so that they would fit better into the process of political decision-making, and particularly into the timetable of budget decisions. He also questioned the extensive use of piece rates in Swedish manufacturing industry (about 60 per cent of all work in the manufacturing sector was paid by piece rates during the fifties and sixties), a system that encourages wage drift in case of the introduction of new technologies. A retreat from efforts to pursue a solidarity-oriented wage policy could in his opinion also contribute to a less inflationary labour market ([62], [63]).

Hansen's main positive contribution to the debate was, however:

(a) a method by which the government might be able to induce employees to accept a wage change consistent with price stability; and

(b) a method to eliminate the price effects of an 'excessive' wage increase that had already occurred ([59], ch. XVII).

Hansen's idea was that the government should use its power over the distribution of income (after taxes) to influence wage changes. In his plan the government should make a decision about the desirable wage increase in the light of expected productivity increases. After that, the government should make public that it wanted the bargaining to wind up by accepting this wage increase. More specifically, the government should declare that if the wage increase was exactly as large, on the average, as the government wanted, the government would allow the wage earners to enjoy the resulting increase in disposable real income, without any attempt from the government to 'take away' additional purchasing power from the consumers. If the wage increase were larger, the government would increase taxes in such a way that the increase in real disposable income for wage earners would actually be *lower* than if the labour unions had accepted the advice of the government.

If, however, wage increases nevertheless became excessive in relation to productivity increases, Hansen proposed a method to eliminate the effects on market prices, without giving up the full employment goal. This method involved a combination of reduced indirect and increased direct taxes. The reduction of indirect taxes (or increase in general indirect subsidies) would eliminate the cost effect of the 'excessive' wage increase (in excess of productivity increase), whereas the increase in direct taxes would eliminate the demand-increasing effect of the wage rise. (To make this policy compatible with the earlier mentioned threat of the authorities to change the income distribution, in this case adversely to labour, the changes in taxation must be regressive.) From this point of view, it would have been quite correct to fight price increases in the forties by low interest rates, appreciation and sales tax reductions – *if* at the same time aggregate demand had been cut back by other means, such as direct income and profit taxation, which as earlier mentioned occurred too late and too little to be efficient.

Hansen also pointed out that there is in general no wage increase that will by itself create equilibrium both on the commodity market and on the labour market. Thus some other economic policy action will always be necessary to guarantee that given increases in productivity and wages would lead to equilibrium in both the labour market and the commodity market. In this analysis Hansen developed ideas that he had expressed in his earlier work, *The Theory of Inflation*, where he analysed the interaction of the factor market and the commodity market in a situation of repressed and open inflation [57]. Hansen's analysis here may be regarded as an extension of Wicksell's cumulative process, particularly as formulated in an article by Wicksell in 1925 [249], in which the process of rising prices and wages was assumed to start from a situation of excess demand for commodities, without Wicksell's emphasis on the difference between the natural and market rate of interest as the driving force.

In fact, this analysis by Wicksell is very similar to Smithies' well-known analysis of demand inflation using the Keynesian 45° diagram [209]. Wicksell showed how a price rise, caused by excess demand for commodities, continued when income receivers obtained higher income via higher prices. As increased purchasing power was created by the price increase itself, the process did not necessarily lead to a new equilibrium position. As Wicksell pointed out, the price increases will stop only when income receivers revise their spending plans by reducing real demand to the full capacity supply of commodities – owing for instance to a rise in real market interest rates or a reduction in the real value of financial wealth (such as money balances).

One of Bent Hansen's contributions in his theory of inflation was to show explicitly how the interaction between the commodity and factor market functions in such a process, and how a quasi-equilibrium of parallel rises of wages and prices might occur. For this purpose he developed his now well-known diagram in which the state of demand in the two markets is depicted simultaneously ([57], ch. VII). In this analysis Hansen distinguished carefully between inflationary gaps in the commodity market and excess demand gaps for factors of production – 'factor gaps'. The signs of these gaps could very well differ in many situations, depending on the real wage rate. By using the same model Hansen also developed a theory of repressed inflation in a system with price control.

Several problems are connected with Hansen's proposed policies for reconciling full employment and price stability. As Hansen himself has pointed out, an upward drift of the average wage level might be difficult to avoid in a labour market that is heterogeneous, in the sense that there is excess demand in some submarkets at the same time as there is excess supply in other submarkets. Stability of the average wage level would in this case require that wage decreases in the latter submarkets fully compensate for wage increases in the former. As wages are sticky downwards, stability of the average wage level is therefore difficult to achieve even if *autonomous* wage increases, i.e. increases not caused by excess demand for labour, could be avoided. However, owing to continuous productivity increases, price stability does not require a stable wage level. But even a rate of increase of average wages in conformity with the rate of productivity increase might be difficult in a heterogeneous labour market.

Another possible criticism of Hansen is that he probably overestimates the authorities' ability to determine the after-tax distribution of income between profits and wages, as well as between different wage-earner groups. Obviously, the general income tax might not be very appropriate for this purpose as there is no close correlation between income bracket and status as employer and employee, nor between union membership and wage level. It has also been argued that to succeed, Hansen's policy would require very skilled and brave politicians. However, this criticism can be directed against any proposal for solving difficult economic policy problems – otherwise they would not be 'difficult'.

Another proposal to reconcile full employment with price stability was made by Anders Östlind [255]. Östlind's idea was to allow relative wages to be determined by negotiated agreements but to have the government assume responsibility for determining the average wage increase. Specifically, the organisations in the labour market would be allowed to bargain over wages, but the government would have the power to reduce all wages afterwards by a given coefficient which would be the same for all employees – a kind of guide-post policy with 'teeth'. An obvious difficulty with this proposal is, of course, that it would give individual unions of employees strong incentives to try to obtain high wage increases, relative to others, without any risks for adverse macroeconomic consequences. Like the proposals by Rehn, Lundberg and Hansen, Östlind's suggestion is interesting *inter alia* in showing how difficult it is to guarantee price stability in a society that wants to avoid both unemployment and centralised detailed government intervention in wage determination.

4 Stabilisation Policy after 1950 – a General Outline

A VERBAL BUSINESS CYCLE MODEL

It is convenient to discuss the performance of stabilisation policy in Sweden against the background of the cyclical pattern in the Swedish economy, which is, in fact, rather typical also for other open west European countries. *Schematically*, the Swedish business cycle may be described by graphic illustration in Chart 4:1. (In principle, we want to describe what might be called the 'pure' cycle, undisturbed by short-term stabilisation policy.) The upswing of the cycle is usually caused by increased international demand for export products, followed by a rise also in imports, induced by the expansion of income and production in the country. Early in the upswing there is also, as a rule, a great increase in inventory investment, in accordance with the predictions of most business cycle theories. The increase in fixed private investment – also predicted by conventional business cycle models – often comes a little later in the boom. (However, in the Swedish setting, the time-pattern for private fixed investment is also considerably influenced by economic policy.) In the early upswing, when there is still unused capacity of both capital and labour within the firms, productivity rises and profits usually go up substantially. Also, the rate of market-induced wage increase – so-called wage drift – accelerates. The rate of price increase, by contrast, tends to accelerate rather late during the course of the upswing; however, if the international boom is connected with considerable price increases in the international markets, the domestic price increases tend, of course, to occur earlier during the boom than otherwise, as was the case in the booms of 1950 and 1969/70.

Rather late during the upswing, the current balance in the

CHART 4:1   Schematic picture of 'typical' business cycle in Sweden

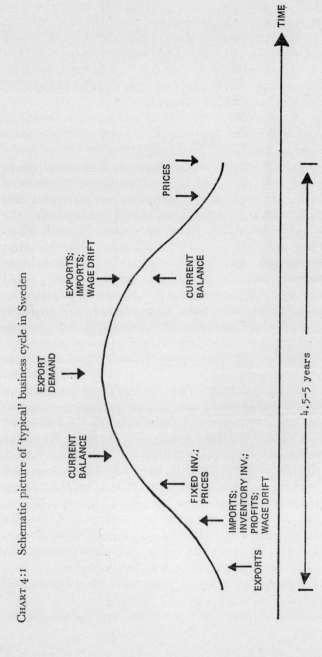

Note: Arrows indicate approximately when the rate of change of a variable typically increases (↑) and falls (↓), respectively.

balance of payments usually turns into a deficit, because of a heavy increase in imports and a retardation in the rate of expansion of exports, both phenomena probably the result of a high domestic capacity utilisation; domestic excess demand for commodities spills over into imports and reduces export incentives, at the same time as the export industries are confronted with shortages of factors of production. For similar reasons the rate of increase in output levels off.

When the international cycle later on turns downwards, export *demand* falls, and the rate of expansion of domestic production slows down still further. However, the rate of expansion of factual exports often keeps the level for a while, or may even experience a new peak (because of backlogs of orders). The rate of expansion of imports goes down, as does inventory investment. The current balance usually improves [126]. Most of the production and sales variables seldom *fall* in absolute terms.

As excess demand for labour goes down, wage drift is reduced. However, the rate of *aggregate* wage increase might still be rather high, owing to bargaining agreements, particularly for wage earners who have lagged during the previous boom, i.e. groups with fixed wage rate systems, such as government employees (see [82], and ch. 8).

It usually takes even longer before the rate of price increase slows down substantially. This is, in fact, a well-known pattern for most industrial countries. As a broad generalisation, we might say that the maximum rate of price increase in Sweden occurs during the first recession year (about one year after the previous peak of the business cycle) and that the minimum rate of price increase takes place during the last recession year, such as in 1949/50, 1953/54, 1959, 1963 and 1968 (see Chart 1:4). It is interesting to note that the rate of increase in *net* consumer goods prices, i.e. excluding indirect taxes, has been no more than about one per cent per year during the last recession year in each cycle (1950, 1954, 1959 and 1968 – the development in 1972 seems to be an exception). Thus, the rate of inflation does seem to slow down considerably by a falling level of economic activity – though with a rather long time-lag (12–24 months).

Closely connected with the fluctuations in output, employment and prices, there is also a cycle in the rate of change in the stock of financial assets, credit and money. There is, as a rule, a strong increase in the volume of credit and money during the recessions and a very low rate of expansion in these variables during booms. This pattern reflects an expansionary fiscal and monetary policy during recessions and a contractive policy during booms. It will be argued in the section on monetary policy (chapter 7) that these fluctuations should probably *not* be interpreted as simple 'causes' of the business cycle, but rather 'enabling factors' for the fluctuations in production and prices.

The anatomy of the cycle can be further illustrated by the statistics on the time-pattern of various components of aggregate demand. This is shown in Charts 4:2–4:4, expressing the yearly fluctuations of various components of GNP, measured as a percentage of GNP during the immediate previous year.

An attempt is made in these (as well as in other) diagrams to indicate the business situations during various years – classified as 'booms', 'recessions', etc. A certain arbitrariness is, of course, unavoidable in classifications of this type, particularly with respect to the exact timing of the denoted periods. Here the labour market situation has been used as criteria for the classifications, more specifically, the difference between the number of vacancies (V) and the number of registered unemployed (U). The classifications of the various periods would not have been much different if instead information from so called 'barometer data' – see below pp. 65-7 – had been relied on (with figures about the fractions of firms with vacancies of skilled labour, or with full capacity utilisation of their stock of physical capital), or if data over the rate of change of output in manufacturing had been used.

Owing to trends in the statistics on vacancies and unemployment, and to *specific* features prevailing in every cycle, it does not seem appropriate to use completely mechanical rules for the classification of the starts and ends, respectively of the various periods (cycles). However, in general booms are said to have started about one or two quarters after every lower turning point for the (V-U) series and to have ended about one or two quarters after every upper turning point. The starting and ending points of recessions are defined in a similar way – *mutatis mutandis*. However, some slight modifications of these general rules have been made in the charts if upswings (downswings) have been particularly rapid or slow, or if they have started from a particularly low (high) level.

As is seen from Chart 4:2 exports (curve A) and inventory investment (B) show a very strong procyclical pattern. The year-to-year fluctuations for inventory investment usually amount to approximately between minus one (or minus two) and plus two per cent of GNP. In the fifties the fluctuations were in about the same interval for fixed private investment (curve C in Chart 4:3), but during the sixties the amplitude may have fallen somewhat for this variable. In fact changes in inventory investment may account for as much as one-third, and fixed private investment for about one-fourth, of the fluctuations in GNP between two consecutive years. It should be observed, however, that the 'import content' of inventory investment may be very high – in extreme booms even approaching unity – and that there is also a considerable import content in private fixed investment (in machines) and in exports – in the case of machine investment on the average probably around 35 per cent, and in the case of exports approximately about 25 per cent. Thus, to a considerable extent fluctuations in inventory investment, and to some degree fixed private investment and exports, influence imports rather than domestic production.

The time-pattern of the various components of GNP is obviously consistent with the generally accepted opinion that exports are more of a leading variable than both private fixed investment and inventory investment (with respect to timing but not to amplitude of fluctuations), and that the business cycle in Sweden is caused mainly by fluctuations in demand for Swedish export products, resulting in a four-to-five-year cycle of about the same kind as in other industrialised market economies (e.g. West Germany) – with booms around 1950/51, 1954–6, 1959/60, 1964/65 and 1969/70.

If GNP is disaggregated further, the instability of the com-

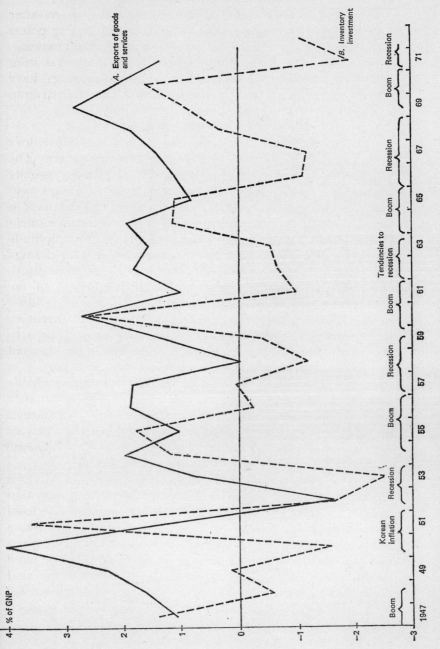

Source: Central Bureau of Statistics: National Accounts.

CHART 4:3 Fluctuations in private investment, public investment and dwellings: per cent of GNP, yearly changes at constant (1959) prices

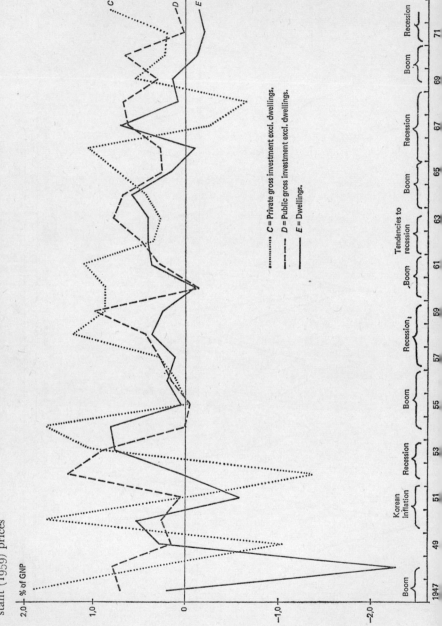

C = Private gross investment excl. dwellings.
D = Public gross investment excl. dwellings.
E = Dwellings.

prices

% of GNP

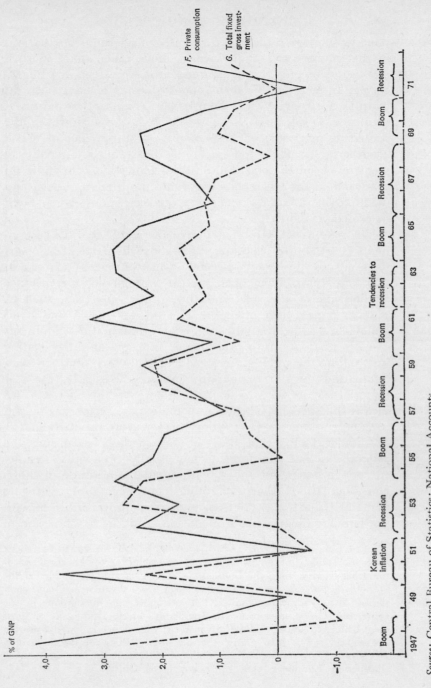

Source: Central Bureau of Statistics: National Accounts.

ponents is more pronounced. Thus, considerable fluctuations in the rate of production increase have taken place in such key sectors as pulp, paper, mining, iron and steel, and engineering. In fact, the Swedish economy seems to have been hit by quite as strong cyclical disturbances as most other industrial countries ([136], pp. 148–54; [138], chs. 3, 5). However, the stabilising properties of the economy – the presence of 'shock absorbers', including the effects of the stabilisation policy – seem to be fairly good, as the disturbances seldom show up markedly in the figures for aggregate production (GNP) and unemployment.[1] (1971 and 1972 are exceptions, when GNP increased very little.)

The reason why GNP has been more stable than its components is, of course, that the fluctuations in particular sectors have not always been completely synchronised. When one or two key sectors have been on the way down, for instance engineering or the steel industry, other industries, such as pulp or paper, have often been on the way up. Usually this behaviour has been a reflection of international developments – with fluctuations in the forest industry usually leading fluctuations in mining, iron and steel, which in turn lead fluctuations in the engineering industry. Basically, the raw material sectors tend to lead the finished goods sectors. This means that the diversification of the export sector has helped to dampen domestic fluctuations in aggregate production.

Another factor that may be regarded as stabilising the economy is that consumption has usually risen quite steadily (except in 1951 and 1971), with smaller amplitude of short-run fluctuations than for other components of aggregate demand (Chart 1:5). This is, of course, quite consistent with the familiar theory that present consumption is a function of

[1] Erik Lundberg has tried to measure what he calls the short-term 'shock absorption ability' of the Swedish economy (including the effects of economic policy) by adding the fluctuations in the various six sectors in the economy *numerically*, the sum being denoted 'gross disturbances', and comparing them with the actual 'net' fluctuations, i.e. fluctuations in the aggregate (GNP). According to Lundberg's study, the ratio of gross disturbances to actual fluctuations in GNP was higher in Sweden during the period 1950–65 than in any other industrial OECD country, indicating a relatively high 'shock absorption ability' of the Swedish economy during that period (Lundberg [136], pp. 153–4; [138], Ch. 3).

the income stream during several consecutive periods, rather than of current income only. However, even though the yearly percentage changes are relatively small for private consumption, they account nevertheless for a considerable part of the year-by-year fluctuations in GNP (Chart 4:4): private consumption constitutes about 55 per cent of GNP, as compared with about 9 per cent for private fixed investment and 23 per cent for exports. In fact, private consumption accounts statistically for about as much of the year-by-year fluctuations in GNP as does total fixed investment – during the sixties even more (Chart 4:4). The good time correlation between these series could perhaps be interpreted as a support for a multiplier theory of income determination, according to which changes in consumption are induced by (actual and preceding) changes in disposable income of consumers, which in turn are 'caused' by fluctuations in investment and exports.

As was mentioned in chapter 1, there has been in Sweden a strikingly parallel development of imports and exports. This observation holds in particular for long-term, but to some extent also for short-term, developments. As a result, Sweden as a rule has not experienced any severe balance-of-payments problems, even though the balance on trade account tends to weaken during boom periods, often by about one per cent of GNP (Charts 4:5A and 4:5B). This weakening of the trade balance, and as a consequence also the entire current balance, in each boom, is presumably caused by the noted tendency for domestic excess demand to 'spill over' on to imports when a very high capacity utilisation is reached in the Swedish economy, usually round about the second year of every boom. In fact, in 1947, a year of substantial domestic excess demand for commodities, the deficit became so large that a balance-of-payment crisis did occur. And even the rather modest deficits in the current balance in 1965/66 and 1969/70 were serious enough to induce the government to introduce a rather restrictive demand management which was extended into the subsequent recessions (1967/68 and 1971/72). It would also seem as if the frequency and the size of deficits in the current balance have increased from the early fifties, up until 1970, mainly on account of a strong negative long-term trend in transfers and services (Charts 4:5A and 4:5B).

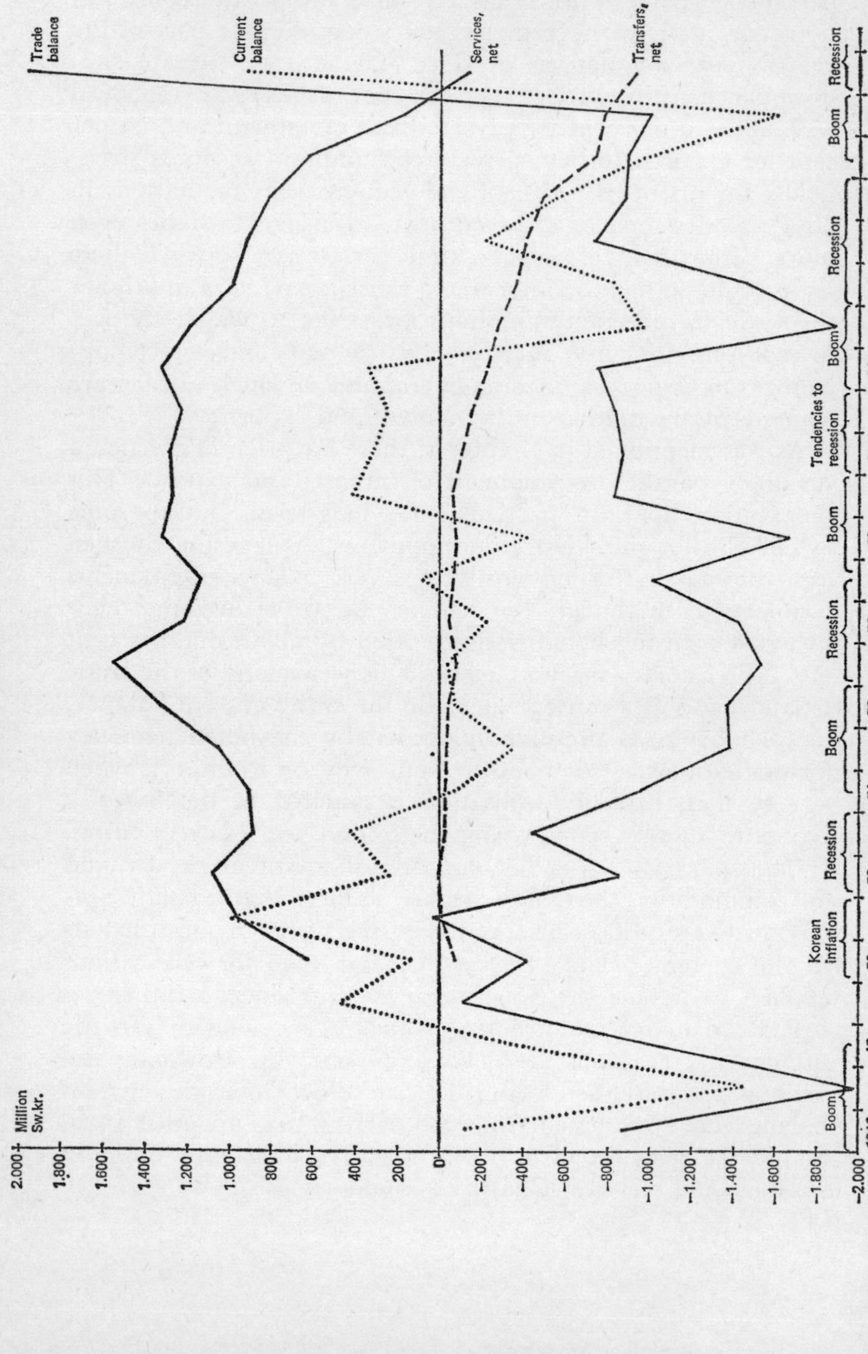

CHART 4·5A Balance of payments: components (million Sw.kr.)

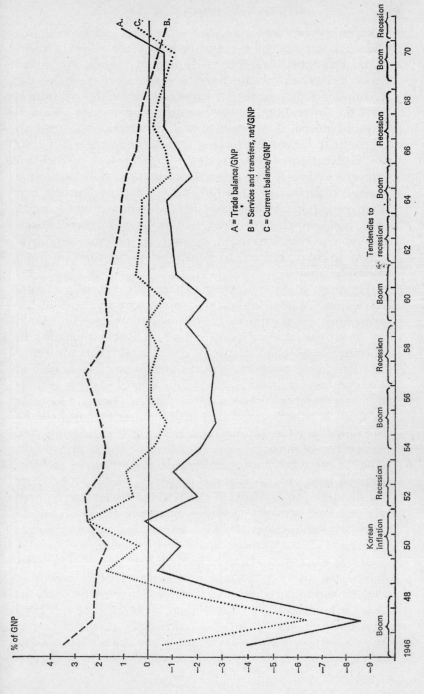

% of GNP

A = Trade balance/GNP
B = Services and transfers, net/GNP
C = Current balance/GNP

A.
C.
B.

Boom · 1946 · 48 · Korean inflation · 50 · Recession · 52 · 54 · Boom · 56 · Recession · 58 · 60 · Boom · 62 · Tendencies to recession · Boom · 64 · 66 · Recession · 68 · Boom · 70 · Recession

Source: The Central Bank of Sweden: Sveriges Riksbank, Yearbook; and *Den svenska betalningsbalansstatistiken* (SOU 1971:31).

The rather parallel fluctuation of imports and exports was also characteristic of the period before the Second World War. Erik Lundberg has attempted to explain the rather 'good behaviour' of the Swedish balance of trade by the favourable development of exports and by the hypothesis that the fluctuations in the Swedish economy are so much export-induced that imports and exports always tend to fluctuate in the same direction ([135], [136], pp. 142–6). As an explanation of the impressive development of Swedish exports, Lundberg has pointed out that the bulk of exports consists of products with a rather high income elasticity, and that the export markets have been dominated by countries with high growth rates (western Europe). Moreover, a considerable diversification of exports on different countries seems to have helped to limit the fluctuations in total Swedish exports.

However, it is necessary to explain not only why exports have risen rapidly, and why imports have changed in the same direction as exports, but also why both have fluctuated by about the same amount in volume. The explanation is, of course, to be found in specific constellations of quantitative relations in the Swedish economy concerning factors such as the propensities to save, invest and import. As a generalisation we might say that, on the average, a 1 per cent increase in GNP in other countries (OECD countries, weighted by Swedish exports to various countries), tends to be connected with a rise of about 1·7 per cent in the exports of Sweden. And for every percentage increase in production in Sweden, imports tend on the average to rise by about 1·8 per cent (Hultcrantz [76]). Thus, if the business cycle is fairly well synchronised between countries, in timing as well as amplitude, we would expect Swedish export and import volumes to change almost proportionally over the cycle.

In the context of a simple, perhaps too simple, multiplier model for an open economy, a parallel development of exports and imports requires that the difference between the marginal propensities to save and to invest, the marginal propensity to 'non-spend', be numerically small relative to the marginal propensity to import: If the autonomous change in exports is denoted by X, the induced change in imports will be $M = X \times m/(m + s)$, where m = the marginal propensity to import and s = the marginal propensity to save minus the marginal propensity to invest. Obviously M is approximately equal to X, if s is small relative to m.

Furthermore, no substantial changes in the terms of trade – defined as the ratio between an index of export and import prices – have occurred to disturb the balance of trade; part of the expansion of this is presumably that raw materials, the prices of which fluctuate more than other commodities, play about the same role on the export and the import side.[2]

Short-term capital movements, moreover, usually seem to have been stabilising rather than destabilising, in contrast for example to the experience of the United Kingdom. Short-term capital tends to flow into Sweden in periods of boom, excess demand and a deficit trade balance, probably because of the then relatively high interest rates and stiff credit rationing in Sweden as compared with many other countries.[3] An exception is the development in 1969, when capital flowed out during the early boom, presumably because Swedish interest rates lagged the development on the Eurodollar market for about half a year. However, what did occur seems to some extent have been simply shifts of foreign assets from the central bank to private Swedish asset holders (firms) [47].

These phenomena probably reflect in part an increased interest-elasticity of capital movements between countries in the late sixties, because of the emergence of an international money and capital market. In principle, the increased flexibility in exchange rates from 1973 might modify this tendency to a higher interest rate elasticity of capital movements. (Sweden has from 1973 pegged to the D-Mark rather than, as earlier, to the US dollar.)

[2] The net balance on current account has been rather close to zero most of the time; otherwise parallel fluctuations in export and import prices would have influenced the surplus (deficit) on current account.

[3] These short-term capital movements show up mainly in the 'residual' item in the balance of payments, which consists partly of trade credit, for which capital movements are free. (However, a considerable part of the 'residual' term is due to errors and omissions in the trade statistics (see Grassman [45];[46]).) For a theoretical and empirical study of foreign trade credit, see also Hansen [64].

ASSESSMENTS AND FORECASTS

The official analyses of the present, and forecasts about the future business cycle situation in Sweden are made by the publicly-owned National Institute of Economic Research (*Konjunkturinstitutet*) and by the Treasury Department. The studies are published in annual reports by the former, and in biannual so-called 'national budgets' by the latter authority. The national budgets may be characterised as a blend of diagnoses, forecasts and programmes, with the emphasis in recent years more and more on the first two aspects.

The main sources of data in the official analyses and forecasts are nowadays (1) inquiries among firms about expectations and plans – including so-called 'barometer data'; (2) national account statistics; (3) plan data from public authorities; and (4) miscellaneous relevant economic statistics, such as data on prices, wages, the labour market situation (unemployment, vacancies, etc.), the credit market situation, the balance of payments, etc.

The methods used are pragmatic and eclectic.[4] As a broad generalisation we may characterise the forecasts for various components of GNP as follows. The forecasts on public investment and public consumption are taken from the 'plan figures' of the public authorities, possibly modified for local authorities by considerations of availability of liquid assets, credit and various factors of production. The forecasts for housebuilding are taken from government plans, because the supply of government credit is strategic for the volume of housebuilding, and because building starts for housebuilding are largely controlled by government agencies. Forecasts for private investment – fixed investment as well as inventory investment – are largely based on the answers to inquiries, somewhat modified by other information, such as the financial situation of the firms and the conditions (expected by the forecasters) in the credit market.

In these analyses, attempts are made to follow the chain of events during the cycle, for example from new orders to changes in raw material inventories, to purchases of raw materials,

[4] For discussions of methods used in assessments and forecasts of the business cycle in Sweden, see B. Kragh ([101],[103], [104]) and E. Lundberg [130].

production, demand for labour, capacity utilisation, changes in
inventories of finished goods, deliveries, etc.

This analysis relies to a large extent on so-called 'barometer
data', which consists of judgements made by the firms. The
judgements are presented as figures on, for instance, what
proportion of firms (weighted by their output) that may have just
experienced or expect positive and what proportion negative
developments in a given variable, or consider some variable
(order stocks, inventories) as too small or too large, respectively
('diffusian indices'). In a way, the barometer method may be
regarded as an empirical application of the methods of the
Stockholm School from the thirties, where economic sequences
for the economy were developed on the basis of expectations and
plans (*ex ante* analysis). The barometer data are probably the
most important type of information used in short-term forecasting in Sweden.

A schematic summary of some barometer data is given in
Chart 4:6 (see O. Virin [251]). In part 1 of the chart, the
vertical axis denotes per cent of firms reporting full capacity
utilisation of the stock of physical capital (the upper curve),
per cent of firms with unfilled vacancies (lower curve) and
the average of the two (middle curve). The other sections
denote 'net' figures on judgements by the firms – computed
as the percentage of firms that are experiencing an increase
in a given variable (such as new orders) *minus* the percentage
of firms that are experiencing a fall in the same variable,
both figures weighted by the production volume of the
firms under consideration. Part 5 of the chart shows the
percentage of firms that regard inventories as too large
minus the percentage of firms that regard inventories as too
small, weighted by the production volume.

The business cycle in Sweden is reflected very clearly in
these diagrams. Of particular interest for forecasting is the
fact that new orders and delivery times lead the production
cycle, making these two variables useful early buisness cycle
signals.

The shaded areas in the chart indicate booms, defined on
the basis of series of production volume and capacity utilisation figures from the 'barometers'. More specifically, in this

particular diagram the *end* of a boom is defined as the time when the curve denoting increase in production reaches a bottom level, or a zero level. This *happens* to occur in all booms recorded in the diagram over the capacity utilisation index at the figure 58 on the vertical axis. The start of the next boom is defined as the time when the same figure is reached again for the capacity variable.

The timing of the business cycle, according to these definitions, differs slightly from the timing of the cycle as suggested by the other diagrams of the present book (which, as earlier mentioned, build on data for the labour market situation).

Also, forecasts for exports are based largely on the judgements by firms in inquiries, although here too the situation on foreign markets as expected by the forecasters also plays an important role. For all these components of aggregate demand – public expenditure, housebuilding, private investment and exports – practically no econometric techniques at all are used in the analyses (except for some simple figures on Swedish export shares in foreign markets). Analytically, we may say that all these variables, in the first round of the analysis, enter the analysis as exogenous, or independent, variables.

The two remaining components of aggregate demand – private consumption and imports – are usually treated in the forecasts as more like endogeneous variables. Both are derived from information on other variables, consumption being regarded as a function mainly of the level and change of income, and import as a function chiefly of the level and composition of domestic expenditure, production and the level of capacity utilisation. These, then, are some of the simple econometric techniques used. However, the forecasts are also modified by various kinds of *ad hoc* considerations, such as price expectations, the availability of liquid assets and the labour market situation (including judgements by the Labour Market Board).

On the basis of all these kinds of information the forecasters try to construct a reasonably consistent picture by a kind of 'iterative process' of analysis, where the various components are adjusted to each other. By using this type of informal approach, forecasting becomes, of course, as much an art and exercise of

CHART 4:6   Some business indicators for Swedish manufacturing

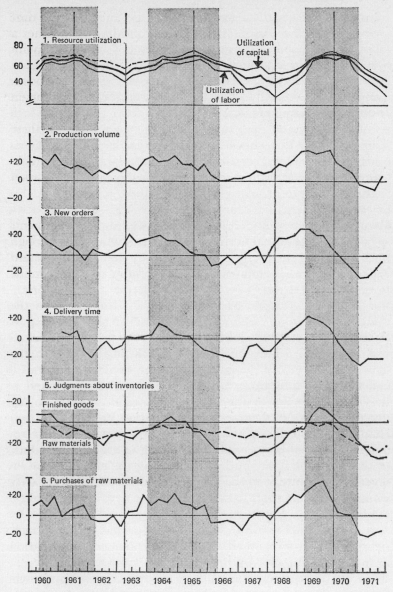

Shaded periods denote booms, as defined in the text.

Source: National Institute of Economic Research: Business Tendency Survey, Dec. 1971 and Sept. 1972.

common sense as of formalised scientific methods. In fact, forecasters in Sweden have shown a considerable scepticism towards 'mechanical' econometric methods, based only on previously observed quantitative relations in the economy. However, partly for experimental purposes, and partly as a complement to these techniques of forecasting, the National Institute of Economic Research has also built a large-scale econometric model for forecasting and policy simulation. Responsible for this work has been Lars Jacobsson [80]. (Some other model-building groups in Sweden are also working on 'complete' econometric macro models in the early seventies.)

It is difficult to make a general judgement about the quality of the assessments and forecasts in Sweden. A characteristic feature has been to underestimate the amplitude of the fluctuations. This observation holds for practically all variables. Such conservatism in official forecasts is in fact rather a general experience in many countries, owing probably to an inclination to try to avoid drastic forecasting mistakes in individual years. Forecasts may in many cases also include elements of wishful thinking, party-policy tactics and possibly also attempts to influence expectations and behaviour in the private sector.

This general feature of Swedish forecasting is illustrated in Chart 4:7 for yearly changes of GNP. It would seem from the chart that the forecasters during the fifties tried to catch year-by-year differences in the rate of change of GNP, but that during the sixties they tended to assume that GNP would change in about the same way every year – a rate of change by about 4 per cent per year. It is tempting to argue, on the basis of this chart, that the authorities during the sixties and early seventies, in contrast to the fifties, have to a considerable extent *abstained* from attempts to catch the year-to-year fluctuations of GNP.

A related feature of the forecasts in Sweden is to underestimate *new* short-term trends in several strategic variables, such as in exports, imports and inventory investment; consequently, there are a great number of 'turning-point' mistakes in the forecasts. There have been eight errors regarding the turning points for GNP and exports, six for fixed private investment and three for inventory investment – out of eleven turning points. (There are difficult problems in the interpretations of these

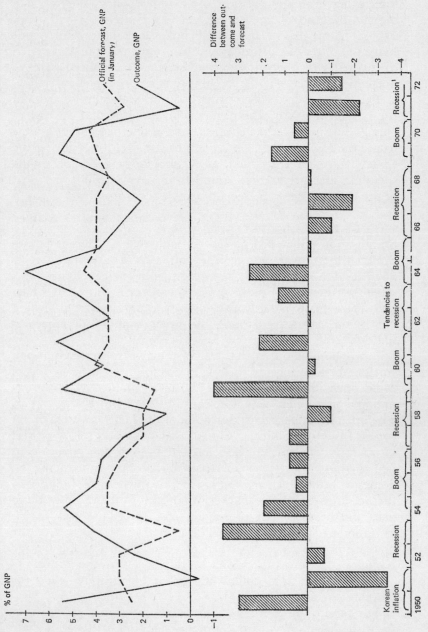

Source: Central Bureau of Statistics: National Accounts; and National Institute of Economic Research: National Budgets (forecatss made in January).

forecasting mistakes, as the economic policy might have *changed* because of the forecasts. See Hultcrantz [76], pp. 156–8.) However, it has usually not taken more than about half a year after the turning points before the mistakes have been discovered, which means that the assessments and forecasts have not entirely ruled out the possibility of counter-cyclical policy.

The forecasts have been quite good for wages and prices. In the case of wages an explanation is presumably that the rate of change has not fluctuated more than a few percentage points from year to year (8–11 per cent increase each year during the sixties). The forecasts have also been fairly good for public spending and private consumption (*usually* within 1 per cent of the correct figures in recent years, except in 1971).

TRENDS IN STABILISATION POLICY
Stabilisation policy has passed through many different phases during the postwar period. The emphasis on different targets has varied, and the policy-mix of instruments has changed. (A schematic picture of main policy measures is shown in Chart 4:8; there is unavoidably a strong subjective element in picking out 'main' measures among the great number of measures undertaken.)

As was pointed out in chapter 2, a policy of repressed inflation was pursued during the forties. It was followed by a period of rapid open inflation in 1950–2, initiated mainly by the international price increases in connection with the Korean War. The open inflation occured in spite of the fact that most direct controls, such as building control and price control, were still in operation. Immediately before, in 1946–9, the government had tried to prevent price increases abroad from influencing the domestic price level, *inter alia*, for the purpose of supporting the attempts of labour market organisations to stabilise (dampen) the development of wages. One technique was to use subsidies to counteract the effects on domestic prices of the increase in import prices when Sweden, following the United Kingdom, devalued the krona by 30 per cent in the autumn of 1949. However, this policy was given up entirely when the Korean War in 1950 inflated world market prices.

The most important economic policy decision of the government at this time was no doubt the decision *not* to appreciate the Swedish krona in 1950/51; this would have been necessary in order to isolate the Swedish price level from the violent price increases in the world market. (Alternatively, we may, with hindsight, say that the 1949 devaluation was too large from the point of view of economic stabilisation.) Instead the Swedish government declared, in contrast to the policy in 1946, that an adjustment to international price increases was necessary – a 'once-and-for-all inflation' – and that full employment would be guaranteed by an expansion of aggregate demand (in money terms) in line with the domestic increase in production costs.

The Korean inflation had a considerable impact on the economic policy debate in Sweden. Bengt Metelius and The National Institute of Economic Research analysed how price increases of imports and exports were spread within the Swedish economy both 'vertically', i.e. through different stages of the production process, and 'horizontally', i.e. to adjacent commodities and markets, above all between commodities that were close substitutes to each other ([156], ch. 4). (The same problem had been analysed theoretically by Hammar-skjöld in the thirties [52]).

The Korean inflation made it clear that isolation of the economy from foreign price influences would require a flexible exchange rate policy. There was a detailed analysis by Bengt Metelius of how such a policy would be implemented, and supported by other policy actions, in a situation where export and import prices increased at quite different speeds ([156], ch. 9). Bent Hansen showed that policy tools other than exchange rates were necessary to guarantee equilibrium in the balance of payments if the exchange rate was used to isolate domestic markets from price fluctuations abroad ([59], ch. XVIII).

The rate of inflation accompanying the Korean War was more rapid in Sweden than in many other countries – 20 and 7 per cent in 1951 and 1952, respectively, for the GNP deflator (very uncertain figures for these years). One reason was that the Korean boom inflated the prices of raw materials in particular, and these at that time played a great role for Swedish foreign trade both on the import and export side. Another explanation for the rapid price increase was that the wage increase reached a very high level during these years – about

CHART 4:8A   Stabilisation policy actions 1945–59 – schematic picture

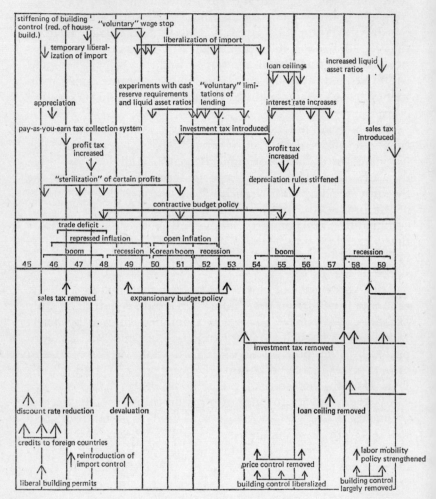

CHART 4:8B   Stabilisation policy actions 1960–71 – schematic picture

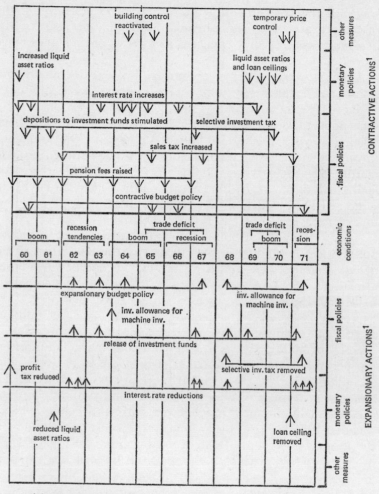

1) In some cases, it is open to some discussion whether an action should be called "contractive" or "expansionary"

20 per cent in both 1951 and 1952. This wage explosion has often been 'explained' as a result of the frustration among employees that had accumulated during the previous wage freeze. A specific reason for the wage explosion was that the wage earners tried to compensate themselves not only for the price increases that had already occurred, but also for the price increase that they expected as a result of their own wage increase.

After the Korean War economic policy was liberalised considerably in the sense that direct controls were gradually replaced by general fiscal and monetary policy (see Chart 4:8). One important step in this direction, which had already been taken in 1949, was carried much further in 1952 and 1954 through the successive liberalisation of foreign trade, initiated mainly by the activities of OEEC. This policy was greatly facilitated, of course, by the creation of the European Payments Union (EPU), which made bilateral balancing of trade no longer necessary.

Another important step in the liberalisation of economic policy was the gradual abolition, during the late fifties, of the licensing control over building. In fact, this had been proposed already in 1951 by the Building Control Committee (of which Erik Lundberg was a member and Lars Lindberger the Secretary [259]). A certain control of the *timing* of building starts was retained, however, through the requirement of permits for building starts from local labour market authorities, the permits being issued on the basis of the local availability of building workers. This control of timing was mainly justified as a method of ironing out seasonal fluctuations in building activity.

Another development in the liberalisation of economic policy was that price control was gradually abolished in the middle of the fifties. It was replaced by a very positive attitude towards price competition, which was supported by a new anti-monopoly legislation. The new policy, hinted at earlier by the Myrdal Commission, was adopted by Parliament in 1955 on the proposal of a government committee headed by Richard Sterner [263]. The policy was supposed to include continuous public studies and reports on the development of prices and margins in the private sector; in practice, there has been very little of this, except possibly in the retail sector. However, a temporary price freeze, lasting about 14 months, was implemented in the 1970 boom. And in 1972 the Government was given powers to introduce future price freezes without the prevalence of extra-ordinary circumstances, a power used to some extent in 1972–4.

General monetary and fiscal policy began to play an increasingly important role in the fifties. Thus, the low-interest rate policy of the forties – heavily criticised by economists such as Bertil Ohlin, Arthur Montgomery, Erik Lindahl and Erik Lundberg, as well as by bankers such as Jacob Wallenberg, Ernfrid Browaldh and Lars-Erik Thunholm – was gradually abandoned after the mid-fifties, though at first rather reluctantly. The shift in monetary policy started with, and has all the time been accompanied by, numerous experiments with direct control of the portfolio policy of the banks and other credit institutions – cash and liquidity ratios, loan ceilings, control of bond issues, etc. (see chapter 7). In this way the excess demand in the markets for commodities, which had characterised the policy in the forties, was replaced by excess demand in the credit market (whereas the government in the forties had supplied practically all credit demanded by pegging interest rates).

Tax policy also came to play a more important role than before. Some attempts made in the forties to 'sterilize' unusually high business profits were repeated during the Korean boom; these 'sterilized' profits were paid back from 1958. Also, profit tax rates, and to some extent depreciation rules, were stiffened in 1955 for the purpose of economic stabilisation.

From about 1960 indirect taxation came to play an ever more important role, by social security fees paid by employers and by the introduction and gradual increase of a sales tax, later on changed to a value-added tax. The value-added tax is currently (1972) 18 per cent. The most important part of the social security fees is the compulsory pension system (the ATP-, or AP-system), introduced in 1960 and designed to guarantee most income earners a total pension amounting to 60 per cent of their previous peak incomes (average of fifteen best years).[5]

[5] However, income earners with an income above 50,000 kronor, i.e. 11,000 dollars, in real terms in 1971 prices will get a pension that is less than 60 per cent of their income; and the more their (average) income exceeds 50,000 kronor the less will the pension be in relation to income.

The social security fees, paid mainly by the employers, were in the early seventies about 10 per cent of the total wage sum. There is also a special tax on the wage sum (i.e. a tax on the use of labour), amounting to 4 per cent from 1973.

Since the pension plan was expected to result in a fall in private saving, a pension fund was created on the basis of pension contributions, paid by firms in proportion to labour costs. As the pension fees during the first two decades of the pension system will be considerably higher than the pension expenditures, the pension funds expand very rapidly. However, the contributions to the pension system have not been used for short-run stabilisation policy; the growth of the fund is therefore mainly of interest from the point of view of long-run policy. Indirectly, the creation of the fund has, however, some importance also for short-run stabilisation policy: if profits are squeezed by the rising pension fees, firms become more sensitive to monetary policy. However, to the extent that contributions are instead shifted to the real incomes of wage earners, pension contributions act as a general contractive force on consumer goods demand – until pensions are paid out on a large scale in the late 1980s (see chapter 9).

Owing to these developments, the total tax rate in Sweden (including social insurance), with respect to GNP, has risen from about 25 per cent in the mid-fifties to about 50 per cent in the early seventies (as compared with a rise from 29 per cent to a little over 35 per cent for the average of western Europe). The total marginal tax rate for the economy as a whole has fluctuated considerably from year to year, probably mainly because of short-run variations in the distribution of income, partly caused by fluctuations in employment. (The range of the fluctuations in the aggregate *marginal* tax rate – with respect to GNP – during the late sixties was 30–50 per cent.)

Another characteristic feature of the Swedish tax system is that income taxes play a relatively large role – they accounted for 67 per cent of total taxes in 1970, as compared with 58 per cent for OECD countries in general.[6] To this should be added indirect taxes, and wealth taxes. At the present time a typical married taxpayer with two children, earning an income of a

---

[6] The following countries are excluded in this sample: Greece, Ireland, Iceland, Japan, Luxemburg, Portugal, Spain and Turkey.

little over 30,000 kronor per year (6700 dollars), has an average income tax of about 34 per cent and a marginal rate of about 60 per cent. For households in the low-to-medium income bracket with income-graduated transfer payments, such as housing subsidies or other types of social payments, the total marginal tax rate, *including* reductions in subsidies when income rises, may well be 80–85 per cent. Thus, compared with most other highly developed countries, Sweden must be characterised as a 'high-tax-economy'.

Another way of expressing all this is, of course, to say that Sweden has very many resources into public consumption and transfer payments, and that public investment is to a large extent tax-financed. For instance, public consumption and transfer payments are, as earlier pointed out, as high as 23 and 18 per cent respectively of GNP.

Some new tools of fiscal policy have also been tried, mainly to influence private investment. Two methods deserve particular attention: (1) taxes on investment expenditure ('investment taxation'); and (2) 'investment funds' for private firms (see chapter 6).

As in the forties, government spending has been more or less successfully varied counteractively for stabilisation purposes. Since the policy has been characterised by strong expansion in recessions, more than by reduction in booms, the public sector has expanded much more rapidly than GNP over the whole period (see chapter 10).

The countercyclical variations in public spending have been integrated with a more and more ambitious labour market (mobility) policy. This policy has been rather selective, since the actions have been undertaken in sectors and geographical regions where demand has been particularly weak. The policy has included public works, so-called 'protected works' and purchases of commodities from private firms, as well as retraining and grants to induce the labour force to move.

One important development in the labour market in Sweden in the sixties is the outflow of labour from certain less industrialised parts of the country, mainly in the north. This is probably partly the result of harder international competition and increased returns to scale in some 'process industries' (forestry and agriculture) but probably also of the 'solidaric wage policy' and of the active labour market (mobility) policy. This has created a rising political resistance among the politicians (and the population) in the northern part of the country at the beginning of the sixties – a 'northern backlash'. As a result, government policy started to put more emphasis than earlier on regional development policy. This policy was reinforced in 1963/64 by a programme of subsidies (mainly of capital costs) and loans to private industries willing to invest in the northern areas of the country. The implementation of the investment funds policy has in recent years been used for the same purpose (see chapters 9 and 10).

The most successful time thus far for stabilisation policy in Sweden seems to have been the period 1955–63, particularly 1960–3. A main policy achievement was to move the expansion of private investment from the boom in 1955–7 to the 1958 recession, though this was not enough to prevent a considerable rise in unemployment in 1958 (Charts 4:3 and 1:7). This was brought about by a battery of actions: investment taxes, loan ceiling for banks, interest rate increases and to some extent investment funds policy (see Chart 4:8). In the 1960/61 boom the restrictive actions were instead taken mainly against public investment and, partly by good luck, against private consumption, via the introduction of a sales tax and pension fees. (A lower rate of the sales tax was applied *also* to capital goods and intermediary products up until 1968, when this part of the tax was abolished for the private sector.) The tendencies to recession in 1962 were fought mainly by an expansion of public investment and housebuilding.

The policy was considerably less successful after 1963. The previously noted tendency for restrictive action to be delayed in booms has been accentuated. Moreover, the wage and price increases, which accelerated during the 1964/65 and 1969/70 booms, resulted in cost increases of quite a long duration. One specific reason for these occasions was that, at the end of both booms, a three-year contract between the organisations in the labour market was signed, where the heated labour market situation, and possibly also the experienced and expected price increases, were reflected. Thus two years of demand–pull inflation were followed by a few years of cost–push inflation – partly a result of the previous demand–pull inflation.

The liberalisation of economic policy in the fifties met with very little opposition – except for the abolition of the low interest rate doctrine. Thus, hardly anybody was arguing openly for more rather than fewer direct controls. However, in step with the removal of many direct controls, new methods of economic policy, using incentives and control of credit, have been developed. In this way, even if the detailed direct (physical) controls of the economy have diminished, other types of intervention have instead been introduced. As will be emphasised later (chapter 8), these new methods tended during the late sixties and early seventies to be used somewhat more selectively than previously – regionally and between sectors – much in line with the earlier mentioned recommendation by Gösta Rehn. During the early seventies, there were also some new demands for more direct regulations, perhaps in particular by some young politicians and economists, with no personal memory of the regulations in the forties and early fifties. It is also of interest to report a temporary, but not very rigorous price freeze from the autumn of 1970 to the end of 1971, in view of the rapid inflation during 1969 and 1970 – a rate of price increase of about 6 per cent during the course of 1970; the year-average increased by 8 per cent between 1969 and 1970. Some of the most important factors behind these new demands for more direct controls have probably been the increased emphasis in recent years on environmental problems, income distribution, regional balance, and accelerating inflation.

The influence of stabilisation policy during the postwar period can probably be seen most clearly on the time path for private investment, public investment and housebuilding (Chart 4:3). The year-to-year fluctuations in private investment (curve C) have been fairly moderate in recent years, as compared with those before the mid-fifties, except for the dip in 1967/68. We are not certain if this relative stabilisation (as compared with that before the mid-fifties) is due to the fact that deliberate attempts to stabilise private investment by monetary and fiscal policy were initiated in the mid-fifties. However, studies of the effects of investment taxes and investment funds policies (chapter 7) indicate that this, at least to some extent, is the case. It is striking to see, for instance, how the expansion of private investment was 'postponed' from the

1955 boom to the 1958 recession, which is difficult to explain otherwise than by the influence of economic policy: the introduction of an investment tax in 1955 (in combination with restrictive monetary policy and building regulations) and the removal of the tax in 1958 (combined with the easing up of other policies towards private investment).

It would also seem that the stabilisation of private investment has been brought about by cutting down the investment booms rather than by succeeding in stimulating an expansion of private investment in recessions. Thus, private investment was 'stabilised' at a rather *low* rate of change during the late sixties and early seventies (Charts 1:5, 1:6 and 4:3), up to 1973.

Moreover, as illustrated by the charts, public investment (curve D) has often moved countercyclically to private investment and exports – 1960/61, 1962/63, 1965/66 and 1967/68. There is also some tendency to a countercyclical pattern for housebuilding (curve E), though less pronounced.[7] As a result, total gross (real) investment, excluding inventories (curve A in Chart 4:2), has since the latter part of the fifties shown a more stable rate of change than earlier, though there have been considerable dips in 1968 and, above all, in 1971.

However, even a superficial inspection of these statistics indicates that expansions in public investment and housebuilding during recessions were as a rule cut off too late during the subsequent upswing (which shows up better in semiannual data) – as in 1954, 1959, 1964 and 1969. And in the recession of 1971/72 the countercyclical pattern in these time series broke down completely. This is one, among many, indicator of a severe deterioration of stabilisation policy in

[7] A countercyclical movement of housebuilding and of investment in public infrastructure was typical also *before* the 1930s (see L. Jörberg [90], pp. 25–6). It should be added that there is a tendency for housebuilding and public investment to move countercyclically also in countries with a minimum of short-run stabilisation policy, as in the United States. A usual explanation has been that the factors of production going to these sectors – labour as well as capital – are partly 'residually' determined, to some extent because of institutional conditions peculiar to these markets, and also because of the high interest elasticity of housebuilding. Thus, the 'invisible hand' of the market mechanism in the United States seems in this respect to give somewhat similar results as those of the quite visible hand of the Secretary of the Treasury in Sweden.

recent years – from 1964, and above all during the cycle in 1969–72. (The analysis of fiscal policy in chapter 5 and 6 will make this point more clear.) Another important point suggested by the diagram is that the violent fluctuations in inventory investment look quite 'undisturbed' by the attempt to pursue a countercyclical policy; the incentives for changing the timing of inventory investment in the investment funds system do not seem appropriate, or large enough, for stabilisation purposes.

The charts also illustrate the obvious point that *if* stabilisation policy succeeds in eliminating the 'big waves' in investment activity the small 'ripples' that remain can to a large extent be identified with specific economic policy actions, such as the above-mentioned pattern for private investment in 1955–1958. Somewhat surprisingly, such identification between policy actions and remaining 'ripples' is sometimes regarded in the international literature as an expression for a failure of stabilisation policy. The question is, however, to what extent stabilisation policy can be given the credit for the elimination of the 'big waves'.

These preliminary comments on stabilisation policy in Sweden have been based on a rather superficial inspection of time series of various GNP components, and on the simple 'verbal business cycle model' presented above (pp. 50–63). Only *slightly* more formalised approaches will be used in the analysis of the effects of stabilisation policy in subsequent chapters. The reason for not using more econometric methods is simply the lack at the present time of reliable econometric policy models in Sweden.

5 General Fiscal Policy

PRINCIPLES

A deliberate counter-cyclical fiscal policy was attempted in Sweden as early as 1933, in the first budget presented by the Social Democratic Secretary of Finance, Ernst Wigforss. It appears that Wigforss was inspired to some extent by the British discussion in the late twenties, in which Keynes and Henderson were most active, concerning the possibility of fighting unemployment by expansionary fiscal policy.[1] However, there are also older 'roots' to the idea about expansionary fiscal policy as a method to fight unemployment, both in Sweden and abroad, for instance discussions in the Fabian Society in the UK.

In an appendix to the budget, Gunnar Myrdal defended the new policy on theoretical grounds [168]. Myrdal's analysis was further developed in his pioneering book on *The Economic Effects on Fiscal Policy* [169] (in Swedish), published in 1934. Another pioneering work in the field of fiscal policy was Bertil Ohlin's *Monetary Policy, Tariffs, Subsidies and Public Works* [178] in 1934 (in Swedish). These works, in fact, formed part of the foundations for the highly celebrated 'Stockholm School of Economics' during the thirties, whereby an embryo to a modern (Keynesian) macro theory was formed along the traditions of Knut Wiksell's monetary theory. (Some of the most important purely theoretical contributions to this development were Gunnar Myrdal's two works, *Pricing and the Change Factor* [165] (in Swedish only) in 1927 and *Monetary Equilibrium* [167], originally an article in Swedish in 1931; Erik Lindahl's *Studies in the Theory of Money and Capital* [111], partly published in Swedish in 1930–1; and Erik Lundberg's *Studies in the Theory of Economic Expansion* [126A] in 1937. Other noticed contributions by the Stockholm School were made by Dag Hammarskjöld, Alf Johansson, Tord Palander, and Ingvar Svennilsson; see [108], [109], [210]).

[1] See Landgren [109], Wigforss [250] and Steiger [210].

The objective of stabilisation policy in the thirties was mainly to *even out* cyclical fluctuations, though at the highest possible employment level. It was believed that this could be achieved by underbalancing the budget in recessions and over-balancing it in boom periods. It was argued by Myrdal and others that a policy of this type was quite consistent with a balancing of the budget over the cycle – a principle that was suggested as a replacement for balancing the budget each year.

This type of counter-cyclical policy was officially recognised in the 1937 budget reform, designed largely by Dag Hammar-skjöld. In this reform, a sharp distinction was made between the budget on current account and the budget on capital account. This division was chiefly designed to highlight the development of the wealth position of the public sector, and the contribution by the government sector to capital formation of the economy. It was also assumed that the financing principles should be different for the two parts of the budget. In normal times, the capital budget should be financed by loans whereas the current budget should be financed by taxes. In boom periods the current budget should, however, be overbalanced, hence part of the capital budget would be financed by taxes; in recessions the current budget should be underbalanced, hence partly financed by loans. However, the war soon made it impossible to follow these budget-balancing principles.

Immediately after the war there was a discussion whether these rather rigid financing rules were an impediment to a rational fiscal policy. Hammarskjöld, in a document in 1946 [53], argued that the rules were somewhat too rigid. He believed that it was not necessary to balance the current account over the cycle, although he wanted to be cautious about under-balancing because of possible effects on the future wealth position of the government sector and on the future tax burden. Welinder [243], too, agreed that the rigid budget rules of 1937 were an obstacle to an efficient policy. But he believed, in opposition to Hammarskjöld, that the issue about the wealth position of the government sector was not very important, compared with the goal of full employment, and that therefore deficits in recessions were not much to worry about even if corresponding surpluses would not arise during booms. His main point was that the problem of the size of the public debt is a purely technical tax issue. (Thus Welinder neglected the aspect that the choice between tax finance and loan finance influences the investment ratio and consequently the time-profile of consumption, and hence 'the tax burden', in terms of consumption possibilities between generations.)

The principles of budget balancing played a great role in the economic policy debate during the fifties. The debate was permanently confused, however, since the politicians geared their arguments sometimes to general economic effects on the society, and sometimes to the effects on the financial position of the government (a balanced budget being regarded as a goal). In general, the government was inclined to refer to macroeconomic arguments when it wanted a surplus on the current budget in boom periods and to budget-balancing principles if a deficit tended to occur during a boom. The opposition, at that time anxious to cut taxes, referred to the existence of a surplus on the current budget when they wanted to give the impression that there was room for tax reductions – hence arguing as if a balanced budget were a fundamental goal.

Both the government and the opposition manipulated the division of the budget between current and capital account to support their respective economic policy positions. Thus, when the government wanted to motivate a more restrictive fiscal policy, it moved expenditure items from the capital budget to the current account to increase the deficit on the latter. The opposition, on the other hand, moved expenditure items from the current account to the capital account, thereby 'creating' a surplus on the current account, which was said to indicate space for tax reductions. Thus the division of the budget into capital and current accounts facilitated tactical political man-œuvres and hampered the fiscal policy debate for many years by focussing it on complicated bookkeeping issues understood by very few and of very little economic relevance.

In the latter part of the fifties, the government talked more about the total budget, current plus capital, which usually showed a deficit, than about the current budget, which often was in surplus. An advantage of this, from the point of view of a rational economic policy discussion, was that the interest thereby was directed toward *all* budget items, and not only those that were recorded on the current accounts. However, at the same time a tactical advantage emerged for the government, as it now became impossible to argue for tax reductions or expenditure increases by referring to a 'budget surplus'. The conventional character of this budget balance concept should also be stressed, however, since on the expenditure side credit to housing is included, whereas pension contributions (in the AP-system) are not included on the revenue side. If the credit supplied to housing were replaced by government-guaranteed loans in the credit market, and if pension contributions were included in the budget, the total 'budget' would be considerably overbalanced permanently, without any change in the impact on the economy of the budget.

During the sixties it became more and more generally accepted among politicians that the purpose of fiscal policy was to balance the economy rather than to balance the budget. However, from time to time the fiscal policy discussion – by all political parties – slips back to the pre-Keynesian notion of 'state-financial' considerations, and hence balanced-budget considerations, such as the argument that an expansionary fiscal policy, by way of lower taxes or higher expenditures, is impossible in a recession because the government would lose revenues, and hence be forced to raise other taxes, cut other expenditures, or increase borrowing.

The most penetrating theoretical analysis of the problem of the budget balance by a Swedish author is found in Bent Hansen's book, *The Economic Theory of Fiscal Policy* [59]. Hansen's analysis is an application to fiscal policy of a general theory of goals and means in economic models. The substance of his general theory is rather similar to Tinbergen's well-known analysis of targets and instruments in economic policy, developed immediately before Hansen's analysis. The difference between the two expositions is mainly that Hansen's analysis was developed along more general lines, in the context of an unspecified system of equation à la Samuelson's *Foundations* [205], whereas Tinbergen used more specified and concrete models along the lines of the Central Plan Bureau in the Netherlands.

As an application of his target-instrument analysis, Hansen showed that the budget balance is neither an instrument of policy nor a comprehensive (unique) indicator of the economic effects of fiscal policy. (Both tax revenues and the budget balance are endogenous variables, influenced by the whole macroeconomic development.) For instance, a given change in the budget balance can be achieved by a great number of different measures (parameter changes) all of which have different effects on basic economic variables such as employment, output and prices, and are themselves affected by those basic variables. (These arguments may also to a large extent be used to criticise the use of a 'full employment surplus' as an indicator of the macroeconomic effects of fiscal policy.)

This limitation of the budget balance as an indicator of the economic effects of fiscal policy had been touched upon already by Myrdal, Hammarskjöld and above all Welinder, though without drawing the full consequences of their observation. The point had been brought up also by Erik Lundberg ([130], ch. IX), although without Hansen's more rigorous theoretical framework. As it is methodologically suspect to analyse the *effects* of changes in endogenous variables, Hansen's conclusion was that an analysis of the budget has to be based on changes in the 'true' parameters of action (instruments) of the government, rather than on changes in the budget balance.

Bent Hansen in his *Economic Theory of Fiscal Policy* also tried to show that the adoption of a goal concerning the budget balance, for instance the goal of a balanced budget, was not a restriction on fiscal policy. His argument was that the introduction of an additional goal meant only that an additional instrument has to be introduced, which naturally follows from Tinbergen–Hansen's theoretical analysis of the relationship between goals and means in a general equilibrium model, according to which it is necessary to use the same number of means as the number of goals.[2] However, against Hansen's line of reasoning it can be argued that there is always a restriction on the number of parameters available to the government, and on the ways in which these parameters can be changed. There-

[2] Hansen admitted that there may be *specific* models where a smaller or larger number of means than goals were sufficient (necessary) ([59], pp. 9–22). As illustrated by analyses by the present author ([117], pp. 151–73; [120], pp. 67–72) and Puu ([194], pp. 56–68), such models may be quite common in economic theory.

fore, there is in reality only a limited number of policy mixes that are politically feasible in a given political situation. If an additional goal is established, such as a given state of the budget balance, the number of politically feasible policy mixes is still further reduced, and might even become zero. Thus, the introduction of a goal concerning the state of the budget will in practice reduce the freedom of action for fiscal policy, and consequently be a restraint for fiscal policy ([115], ch. 1).

Another application of Hansen's target-instrument analysis was to demonstrate that the various economic policy actions must be co-ordinated if the policy is to be successful. Hansen's analysis was partly a polemic against Erik Lindahl, who wanted the Central Bank to be responsible for the price level while the government should take the responsibility for the employment level ([112], [265], a public report with Lindahl as co-author). The basic reason for Lindahl's position seemed to be that he did not believe that the political leaders had the courage to take effective anti-inflationary action. For these reasons he wanted an 'independent' Central Bank with responsibility for the price level only. Hansen tried to show how an explosive cobweb cycle for prices and employment may arise if the Central Bank acted in order to reach one goal, for instance price stability, whereas the Treasury tried to achieve another goal, such as full employment: one policy measure would disturb the other. The conclusion was that monetary and fiscal policy had to be co-ordinated in order to reach the double goal of full employment and price stability in an efficient way. (Such problems owing to an unco-ordinated monetary and fiscal policy à la Lindahl would be rather limited if monetary policy has *relatively* stronger effects on the price level than on the employment level – as compared with fiscal policy. This statement is, of course, a simple application of Robert Mundell's 'principle of market classification' – or 'the assignment problem'.)[3]

[3] Compare Mundell's demonstration (in 1962) of how poorly co-ordinated monetary and fiscal policy may create instability, the targets being internal and external balance [163]. However, whereas Hansen argued for a co-ordinated economic policy, in the context of fully informed politicians, Mundell's analysis may be regarded as an attempt to develop a dynamic 'trial and error' process of policy when only 'limited information' (i.e. ignorance) prevails among the policy-makers.

THE RECORD[4]

Hansen's theoretical work inspired the development of methods for empirical studies of the economic effects of fiscal policy in Sweden in the postwar period. The approach of these studies – the first one in 1956 by the present author [115] – was to analyse separately all parameter changes in the government budget on the revenue and expenditure sides and to specify the *direct effects* of each parameter change on the demand for consumer goods and capital goods. The 'direct effects' were defined as the *ceteris paribus* effects, i.e. the shifts in the demand curves in the markets for consumer goods and capital goods. After that, these *ceteris paribus* effects of all separate parameter changes were added for each market. (In the context of a simple Keynesian multiplier model, we may say that the studies specified the multiplicand of the effects of changes in the government budget. See also [61], [65], [150].)

If studies of this type are applied to the policy in the thirties it is easily shown that the role of fiscal policy for the revival from the recession was in reality quite insignificant (as pointed out in chapter 1). In fact, the magnitude of the stimulating (direct) effects on aggregate demand of the expansionary fiscal measures was not more than about 1 per cent of GNP. This should be compared with the 'need' for expansion, which is indicated by the fact that unemployment probably was about 20 per cent, and hence the economy was very far from full capacity utilisation (in 1933). (One reason for the failure to achieve strong expansionary effects in the economy by fiscal measures was that the designed expansion of building construction was wrecked by a country-wide strike in the building sector in 1933.)

For the postwar period a more vigorous fiscal policy can be reported. In Chart 5:1 an attempt is made to estimate the immediate (direct) impact effects of fiscal policy on aggregate demand (the 'multiplicand' in the context of a simple Keynesian multiplier model) – including both the effects of discretionary actions (changes in tax rates and in public real expenditures) and the automatic stabilisers (mainly on the revenue side) – as well as their combined net effects. All effects are expressed as

[4] An historical review of fiscal policy actions for stabilisation policy purposes in Sweden, during the post Second World War period, is found in Lars Matthiessen [150].

percentages of GNP (in the previous year). In estimating the effects on private consumer goods demand, a consumption function of the following type has been used ([122], [150]), which in fact means that the time-lags in consumers' response to policy changes are incorporated in the analysis:

$$C_t = 0.43\,\Upsilon_t + 0.58C_{t-1} - 878.90$$
$$(5.21)\quad (6.27)$$
$$\bar{R}^2 = 0.998$$
$$D/W = 1.98$$

Υ_t being real disposable income and C_t consumption (for period t).[5]

As the figures for public expenditures are taken from the national accounts, the analysis will in principle take account of *all* basic time lags in influencing aggregate demand – the recognition lag, the decision lag and the effect lag. The quantitative estimates do not include effects of fiscal policy on private investment; actions designed to influence private investment have instead been indicated 'qualitatively' by arrows in the diagram – arrows pointing up denote expansionary actions and arrows pointing down denote restrictive actions.

The reason for using this rather primitive analytical technique is that no sufficiently reliable econometric models exist so far for Sweden (or, I think, for any country). Thus the analysis may be regarded as a substitute for an econometric approach – with a combination of, on the one hand, a quantitative estimate of *direct* impact effects on private consumption and public spending on goods and services, and on the other hand a *qualitative* analysis of the direct effect of actions undertaken to influence private investment.[6] The statistical

---

[5] In the case of *temporary* (one-period) changes in disposable income the marginal propensity to consume would presumably be much smaller than 0.43.

[6] Somewhat similar analyses have been presented for the US by E. Cary Brown [27] and Richard Musgrave [164], though with simpler consumption functions – of the form $C_t = f\,(\Upsilon_t)$. Whereas Brown's analysis was confined to the effects of discretionary actions, i.e. parameter changes, the Swedish studies also include the effects of the budget as a built-in stabiliser, i.e. the effects of automatic changes in endogenous variables in the budget. The

CHART 5:1   Impact effect on aggregate demand of fisca

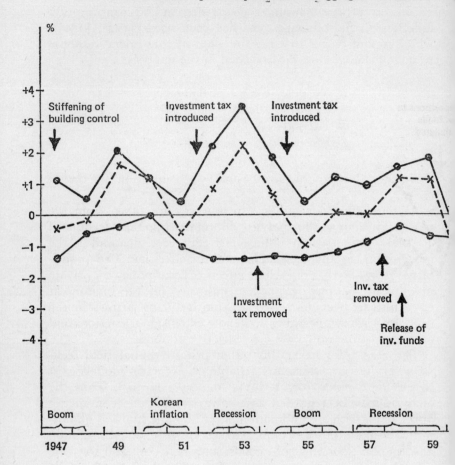

Source: Government budgets; official documen
National Accounts (calculatic

latter effects were defined as the difference between the actual development of the economy in a period and the hypothetical development in the case where no budget items were endogenous variables in the economic system, i.e. where the marginal tax rates were zero. Musgrave, like Bent Hansen, has used a multiplier to get the total effects on GNP.

olicy, per cent of GNP; real value estimates; yearly data

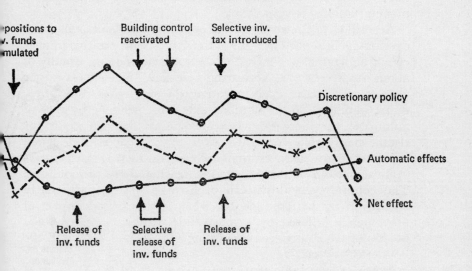

positions to
v. funds
mulated

Building control
reactivated

Selective inv.
tax introduced

Discretionary policy

Automatic effects

Net effect

Release of
inv. funds

Selective
release of
inv. funds

Release of
inv. funds

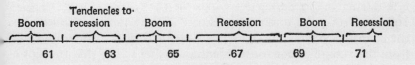

| Boom | Tendencies to· recession | Boom | Recession | Boom | Recession |

| 61 | 63 | 65 | ·67 | 69 | 71 |

m Parliament; Central Bureau of Statistics:
Lars Matthiessen [150])

computations presented here have kindly been supplied by
Lars Matthiessen [150].

The analysis includes both central and local government
activities (excluding the small groups of publicly-owned corporations). Pension fees are treated as indirect taxes, assumed
to be shifted on to households (by way of prices or wages). As

the central government in fact tightly controls the volume of housebuilding – by credit supply over the budget – variation in housebuilding has been treated as a fiscal policy instrument. (The situation has changed in the early seventies; see pp. 102–4.) By contrast, public credit transactions and monetary policy are not included in the diagrammatic analysis. (For an analysis of monetary policy see chapter 7.)

According to Chart 5:1, fiscal policy in Sweden has shown a counter-cyclical pattern most of the time – with positive impact effects on aggregate demand of discretionary actions usually of about 2 per cent of GNP during recessions, and effects rather close to zero (occasionally negative) during booms. The 'automatic stabiliser' on the demand side – for instance by way of automatic tax increases when income in the private sector rises – has varied very little over time. If actions designed to influence private investment are also considered, the counter-cyclical pattern of the policy is somewhat more pronounced. The counter-cyclical pattern of fiscal policy is particularly obvious in the period 1958–62, when the measured impact of fiscal policy differed by a magnitude of about 3 percentage points (of GNP) between recessions in 1958 and 1962 and the boom in between.

However, the same weakness emerges from the analysis as was suggested by Charts 4:2 and 4:3 in chapter 4 – expansionary actions undertaken during recessions tend to be cut off too late during the following upswings, in 1947, 1950, 1954, 1959, 1964 and 1969. An interesting feature of the analysis is also that the counter-cyclical pattern seems to have been less pronounced from the 1964/65 boom onwards than earlier; thus, this analysis too suggests a 'deterioration' of the policy in recent years. For instance, during the 1964/65 and 1969/70 booms the restrictive actions were much weaker than during the 1960 boom, when policy was both strong and well-timed. And during the first recession years after the last two booms (hence in 1966 and 1971) the policy seems, in fact, to have been more *restrictive* than during the previous booms.

Thus, in summary, fiscal policy seems to have exerted a counter-cyclical influence on the economy during most of the postwar period. The restrictive actions have been considerably delayed in the booms, however. And from 1964 the counter-cyclical pattern has hardly been discernible. Not only have the restrictive actions been weak and delayed in booms (1964, 1969) and the expansionary action rather weak also in recessions (such as 1966) but the policy on some occasions is probably best characterised as 'procyclical' (1966 and 1971).

6 Innovations in Fiscal Policy

An important objective in Swedish economic policy in the postwar period has been to control the level of aggregate investment. These attempts have, at least occasionally, met with some success (chapters 1, 4 and 5). We can hardly say that any explicit and uniform theory of investment lies behind these policies.

In the conduct of economic policy directed towards investment, private investment has been influenced mainly by incentives and credit restrictions, particularly after the liberalisation of building control at the end of the fifties. Public investment, on the other hand, has been controlled by direct administrative means and housebuilding mainly through the supply of government credit via the state budget.

THEORETICAL DEVELOPMENTS

In the thirties the single most important policy action to influence private investment – in addition to the 'accidental' devaluation – was presumably the introduction of free depreciation rules in 1938. The main arguments for this change were probably long-run efficiency aspects rather than short-run stabilisation aspects. (Swedish short-run fiscal policy in the thirties was concerned mainly with public works and to some extent private consumption.)

In the postwar period, by contrast, policies directed towards private investment have been geared more to short-run stabilisation aspects, i.e. to influencing the *timing* of private investment – often, in fact, implying a neglect of the long-term consequences for private investment. This is the case for short-run monetary and fiscal policy actions as well as for the stiffening of the depreciation rules in 1955. The latter reform was largely justified as a way of making private investment more sensitive to stabilisation policy – monetary as well as fiscal.

The simple basic idea behind all these reforms and policies has obviously been that the *timing* of private investment can be modified by changes in investment costs, and hence profitability, as well as by changes in 'liquidity', the latter concept referring to the availability of both internal funds and credit. It is difficult to say to what extent the reforms have been influenced, directly or indirectly, by developments in economic theory. The economists of the 'Stockholm School' in the thirties certainly developed sophisticated, though rather esoteric, theories about factors influencing private investment. For instance, Myrdal ([165], [167]) and Svennilson [213] constructed a theoretical framework for investment analysis in which expectations and uncertainty about future prices and demand conditions played a central role, and where Myrdal's new concepts *'ex ante'* (expected or planned magnitudes) and *'ex post'* (actually realised magnitudes) were strategic. Svennilson's analysis may be regarded as a forerunner of what is nowadays called 'dynamic programming', as formulated by, for instance, R. Bellman [16].

However, of more immediate relevance to problems of stabilisation policy is the point made by Tord Palander at the beginning of the forties, in a critical examination of Myrdal's investment theory: 'What is neglected in Myrdal's analysis is that, for an investment to be made at a particular time, it is not only necessary that it is regarded by the entrepreneur as profitable at the time [i.e. in Myrdal's terminology, as getting a gain from investment], but also that the time is regarded by the entrepreneur as the *best possible* for carrying out this investment. In this respect Myrdal is in numerous and famous company which includes Keynes, amongst others.' ([190], p. 33.) Obviously Palander's line of thought has immediate relevance for the objective of Swedish stabilisation policy in the postwar period to create incentives for firms to change the timing of their investment expenditure.

Whereas the stress on the profitable aspect of investment decisions, as well as on the acceleration principle (emphasised by Lundberg in his 1937 thesis [126A]) is in line with the main stream of economic theory, the source of the emphasis on the importance of internal funds and the availability of credit is more uncertain. However, Svennilson stressed the liquidity aspects of investment planning in his study of 1938 [213], and in the middle fifties the importance of internal funds was emphasised by Lars Lindberger [125]. Lindberger's basic ideas, in fact, were rather similar to what later has been called 'the residual funds theory' of investment behaviour, as formulated, for instance, by Meyer and Kuh [157]. However, though Lindberger developed his approach against the background of empirical macro relations for Sweden, there was hardly any rigorous statistical testing of the hypothesis in Lindberger's study.

The concept of the importance of internal funds for investment behaviour was stressed also by Erik Lundberg in the early sixties ([131], ch. 10). In his work the notion that firms prefer internal funds was expressed mainly by the assumption that the required rate of return is higher for borrowed funds than for internal funds, the reason being that the risk of a project rises with the ratio of borrowed to internal capital.[1] The author of the present book has tried to integrate the notion of a preference for internal funds with a general theory of the firm, by assuming that the firm does not maximise profits but rather a preference function in which, beside profit, various types of assets and debt enter as arguments, debt being regarded as a 'disutility' (debt aversion) ([117], ch. 3; [120], sect. II).[2] On the basis of this approach, the availability of internal funds will have importance for investment behaviour even if there are no imperfections in the credit market, in the sense that every firm can obtain whatever funds of credit it desires at a given interest rate.[3]

[1] Lundberg's approach is somewhat similar to the one earlier followed by, for instance, E. Hoover [75] and J. Duesenberry ([36], ch. 5). Lundberg also incorporated an idea from Modigliani and Miller [160] that the financial policy of the firm depends on how different alternatives influence the capital value of the firm in the hands of shareholders.

[2] This approach was inspired mainly by J. Marschak [149] and L. Klein ([95], pp. 27–32).

[3] Other contributions to investment theory have been made by Guy Arvidsson ([12], [13]) and Björn Thalberg ([228]–[230]). Arvidsson has tied together short-run production theory with traditional investment theory, and Thalberg has developed the theory of the market for capital goods, along lines suggested by Haavelmo, where delivery time is determined endogenously together with capital goods prices and investment volume. Thalberg has also integrated his model of the capital goods market

INVESTMENT TAXES, INVESTMENT SUBSIDIES AND INVESTMENT FUNDS

In the Swedish attempts to stabilise private investment, two fiscal policy 'innovations' are of particular interest – taxes on investment expenditure and investment funds policy. As both methods seem to be quite promising ways of influencing private investment, a comment on their principles as well as on their actual use in Swedish economic policy is appropriate.

General investment taxes have been used during two periods in Sweden, 1952–3 and 1955–7, amounting to 12 per cent of investment costs. The tax rate was applied to gross investment in building and machinery, excluding housing and most public investment. Investment taxes were deductible for income tax purposes. As the income tax rate for corporations has varied around 50 per cent in Sweden, the *net* (after tax) investment tax rate was about 6 per cent in the two periods.

Two empirical studies were made in Sweden, using the questionnaire technique, of the effects on investment in industry of the 1955/56 investment tax – one study by Guy Arvidsson [6], the other by Krister Wickman [247]. According to these studies, planned investment by industry was reduced by 5–6 per cent in 1955 and a little less in 1956 owing to the introduction of the investment tax in 1955. The effect of the investment tax, which was declared to be temporary, indicates a short-run *price* elasticity of investment expenditure of about one half.[4] Another interesting feature of the studies is that about one-third of the firms reacted rather quickly – within a year – with cuts in their investment.

In the recession of 1958, when the investment tax was removed, private investment expanded considerably (see Chart 4:3). However, there are no studies of the extent to which this was the effect of the removal of the investment tax and other policy measures, such as an easing of the building regulation and monetary policy or possibly the release of 'investment funds'.

---

into Keynes's and Goodwin's macro models. Arvidsson [7] and Thalberg [227] have also studied how the relationship between interest rate elasticity of investment spending and durability is influenced by eliminating certain *ceteris paribus* assumptions.

[4] The 12 per cent tax reduced demand by about 5–6 per cent.

Since 1958 the authorities have relied on investment funds policy rather than on *general* investment taxes to influence private investment. However, extra investment allowances have also been used at several occasions since the mid-sixties (1964, 1968, 1971–2) to influence private investment. Moreover, a *selective* investment tax has been used on building investment in the service sector and for municipalities (1967, 1968, 1970–1).

The investment funds system had been introduced in 1938, but did not play any role of importance until after 1955, when the system was reformed. With this system, corporations and certain other types of firms are allowed to set aside as an investment reserve fund a certain fraction, 40 per cent, of profits before tax. This investment reserve is exempt from taxation, but 46 per cent of the sum has to be deposited in a blocked account with the Central Bank (with no interest rate); the rest is available to the firm. By certain tax advantages, firms are stimulated to make appropriations to investment funds and to utilise them for investment in recession periods. The idea is, as in the case of temporary investment taxes, to induce firms to change the timing of their investment expenditure from booms to recessions.[5]

The basic incentive in the investment fund system is that firms are allowed to deduct new additions to the fund from their current profit for purpose of profit taxation and that profit tax does not have to be paid when the funds are later used for investment purposes, provided they are used at a time that is accepted by the authorities. Thus, the investment fund may be characterised as an appropriation, free of tax, for investment in the future. The immediate advantage to the firm is a certain gain of liquidity; the alternative to deposi-tions of 46 per cent of the appropriations to blocked accounts in the Central Bank is to pay profit taxes, presently amounting to 54 per cent. The main incentive, however, is that the in-vestment funds, still free from taxes, later may be used for investment expenditures. Moreover, if the funds are used at a time when the government finds this appropriate from the point of view of economic stability, the firm is allowed to make an additional deduction from profits of 10 per cent of

---

[5] For a presentation and analysis of investment funds policy, see Eliasson [39], Edenhammar and Johansson ([37], [85]), Matthiessen [151].

the amount taken from the investment funds. Thus, the system implies tax deductions by depreciation charges in excess of 100 per cent (in fact by approximately 110 per cent) of the investment cost – in addition to the previously mentioned immediate liquidity gain.

Hence, the idea of investment funds is similar to that of accelerated depreciation. In both cases there is a liquidity gain as well as a profitability gain. We may say that the system is approximately equivalent to free depreciation in advance of an investment made during a stipulated 'release period'. The firm obtains a 'tax-subsidy' that amounts to the value of the tax reduction (owing to the deposition and the 10 per cent investment deduction) *minus* the capital value of future tax increases owing to lost opportunities of 'normal' depreciation deductions.

If a firm chooses to use its investment funds without permission of the authorities, which it can, the fund is subject to the usual profit taxation, and there is also a special penalty tax imposed by the addition to taxable income of 10 per cent of the amount taken from the investment fund.[6]

As an indicator of the potential importance of investment funds policy, it may be mentioned that in 1970 the funds amounted to 4000 billion kronor (about 890 billion dollars), compared with a total of gross investment by private manufacturing industry of about 6900 billion kronor per year and about 14,400 billion kronor for total private gross investment (excluding investment in housing).

The government has permitted firms to use their investment funds under favourable conditions during four main periods – 1958/59, 1962/63, 1967/68 and 1971/72. The releases of investment funds have each time been of about the magnitude of 5 per cent of total private investment, with releases spilling over occasionally into the first boom year as well (1960, 1964, 1969) (see Table 6:A). In 1958 and 1959 private investment increased by 7 per cent each year, in spite of obvious tendencies to a recession. However, no empirical study is available of the extent to which this development was the result of the investment funds policy rather than of other measures, such as the

---

[6] The firm can use 30 per cent of the deposition (the so-called 'free sector') freely after five years, however.

Table 6:A

Yearly releases from investment funds

Year	Swedish kronor (millions)	Per cent of total private investment
1956	0·6	0·2
1957	0·2	0·01
1958	29·9	0·54
1959	308·8	5·09
1960	381·0	5·41
1961	172·4	2·12
1962	170·6	1·96
1963	644·6	7·01
1964	313·6	3·15
1965	227·5	2·03
1966	302·9	2·34
1967	536·3	4·11
1968	1421·2	11·47
1969	730·4	5·63
1970	368·7	2·58
1971	988·5	6·82
1972	1021·9	6·52

☐   denotes main 'periods of release'.

abolition of the investment tax and a shift to an easier monetary policy. There seems to be general agreement, however, that the release of funds lasted for so long that a substantial part of the investment expenditure generated by the action came at the beginning of the next boom (end of 1959 and beginning of 1960).

The effects of the release of investment funds in 1962/63 and 1967/68 have been studied empirically by the use of a questionnaire technique ([39], [200]). According to one study, there was a well-timed *net* effect (compared with the hypothetical case without a funds release) on private gross industrial construction during the ten-month period July 1962–April 1963, amounting to about 15 per cent of total annual industrial construction. There was also, during a five-month period, a

CHART 6:1 Effects of investment fund releases in manufacturing industry (seasonally adjusted, figures in constant prices)

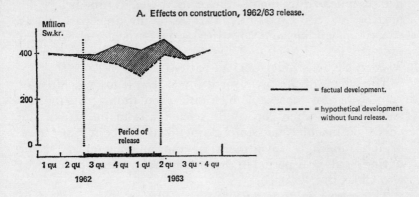

A. Effects on construction, 1962/63 release.

—————— = factual development.

- - - - - - = hypothetical development without fund release.

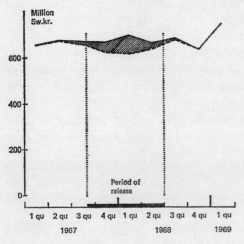

B. Effects on machine investments, 1967/68 release.

Source: National Institute of Economic Research: Investment Funds in Operation (Occasional Paper 2, 1965); and Investment Funds – The Release of 1967 (Occasional Paper 5, 1971).

net increase in orders placed for machinery and equipment of about 5 per cent of total annual industrial machinery investment. That the timing of the policy was good from the point of view of the business cycle is indicated by a finding of the study that the net effect reached its maximum in the middle of the recession at the beginning of 1963, nine to ten months after the announcement of the release of the funds. The effects had disappeared by the middle of 1963, well in time before the next boom. (See Chart 6:1, Part A for the time path of the effects on building and construction investment.) However, a problem for all such policies is that building activities in Sweden have a strong seasonal pattern.

The effects of the investment funds release for machines in 1967 were also successful, including good timing; during the four quarters when the funds release was in operation, the effects on machine investment amounted to about 7 per cent of total machine investment in the manufacturing sector during a half-year period in the middle of the release period (see also Chart 6:1, Part B).

The release in 1971/72 was on a more selective basis than earlier releases, and it also involved less favourable terms for firms. There are presently no empirical studies available of the effects.

PUBLIC INVESTMENT AND HOUSEBUILDING
The most important component of stabilisation policy in Sweden has probably been variations in public spending on goods and services. It has often been argued in the international discussion that short-run variations in public spending do not, in practice, constitute a very useful tool for economic stabilisation. In the case of *current* spending there is probably some truth in this observation, though it should be possible, and in Sweden it has to some extent been possible, to speed up, or even to slow down, *the rate of expansion* of programmes that have already been planned.

More importantly, counter-cyclical variations in public investment spending should be much easier. The technique used in Sweden to make public investment a useful tool of short-run stabilisation policy is rather similar to the techniques used to influence private investment. The *decision lag* has been reduced by keeping a ready shelf of public investment projects and by the right of the government to vary investment spending up and down (in practice by at least 10 per cent), during the course of the budget year, without previous consent of Parliament. This means, in fact, that the decision lag does not have to be longer than the time it takes for the government to judge the conjuncture situation and take action.

The *effect lag* has been reduced by giving various public authorities incentives to prepare continuously an 'actual' shelf of ready projects; most government agencies (except possibly the university system!) nowadays know that if they do not have ready projects when the next recession comes, other agencies will be allowed to fill the vacuum for increased public investment, which means that the agency in question might have to wait for another recession to implement its projects. The *scope* of the actions can also be made reasonably large by holding a sufficiently large shelf of projects. In boom periods, contractive effects can, in principle, be achieved mainly by postponement of new orders and launching of projects; thus in this situation the effect lag would be expected to be more of a problem.

The government has also tried to use counter-cyclical variations in housebuilding as a component of aggregate demand management. The techniques have, as already mentioned, been to regulate the supply of credit to housebuilding, which is largely financed by government credit, and also to influence the timing of housebuilding by the system of building starts, administered by the Labour Market Board according to the local availability of building workers, mainly as a method to even out seasonal fluctuations in housebuilding. A prerequisite for this policy has been that there was a permanent excess demand for housing (owing to rent control), which means that increased building during recessions has not created problems of empty apartments in new houses. However, such problems would occur as soon as there is a tendency to equilibrium in the market for new apartments. This seems, in fact, to have occurred in the early seventies. In a market with equilibrium for new apartments, new techniques would be required to use housebuilding as a tool of counter-cyclical economic policy: for instance subsidies for house construction in recessions, and taxes (or *reduced* subsidies) during booms.

There are other problems, too, connected with heavy cyclical fluctuations in housebuilding. For instance, there is a risk that costs are increased when housebuilding is rapidly expanded, and that these cost increases are not reversed in periods of reduction in housebuilding. It is therefore possible that the rate of inflation in the housebuilding sector is increased by aggressive counter-cyclical policies in this sector. Maybe there is also a risk that such cost increase can spread to other sectors of the economy by way of competition for labour as well as by union demands for 'compensation'.

As was suggested by Charts 4:2–4:4 (in chapter 4), it would seem that the authorities have to some extent succeeded in moving public investment counter-cyclically to private investment, exports and inventory investment; it is of interest to note that this counter-cyclical pattern is most pronounced for local governments, which are influenced by monetary policy, building start restrictions and the earlier mentioned selective tax on building investment. There has been a counter-cyclical pattern also for public consumption by municipalities (L. Matthiessen, [150]). The counter-cyclical pattern is less pronounced for housebuilding. In 1971 the counter-cyclical pattern broke down completely for the entire public sector, including housebuilding. (Some of the reasons seem to have been delayed restrictive policies to fight the rapid inflation starting during the previous boom, balance of payments problems in 1970, and simply lack of skill of the policy.)

LABOUR MOBILITY POLICY AND PUBLIC WORKS

Labour market policy is another area of budget policy in which new tools have been tried in Sweden during the postwar period, in particular since the 1958 recession. The development in this field has very much followed the ideas of Gösta Rehn, with the emphasis, particularly during the first ten years, on methods to increase labour mobility, such as activities of the public labour exchange boards, financial help to people who move from one job (place) to another, organisation and financial help of retraining, etc. However, in recent years there has also been increased emphasis on various types of job-creating activities – protected works and subsidies to the employment of the handicapped.

From 1956 to 1971, the budget of the Labour Market Board rose from 125 to about 2000 million kronor in current prices. In 1971 this is slightly more than 1 per cent of GNP, as compared with 0·2 per cent of GNP in 1956. Direct 'job-creating' activities nowadays account for about half of this expenditure (45 per cent), of which 15 percentage points are on traditional public works and 30 percentage points on new types of public works, so-called protected works, designed mainly for people who have difficulties in obtaining jobs in the open labour market. The other half of the expenditure may be classified broadly as 'adjustment activities' (mobility increasing policies, retraining etc.) and administration costs.

Another way of expressing the importance of various programmes is to look at the number of persons engaged in them. At the present time (1972) about 1 per cent of the labour force is more or less continuously engaged in public works or 'protected works', and another 1 per cent is engaged in retraining organised by the Labour Market Board. The amounts are more dominated by long-term trends and seasonal fluctuations than by the business cycle. These activities together account for about 1·5–2·0 per cent of the labour force in the early seventies, as compared with about 0·5 per cent in the early sixties (Chart 6:2 and Table 6:B).

Table 6:B
Number of persons in public works, in protected works and retraining (yearly averages)

	1966	1967	1968	1969	1970	1971
Public works	4,664	5,433	6,826	4,332	3,197	4,743
Protected works & public works for special groups[a]	14,480	19,987	27,916	29,419	33,415	38,969
Retraining	18,846	23,549	29,593	31,564	33,882	39,425
Total	37,990	48,969	64,335	65,315	70,494	83,137

[a] Such as handicapped and elderly people with special employment difficulties.

Figures on government spending, or the number of people engaged, are a very incomplete indicator of the importance or costs of these various activities. The economic costs for the society of public works and protected works is of course much smaller than the government spending, as a production result is obtained. Their total economic costs may rather be estimated as the difference between the return (value added)

CHART 6:2 Labour force taken care of by Labour Market Board (per cent of labour force according to Labour Force Studies (AKU))

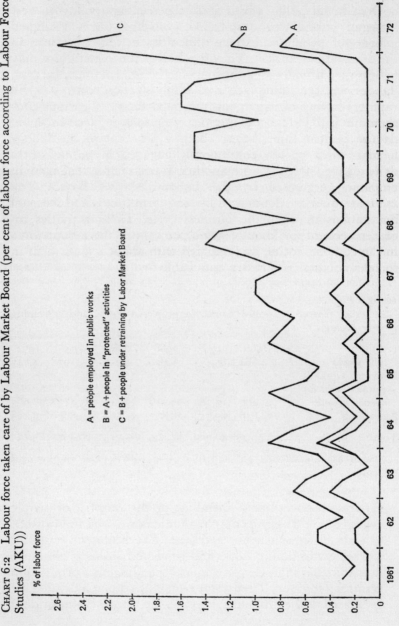

A = people employed in public works

B = A + people in "protected" activities

C = B + people under retraining by Labor Market Board

Source: Labour Market Board: Labour Force Studies, and Central Bureau of Statistics.

of the factors of production in public and protected works, and in alternative uses, which in some cases might be zero. Occasionally, the value added might of course be zero (or negative) also in public works; there may be some 'social benefits' of the employment effects in such cases, however.

Several different goals lie behind the activities denoted 'labour market policy': (1) to give the unemployed work rapidly; (2) to help them obtain new skills; (3) to compensate them financially for adjustments forced upon them by the development of the economy; (4) to make it possible to keep a high level of employment without increasing aggregate demand so much that excess demand emerges in high-employment sectors (i.e., labour mobility is designed as a method to make it easier to reconcile full employment and price stability); (5) to facilitate the rate of structural change of the economy. There is hardly any doubt that the policy has made important contributions to solving the first three social and distributional problems. It will be discussed later (chapter 8) whether the policy has also helped to solve the remaining two problems.

7 Experiences of Short-Term Monetary Policy

THE RECORD

The history of Swedish short-term monetary policy after the Second World War might be divided schematically into three periods (long-term financial problems will be discussed in chapter 11):

(1) *1945–50*: pegged interest rates and an easy ('passive') monetary policy;
(2) *1950–55*: attempts to pursue a tight monetary policy at low interest rates and with direct controls in the credit market;
(3) *1955–* : more and more reliance on 'high' and flexible interest rates, still with a number of credit market regulations.[1]

Monetary policy in Sweden during the first years after the war followed the same general pattern as in most other countries. The stabilisation of the interest rate at a low level, about 3 per cent for long-term government securities, and consequently also for private bonds was the main goal (Chart 7:1). The arguments for this policy were about the same as in most other highly developed countries. Thus, reference was made to various 'undesirable' side effects of higher interest rates: effects on the distribution of income and on the interest cost of the government debt, 'disturbances' on the credit market (falling asset prices and increased uncertainty about such prices), etc. However, particular importance was attached to the fact that in a regulated economy (with price control based on production costs), higher interest rates result in

[1] For an empirical survey of monetary policy in Sweden see K. Kock [96].

CHART 7:1 Discount rates and interest rates on manufacturing bonds

A = Official discount rate

B = Interest rate on manufacturing bonds (chained to new series in 1971)

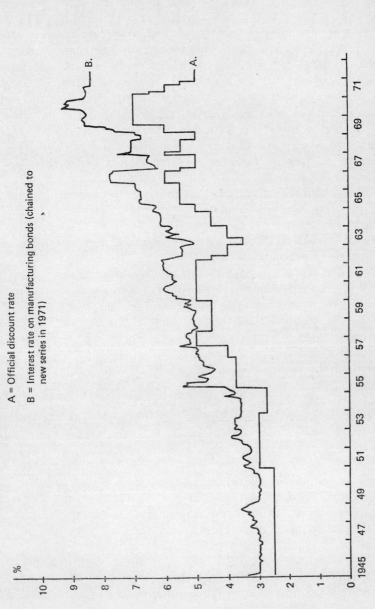

Source: Central Bureau of Statistics: Monthly Digest of Swedish Statistics; and Central Bank; Sveriges Riksbank, Yearbook.

price increases via higher production costs. In particular, reference was made to the effects on rents and agriculture prices, which have been controlled during the entire postwar period.

It was also alleged that small and moderate interest rate increases are without much importance for aggregate demand, whereas large interest rate increases could not be accepted because of the above-mentioned 'undesirable' side effects. Sometimes it was argued, rather inconsistently, that interest rate increases could result in unemployment. (It is not clear if the reason would be a sudden increase in the interest rate elasticity when rates reached a certain, rather high, level or if some collapse in 'business confidence' was assumed to take place in the economy with high interest rates.)

It was also said that monetary policy is too general ('blind') in its effects, as it hits sectors where no reduction of expenditure might be desired by the authorities, such as housebuilding. For these reasons direct controls of demand were regarded as a superior method.

On the basis of considerations of this kind, a very passive attitude towards monetary policy was taken by the authorities during the first years after the Second World War. To begin with, the Central Bank argued that it could not influence interest rates effectively, not even those on government securities, but had to follow the market-determined development of the rates in accordance with the prevailing interest rate expectations of the private sector. This argument was put forward mainly by Dag Hammarskjöld ([54], [55]), Under-Secretary of the Ministry of Finance and Chairman of the Board of the Central Bank, in defence of a reduction in interest rates early in 1945. Hammarskjöld's argument was strongly, and certainly correctly, criticised by Bent Hansen [56] in a polemic between Hansen and Hammarskjöld in *Ekonomisk Tidskrift*. As pointed out by Hansen, the Central Bank has means at its disposal to change these expectations – discount policy and purchases and sales of government securities, i.e. open market operations.

When banks started to monetise their vast holdings of government securities in 1946 for the purpose of expanding private loans, the Central Bank abandoned its passive attitude to interest rates and resisted the market forces tending to pull up interest rates. In fact, the Central Bank, by buying up all securities supplied to the market, pegged the interest rate for government bonds at about 3 per cent. Thereby the Central Bank took a passive attitude towards the *supply* of private loans (rather than as earlier to the interest rate) and consequently towards prevailing tendencies to excess demand for commodities and labour. The position of the Bank was that these events were the result of too soft direct controls and too expansionary fiscal policy, whereas the policy of the Central Bank was regarded as having very little to do with these developments. In fact, the authorities regarded its policy as quite adequate to the existing situation: 'The experiences of the past year indicate that the Central Bank has in the main been able to accomplish the stabilisation of the long-term interest rate and has thereby preserved an important first condition for the government's general economic policy.'[2]

The view of the Bank continued to change, however, probably to some extent in response to heavy criticism from economists, members of the opposition and bankers, who argued that the inflation and the associated deficit in the balance of trade were partly caused by the easy monetary policy. In particular, they pointed out that the abundant availability of money and credit was of crucial importance for the increase in spending even if small interest rate increases had no substantial effects on the volume of expenditures. (The *theory* behind this point is developed below.)

However, the Bank had admitted already in 1948 that a more restricted availability of credit could contribute to price stability. This meant that the Central Bank faced a dilemma: how to restrict the volume of credit without raising the interest rate? This problem was clearly formulated in a report by the Banking Committee of Parliament, to which the Central Bank is responsible: 'In the course of the past year the Riksbank has been faced with a difficult problem of simultaneously keeping the market easy enough to maintain the desired rate of interest but tight enough to reduce the volume of credit'

---

[2] Statement by the Banking Committee of Parliament ([257], p. 12). For a lively discussion of the policy statements by the Central Bank during this period see Erik Lundberg ([130], pp. 138–43).

([257], p. 12). To resolve this dilemma the Central Bank tried on various occasions to limit the expansion of bank advances by 'voluntary agreements' with commercial banks about cash reserves, liquid asset ratios and the volume of loans (such as in 1947, 1948, 1950 and 1952).

However, the policy was difficult to implement in periods of heavy demand for credit, as banks were very liquid and unwilling to abstain from possible profits in connection with loans to the private sector. The Central Bank made some minor attempts to support its policy by small increases in the discount rate (in 1950) and by accepting a slight upward slide in other interest rates (Chart 7:1). However, the Bank retreated rather rapidly to purchases of government securities to prevent a further upward drift of interest rates.

An attempt was made in 1951/52 to strengthen the power of the Central Bank by a law according to which the government could give the Central Bank the right to forbid interest rate increases and to fix maximum interest rates on loans and minimum interest rates on bank deposits. The law was never invoked, but with it as a vague threat in the background commercial banks became willing to follow the 'voluntary agreements' about cash reserve requirements and liquid asset ratios more rigorously than before. At the same time the Central Bank was given the power to control the amounts of and interest rates on bond issues by municipalities and private firms, by a system of compulsory applications for potential issuers of bonds. This control of bond issues has been one of the basic tools of monetary policy during the last decade – the so-called 'bond queue'.

With these new powers, the Central Bank finally succeeded in restricting lending by banks and a number of other credit institutions (credit intermediaries). A restrictive monetary policy, with stiff credit rationing at low interest rates, was thus applied in 1952/53 and, above all, in 1955/56. In the latter period a definite break with the low interest rate policy occurred, however, shortly after a change of manager of the Central Bank; (a *tendency* to a new interest policy may be discerned already in 1954 through an issue of a 4 per cent government loan). At about the same time, direct control of the volume of bank loans was introduced through a ceiling on the total of bank advances. The policy was implemented by a 'voluntary' agreement between the Central Bank and commercial banks, implying a reduction of the total of bank advances by 1 per cent within one month (compared with the credit volume at the end of July the same year). In 1956 there was a new agreement that the total of advances would be reduced by a further 5 per cent within four months.

The reduction in credit supply, in combination with sticky interest rates, resulted in a heavy excess demand for credit in the middle of the fifties, and hence in stringent credit rationing. In combination with other measures, such as an investment tax and direct control of construction, the boom in private investment was kept within a rather limited margin (Chart 4:3). As pointed out earlier, the authorities succeeded in postponing, to some extent, the investment boom to the next recession (1958), which must be regarded as a considerable achievement of economic policy at that time.

Since the middle of the fifties monetary policy has been extensively used as a tool in stabilisation policy. A typical feature of the policy is that a vast variety of methods have been used – discount rates, open market operations, cash reserve requirements, liquid asset ratios, other portfolio ratios, bond issue control and occasionally also ceilings on bank advances (1955-7 and 1970). The increased reliance on monetary policy during the last decade, particularly to fight inflation, is indicated by the increased fluctuations in interest rates, on a rising trend (Chart 7:1). Another indication is that the real quantity of money held by the private (non-banking) sector fell considerably during periods of tight monetary policy (Chart 7:2).[3] It is also of interest to note that interest rate policy in later years has been more and more motivated by balance-of-payments considerations. (However, *to some extent* balance of payments considerations seem to have influenced interest rate policy already during the 1958 recession.)

While long- and medium-term capital movements are subject to exchange control, there seems to be a belief among monetary authorities that short-term capital movements, such

[3] The real quantity of money is here defined as the real value of currency, demand deposits and time deposits held outside the banking sector, as a fraction of GNP.

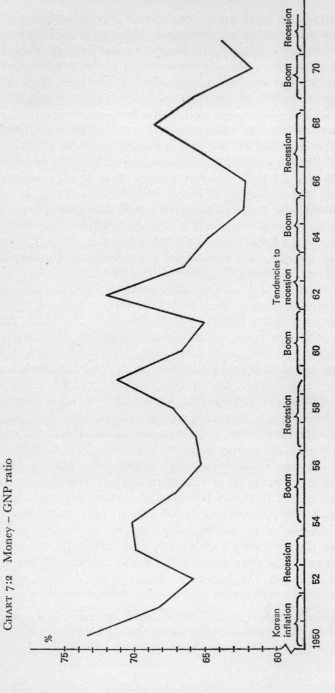

CHART 7:2   Money – GNP ratio

Source: Central Bureau of Statistics: National Accounts; and Central Bank; Sveriges Riksbank, Yearbook.
Note: Money defined as currency, demand deposits and time deposits held outside the banking sector.

as trade credits, are rather sensitive to interest rate policy. A dramatic example of the increased assignment of interest rate policy to the balance-of-payments situation (à la the well-known policy proposals of Robert Mundell) is the increase in interest rates – in the midst of a recession – in December 1967, immediately after the British devaluation, to counteract a capital outflow during a period of rising interest rates abroad and 'nervousness' (exchange speculation) on the international exchange markets. In the process, about one-fifth of the exchange reserves in Sweden ($200 million) disappeared during the course of a few weeks. The international mobility of short-term capital was again illustrated in early 1969, when the interest rates in Sweden lagged behind the interest rate increases on international markets: again, about 200 million dollars of exchange reserves disappeared during a rather short period of time. However, it would seem that the reduction in exchange reserves, as earlier pointed out, was partly balanced by increased holdings of foreign assets by private Swedish firms [47].

In spite of much higher interest rates in the booms of the sixties than in the boom of the fifties, the degree of credit rationing seems to have been severe also in the sixties. An explanation is probably that the expected real interest rate after tax – i.e. the nominal rate, after tax, deflated by the expected increase in consumer goods prices – may not have increased as much as the nominal interest rate before tax. In fact, as profit taxation is about 50 per cent and personal income tax rates even higher, interest costs are deductible, and people have reason to expect a yearly price rise of 3, 4 or 5 per cent, the real interest rate after tax in Sweden is scarcely above zero.[4] Thus, the real interest rate after tax is rather lower than during the depression of the thirties. It is therefore not surprising that excess demand for credit has been considerable in boom periods.

[4] An interest rate of 8 per cent, a tax rate of 50 per cent, and a rate of expected price rise of 4 per cent make the real interest rate after tax about 0 per cent. If the wholesale price index, which during the last ten years has risen by about 2 per cent, is instead used as deflator, the real interest rate after tax will be about 2 per cent. It should be added that uncertainty is attached to price expectations, and that the tax rate often has a symmetric effect on the revenue side.

A schematic picture of monetary policy in the postwar period in Sweden is given in Charts 7:1, 7:3 and 7:4, showing interest rate changes, percentage changes in the quantity of money and percentage changes in the stock of credit obtained by the business sector from the organised credit market.

If evaluated by interest rate changes, monetary policy shows (if the effect-lags are not *very* long, in fact no more than one-and-a-half or two years) an anticyclical pattern from the mid-fifties, when the policy of pegging interest rates was abandoned. It is interesting to note that monetary policy, as opposed to fiscal policy, has been quicker to change during booms than during recessions. As a generalisation we might say that, while fiscal policy has tended to lag in upswings, monetary policy has tended to lag in downswings. There is also a rising trend for interest rates over time. This is presumably partly a deliberate attempt to adjust the general interest rate level (over the entire cycle) to a long-run level that reflects prevailing price expectations, but also partly a result of the necessity to adjust interest rates to rates abroad for balance-of-payments reasons, particularly after 1965 when balance-of-payments problems began to emerge.

The diagrams for the quantity of money and the amount of credit to business (Charts 7:3–7:4) show about the same pattern as for interest rates. With budget deficits and expansionary monetary policy during every recession – and a boom after every recession in a four-to-five-year cycle – there is of course, for reasons of simple arithmetic, a peak in the rate of change in the monetary variables one or two years before every period of economic expansion and a trough about one or two years before every period of economic contraction. This pattern will, of course, emerge regardless of what the 'ultimate' causes of the fluctuations are – changes in export demand, autonomous shift in private investment, public spending on goods and services (or 'sun spots', for that matter). If we accept that the fluctuations are mainly caused by shifts in international demand for Swedish exports, we could have a good illustration of the risk of interpreting a systematic statistical correlation with time lags between two variables – in this case financial variables and economic activity – as a causal relation, with the first type of variables asserted to

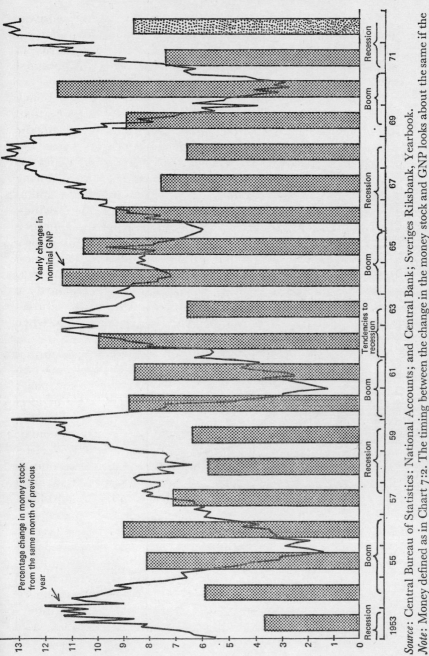

Source: Central Bureau of Statistics: National Accounts; and Central Bank; Sveriges Riksbank, Yearbook.

Note: Money defined as in Chart 7:2. The timing between the change in the money stock and GNP looks about the same if the rate of change in the money stock is instead defined as seasonally-adjusted change from previous month. However, it is very difficult to obtain a reasonably good ('smooth') seasonal adjustment of this variable in Sweden.

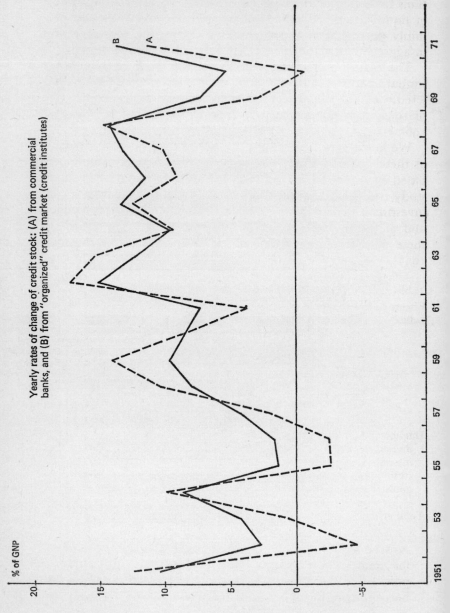

CHART 7:4 Fluctuations in the credit stock to the business sector

% of GNP

Yearly rates of change of credit stock: (A) from commercial banks, and (B) from "organized" credit market (credit institutes)

cause the change in the latter. However, even if changes in the quantity of money are not regarded as 'causes' of fluctuations in aggregate demand and nominal GNP, the expansion of liquid assets, including money, during recessions can certainly be regarded as an 'enabling' factor for the expansion in aggregate demands and GNP during the ensuing booms.

The diagram of changes in the credit stock gives a rather similar pattern, though here monetary policy, or rather 'credit' policy, would seem to have been much more restrictive in 1952, 1955/56 and 1969/70 than in the booms of 1960 and 1965 [164A].

We know very little about the effects on aggregate demand of these policies. There are some empirical studies, however, based on questionnaire techniques. One is the earlier-mentioned study (chapter 6) by Arvidsson and Wickman of the effects on investment expenditures in manufacturing of monetary policy and of the investment tax in 1955/56 period. The results of these studies are summarised in Table 7A ([267], autumn 1957).

Table 7:A

Effects on investment in manufacturing of investment tax and interest rate policy – as estimated by questionnaire studies

	Reduction in investment in 1955 (%)		Reduction in investment in the two-year period 1955/56 (%)
	According to 1955 study	According to 1956 study	According to 1956 study
Due to:			
investment tax	5·8	5·0	3·2
interest rate increase	0·8	0·7	0·7
stiffer credit rationing	3·9	6·9	9·1
undistributed effect	3·5	1·7	1·0
Total effect	14·0	14·3	14·0

As seen from the table, the 1956 study gives stronger effects for credit rationing (in 1955) than does the 1955 study. A possible explanation is that the tighter credit policy had been in force for only two months when the 1955 study was made, whereas the investment tax had been in force for about half a year.

The results reported by the studies are quite consistent with other types of information. More specifically, we know that *actual* investment by industry (*ex post*) was about 15 per cent lower than planned investment expenditures (*ex ante*), reported regularly in the survey undertaken by the Board of Commerce (Kommerskollegium), immediately before the policy measures were undertaken.

(These results have been challenged by Gunnar Eliasson in an econometric study [40]. The result of his study is that the effects were both delayed (by about one year) and of smaller magnitude than according to the studies by Arvidsson and Wickman.)

According to these studies, monetary policy reduced investment expenditures in manufacturing by about 5–7 per cent during the first year and by about 10 per cent during the two-year period, with the main effects emerging from stiffer credit rationing rather than from the modest increase in interest rates (by about 1 percentage point for industrial bonds).

There is also a study using questionnaire techniques by Lars Jacobsson of the effects of monetary policy in the 1969/70 boom and the 1971 recession. According to this study the restrictive credit policy would have reduced the investment expenditures in manufacturing by 3 per cent in 1969 and 8 per cent in 1970. Again, the credit rationing is reported (by the firms) to have had much stronger effects than the interest rate increase that did occur (by a little more than 2 percentage points for industrial bonds, from spring 1969 to autumn 1970).

The effects were (according to all studies) concentrated in small and medium-sized firms (except for firms with fewer than 10 employees, which were not much effected). For instance, quite strong effects were reported in 1970 for firms with 10–49 employees (a reduction in investment spending by 12 per cent) and above all for firms with 50–199 employees (22 per cent reduction) [79].

It may also be possible to obtain some information about the strength of 'pure' interest rate effects on investment expenditures on the basis of the studies of the effects of investment taxes and investment funds. Assuming that an interest rate change that affects the capital value of an investment in the same way as the investment tax also has the same effect on investment spending, we can calculate that 1 percentage point change in the long-term interest rate should have influenced investment spending in manufacturing by 1–5 per cent in the 1955/56 boom, by about 2 per cent in the 1962 recession and by 1 per cent in the 1967/68 recession (see pp. 130–4 and reference [120A]).

Thus, it would seem that the Swedish studies on the effects of monetary and credit policy as implemented in Sweden give support neither to those denying the effects of monetary and credit policy nor to those who argue that such policies have great effects even in *very* 'small doses'.

THE CRITICISM

By the shift to restrictive monetary policy in the middle of the fifties, still at rather low interest rates, the previous excess demand for commodities and labour was succeeded by excess demand in the credit market. However, in spite of the activation of monetary policy, many economists went on criticising the monetary policy pursued, mainly because of the prevalence of credit rationing, in particular as a more or less permanent method of pursuing a tight monetary policy in booms. Thus, considerable criticism was directed against the policy, particularly by Erik Lundberg, Bengt Senneby and Bent Hansen.

The Lundberg–Senneby criticism [143] went along two main lines:

First, control of the volume of credit issued by credit institutions may be a poor instrument for monetary policy owing to the fact that the relationship between the credit volume and aggregate demand (for commodities and services) is rather weak. In particular, Lundberg and Senneby emphasised that a given aggregate demand in the economy can be combined with a varying volume of credit, depending, for instance, on how saving and investment are distributed between households, firms and government. For example, the greater the fraction of saving performed by households and government, the larger is the volume of credit necessary in order to transfer financial surpluses to the business sector from the other sectors.

Moreover, the more the distribution of saving deviates from the distribution of investment *within* the business sector, the larger is the credit volume necessary to finance a given investment programme. (This problem concerning the relationship between, on the one hand, the distribution of saving and investment, and on the other, the credit volume had earlier been thoroughly analysed theoretically by Börje Kragh ([99], ch. II).) Lundberg and Senneby also argued that in a process of 'profit inflation' a rise in investment might, in fact, be compatible with a *reduced* credit volume. On the other hand, in a deflationary situation, with a rise in unplanned inventories the demand for credit might have to *rise* to carry the increased inventories and at the same time to finish already-started investment projects.

Their conclusion seemed to be that the credit volume is both a poor *instrument* of economic policy and a poor *indicator* of the effects of monetary policy. This recalls Bent Hansen's arguments against regarding the budget surplus as a tool, or an indicator, of fiscal policy: the volume of credit, as well as the budget balance, is an endogenous variable in the economic system, which is strongly influenced by a number of different parameters, including various policy instruments, as well as by other endogenous variables.

A second criticism by Lundberg and Senneby was that reliance on credit rationing rather than on high interest rates could in the long run be disruptive to the allocation of resources. The idea was, of course, that in the allocation of credit, considerations of profitability were often replaced by other types of considerations, such as traditional relationships between lenders and borrowers (for instance, one firm lending directly to another) and, in the case of the control of bond issues, by the turn in the bond queue (at the Central Bank, or at the private banks when the Central Bank, as in Sweden, left them to administer the queue). There was also a risk of compartmentalisation, i.e. of dividing the credit market into a number of submarkets with quite different interest rates in each market, and also a risk that firms with large internal funds, owing to a good *historic* profit record, would be induced to invest internally in low profit projects rather than supply the funds to the credit market. Lundberg and Senneby also argued that credit rationing creates a new type of uncertainty in the economy – uncertainty whether credit can be obtained at all in the future – in addition to uncertainty about interest rates, collateral, etc. This would mean that a new influence on the allocation of investment would emerge – an influence distorting the pattern corresponding to economic efficiency.

Lundberg and Senneby concluded that a flexible interest rate policy was desirable both from the point of view of stabilisation policy and from the point of view of allocation of resources. They admitted, however, that a sudden reduction in the volume of credit, or a credit freeze, may be efficient as a short-run brake on an acute investment boom, before other measures can be implemented, even if the connection between the level of credit and total expenditure is rather loose. The disadvantages of this method would, however, in their opinion, increase with time.

These arguments were later further developed by Lundberg in a study of investment criteria and rates of return in Swedish business firms ([131], ch. 10). Lundberg connected the great differences in rates of return, 'required' as well as actual, that were found in this study with the imperfections in the credit market (to a large extent a result of the monetary policy), with the high degree of self-financing in the business sector, and with the primitive calculation methods employed by many firms.[5]

Bent Hansen, too, was willing to accept a credit freeze as a short-run device in an acute investment boom [58]. However, he argued that flexible interest rates would give the credit market better properties as a built-in stabiliser than would a regulated market with a loan ceiling. Hansen tried to show this by a number of examples of disturbances in the economic system, from a credit market with flexible interest rates in one case to pegged interest rates and a controlled credit volume in another. One of Hansen's examples was a situation in which household saving increased and, as a consequence, business income tended to fall. In such a situation, a flexible credit market would automatically transfer increased saving

[5] The existence of rather primitive calculation methods by Swedish firms, implying in fact a very high time-discount, is confirmed in a study by Renck [199].

into credit supply, partly long-term. The lower interest rates that follow would induce an increase in fixed investment and also help firms to carry additional inventories, which would be favourable from the point of view of economic stability. If the volume of credit was fixed in such a situation, no such built-in stability effects in the credit market would help to restore the stability of output.

Whereas Lundberg–Senneby and Hansen gave arguments for a freer interest rate policy in general, Guy Arvidsson developed a proposal for reconciling controlled interest rates on 'priority credit' (mainly government securities and housing loans) and free and flexible interest rates on other types of credit ('private loans') ([9], pp. 123–7). The technique – well known from discussions in other countries – would be to isolate the markets for government securities and mortgage bonds by portfolio rules for credit institutions. The main original idea in Arvidsson's proposal was to create incentives for banks to charge 'equilibrium' interest rates on other types of credit, either by high cash reserve requirements or by high interest rates on bank deposits, and possibly also by taxes on deposits. Such actions would also, if properly adjusted, keep down the profits of the banks, in spite of high loan rates.

LESSONS OF SWEDISH MONETARY POLICY EXPERIENCE
Besides the general problems connected with severe credit rationing, what have been the main lessons learned from monetary policy experiments in Sweden?

First of all, it has proved difficult to pursue a tight monetary policy without flexible interest rates. This is presumably the reason why a flexible interest rate policy has come to be more and more accepted. Of course, such difficulties are predicted by theoretical considerations. The occurrence of queues, tendencies to 'grey' markets and difficulties in finding efficient criteria for the distribution of credit are effects of price control and rationing that can be inferred from the simplest type of price theory.

Cash reserve requirements and liquid asset ratios also give rise to obvious problems. For instance, the effectiveness of cash reserve requirements is impaired if banks can go on expanding private loans by unloading their holdings of government securities. This may be a problem even if interest rate flexibility is accepted, but the problem becomes particularly severe, of course, if banks are able to obtain additional cash reserves via Central Bank purchases of unloaded government securities, necessary to the pegging of the interest rate. In fact, it might be necessary for the authorities to accept such a decline in bond prices so that expectations of a future rise develop, thereby creating expectations of large future capital gains from continued holdings of government securities (the 'locking-in argument').

It was mainly this problem of the unloading of government securities by banks that induced the Swedish monetary authorities to rely on liquid asset ratios (secondary reserve requirements) rather than cash requirements as a tool of monetary policy. However, secondary reserve requirements are also afflicted with severe problems. One such problem is that it is difficult to fix the rules so that the bulk of banks' holdings of government securities is efficiently locked in. Because of the unevenness of holdings among different banks, some of them may have excess liquidity and they will in fact be more willing to sell out when liquid asset ratios have been raised than when interest rates have been raised via open market operations (as an increase in interest rates of banks brought about by open market operations increases the willingness to hold such assets). Moreover, in a system with very few banks (branch-banking), such as that in Sweden, an individual bank can usually expect that at least part of the deposits created by purchases of government securities will wind up as deposits in the bank itself. This means that if the bank buys government securities, the capacity of the bank to increase its supply of *private* loans will in fact *increase* (as the amount of actual liquid assets will then increase by a larger amount than 'required' liquid assets, the latter rising only by a fraction of the expanded asset holdings).

Thus, whereas a main problem with cash reserve requirements is that banks can avoid the intended consequences (on the supply of private loans) by *selling* government securities, they can avoid the consequences of liquid asset ratios by *buying* government securities. Theoretically these difficulties could be mitigated by successive increases in cash reserve requirements and liquid asset ratios along with increased cash reserves and liquid assets, respectively, for banks. However, such policies require considerable skill to be successful.[6]

A special motive for secondary reserve requirements has been to induce banks to supply housing loans to an amount consistent with the housebuilding plans of the authorities. The government has not as a rule, particularly not in the fifties, accepted interest rates on housing loans high enough to induce capital market institutions to satisfy the demand for housing loans. Instead the monetary authorities have tried to guarantee credit to housing by including mortgage bonds among legal secondary reserves, and also by 'voluntary' agreements with credit institutions.

However, in spite of the attempts to persuade the capital market institutions to hold mortgage bonds, crises in the financing of housebuilding have occurred from time to time (e.g. in 1966), with the result that housebuilding plans have not been fulfilled, apparently partly because of a lack of housing credit. But in the Swedish system, with most housebuilding partly financed by the government, and with secondary reserve requirements for credit institutions, it would not be difficult technically to solve this financing problem. The conclusion must therefore be that, apart from some technical deficiencies in policy, the authorities (the government and the Central Bank) have not been willing to enforce the original housebuilding plans of the authorities themselves, presumably in order to keep down the level of total expenditures in the economy during inflationary boom periods (such as 1965/66).

Another interesting experience of monetary policy in Sweden is that it indicates the limitations not only of credit rationing and quantitative controls of the credit supply, but of the reliance in general on *control of liquidity* rather than on interest rates. For if a very expansionary monetary policy is pursued in a recession, firms, households and credit institutes will be flooded with liquid assets during such periods. The same holds if increases in financial assets are created by budget deficits during the recession. This means that it takes a very long time before a restrictive liquidity and credit control 'bites' in the

---

[6] There is a discussion of various problems connected with cash reserve requirements and liquid asset ratios in [117], ch. 7.

next boom. The 'braking distance' for monetary policy will be very long if the policy relies on control of liquidity and credit volume rather than on heavy interest rate fluctuations. (See E. Lundberg [141], pp. 30–8.)

In fact, if firms and households in previous booms have experienced credit regulations, they will, during recessions when monetary policy is lax or expansionary, increase their liquidity for the very purpose of being 'immune' from credit restriction in the next boom. Thus, when firms have learnt the 'regular' policy pattern, a policy of liquidity control and credit rationing will induce firms to make *financial* investments rather than investments in real capital during recessions. These problems could at least partly be avoided if monetary policy instead relied more on heavy fluctuations in interest rates between booms and recessions, or on tax-subsidy programmes, to influence investments.

MONETARY THEORY

If the focus of our interest is switched from monetary policy to monetary theory, what are the main features of the theory of monetary policy in Sweden? Naturally, in the theoretical discussion, too, there has been considerable emphasis on the availability of credit, and hence on the behaviour of lenders, rather than on the interest rate as a cost factor. The Swedish version of the availability theory was originally developed in the late forties by private bankers educated in economic theory, such as Jacob Wallenberg ([239], [240]), Ernfrid Browaldh [26] and Lars-Erik Thunholm ([231]–[234]). A typical element in their approach was to regard credit supply as a necessary, but not sufficient, condition for the inflationary process that was going on. Even though they believed that certain long-term investments were sensitive to interest rates, they argued that the most important effects of monetary restraint were due to stiffer credit standards and more severe credit rationing – a line of thought from Keynes's classic, *A Treatise on Money* [93].

The effects of a fall in the capital value of assets on spending and lending were also part of the argument. Sometimes it was argued, too, that the reduction in the quantity of money that followed a tight monetary policy has *direct* effects on expenditure, i.e. a 'real balance effect' – a kind of asset-effect of a change in the quantity of money: 'You do not save on what you have in surplus – money' (J. Wallenberg ([240], year 1950)).

Erik Dahmén, in an article in 1952 [29], systematised and elaborated the ideas of this Swedish availability approach. In addition to clarifying various points about the exercise of credit standards and the importance of availability of credit for investment expenditures, Dahmén in particular stressed the increased liquidity preference among banks and firms in a situation when the future price and availability of funds become more uncertain owing to a discontinuation of the policy of pegging interest rates. The present author ([117], chs. 3, 7) later tried to clarify the distinction between interest rate effects and availability effects. One conclusion was that it may be misleading to treat credit availability as something completely distinct from interest rate effects. If a loan applicant is refused (further) loans from one lender he may turn to others, provided he is willing to pay the interest rates required by these. Thus, only when a loan applicant is refused credit in the section of the credit market with the highest interest rate in the whole market is it possible to refer rigorously to credit availability effects as something completely distinct from interest rate effects. This does not mean that references to 'availability of credit' are nonsense. It only implies that credit availability *in particular channels* has to be analysed simultaneously with interest rate effects.

An econometric attempt has been made by Gunnar Eliasson to study the effects on investment of various monetary and financial factors [40]. According to this study, investment expenditures are considerably influenced by the access to the bond market ('the bond issue permits') and also by the availability of liquid assets of firms. Eliasson did not obtain any indication of influences on investment expenditures of the volume of commercial bank advances. (Eliasson used a combination of an accelerator and residual-funds model, somewhat similar to a model by Meyer and Glauber [158].)

Apparently, many of the ideas of Swedish bankers in the late forties recall the American availability theory, as developed at the beginning of the fifties by economists connected with the Federal Reserve System ('the Roosa doctrine'). There are some differences between the two availability theories, however. One such difference is that the Swedish availability theory did not, like the American version, focus so much on the effects of *very small* interest changes for government securities on the supply of private credit. (It was in fact assumed in the American availability theory that the *cross*-elasticity of supply of private credit with respect to interest rates on government securities is high [116].) Rather than focusing on the effects of interest rate changes on the supply of private credit, the main idea in 'the Swedish Availability School' was to regard the supply of private credit as a function of bank reserves – the well-known idea of credit expansion multipliers.[7] In the policy-oriented part of the Swedish availability debate the focus was to a large extent on 'direct' ways of controlling the supply of credit – secondary reserve requirements, portfolio management regulations and ceilings on bank advances.

It is also of interest to note that monetary theory in Sweden has usually attached very little importance to the quantity of money. This is an old tradition dating from the time of Wicksell, who emphasised interest rates and not just the quantity of money. Lindahl [111] went much further along this line; in his monetary theory the quantity of money hardly entered at all. The same can be said about Ohlin's loanable funds approach, in which the effects on the real sector (i.e. the market for commodities, services and factors of production) were transmitted only via interest rates ([181]–[183]). Ohlin, as well as other economists of the Stockholm School, energetically criticised the quantity theory of money by arguing that the volume of money in reality has no direct influence on spending plans. In the same tradition, money is not introduced in Bent Hansen's theory of inflation [57].

As credit supply rather than the quantity of money has been regarded as the strategic variable for monetary policy, the emphasis in policy has been on the asset side of the credit

[7] Dahmén may be regarded as an exception; and he referred explicitly to the American availability theory.

institutions' balance-sheets, rather than on their liability side. This is presumably a reason for the de-emphasis on open market operations, and for the emphasis on methods to control the level of credit more 'directly', such as by loan ceilings, liquid asset ratios and portfolio requirements. Even though there is, of course, a correlation between, on the one hand, the credit volume extended by credit institutes and on the other hand the quantity of money and other liquid assets among households, we may say that the authorities have mainly pursued 'credit policy' rather than 'monetary policy'.

Therefore it has been regarded important to control the *credit volume* of all credit institutions, not just commercial banks (whose liabilities partly serve as money). In this respect Swedish monetary policy thinking has followed the same lines as the British Radcliffe Report, which also has emphasised the importance of considering and influencing various types of credit institutes, not just banks. In accordance with this tendency, studies of the credit market in Sweden have, with the help of credit matrices, dealt with the entire flow of credit funds in the economy, rather than confining the interest to commercial banks, even though *practical* monetary policy has concentrated on the *organised* credit market, with the main effects on the credit value of *commercial banks* (see Chart 7:4). The 'need', or demand, for a credit flow from one sector to another that emerges from such analyses may then be compared with the propensities of various sectors to finance deficits and to allocate surpluses (portfolio management). As an end result, a certain test of 'consistency' between financial flows and expenditure plans is thereby obtained for broad aggregates of the economy.[8]

COMPARISON BETWEEN INTEREST RATE POLICY, INVESTMENT TAXES AND INVESTMENT FUNDS POLICY

Both investment taxes and investment funds policy work somewhat similarly to monetary policy – via profitability as well as via liquidity. There are, however, some differences between the techniques that are worth noting. It is convenient to compare the two fiscal methods by contrasting each one

[8] This type of analysis has been performed mainly by Guy Arvidsson [5], Börje Kragh ([100], [102]) and Erik Karlsson [91].

with interest rate policy. However, it is rather difficult to translate the profitability effects of investment taxation and investment funds policy into 'interest rate equivalents' in a general way; the outcome of a translation of that kind depends *inter alia* on the durability of the investment project and on the timing of the income generated. But it is obvious that investment taxes and investment funds policy, such as have been implemented in Sweden, have profitability effects that are considerable compared with the effects of interest rate variations of the magnitude usually practised in Sweden (and other countries, for that matter) during the postwar period; this is so in particular for short- and medium-term investment. (These points are developed in the indented paragraph below.)

A removal of investment tax of 12 per cent is, in the context of a conventional investment calculation, equivalent to a 6 per cent subsidy of the costs of investment (if the tax is deductible for tax purposes and the tax rate is 50 per cent). A release of investment funds implies an even stronger subsidy. The present value of a fund release can, in rather 'normal' cases, be estimated at the magnitude 10 per cent for machine investments and 35–40 per cent for building investment. Thus, investment fund releases may be regarded as subsidies of investment in machines by about 10 per cent and in buildings by about 35–40 per cent – for firms that invest by way of accumulated investment funds. As in the case of interest rate policy, we would expect investment funds to have stronger effects on long- than short-term investment, contrary to investment taxes. We would also expect the effects of investment taxes to be even stronger if the tax is expected to be *temporary*, as in this case there will be a 'substitution effect' between periods, making it profitable to postpone a planned investment to a period free of investment taxes. When comparing with interest rate policy it may also be worth noting that the cost effect of an investment tax is obvious and easily detectable by the firm irrespective of whether the investment is financed by internal or borrowed funds. By contrast, it is often asserted in monetary policy discussion that interest rate increases mainly influence investment with borrowed funds.

Suppose that the interest rate for an investment project, financed by credit, is reduced during one year and then returns to the initial level. To influence the profitability of the project as much as it would be reduced by a one-year removal of an investment tax of 12 per cent, the interest rate reduction obviously has to be 12 percentage points. To get the same profitability effect by interest rate policy as by the utilisation of investment funds, an interest rate reduction by 60–80 percentage points would be required in the case of a building investment with a service life and depreciation time of 50 years. It should be observed that these figures refer to *temporary* (one-year) changes in interest rates.

If the investor pays the lower interest rate for a longer period, the profitability effect of the interest rate reduction will be larger, of course, compared with the investment tax and investment funds effects. Assume an investment project with constant cash flow over time. Suppose further that the internal rate of return is 8 per cent (before tax). In this case a removal of a 12 per cent investment tax and an investment funds policy such as practised in 1962/63 would be approximately equivalent in terms of profitability effects to the following permanent interest rate reduction (percentage points):

Service-life (and depreciation time) of capital goods (years)	Investment tax (%)	Investment funds policy (%)
5	5	8
10	4	7·5
50	1	7

(Machines are usually written off in five years and buildings in twenty-five to fifty years in Sweden.) The figures for investment funds policy refer to the case when investment funds deductions result in a loss of normal tax depreciations. (The comparison does not include the immediate liquidity (and, attached profitability), gain when 46 per cent of the appropriation is deposited in the Central Bank rather than 54 per cent of profits being paid as taxes. And the figures do not include the special tax advantages in the 1960/61 boom for firms depositing 100 per cent of their appropriation to investment funds in the blocked accounts in the Central Bank.)

Thus, investment taxes seem to 'correspond' to interest changes of about 4–5 percentage points (for machines) and investment funds releases to interest rate changes of about 7–8 percentage points.

According to earlier-mentioned empirical studies, the investment tax in 1955/56 reduced private investment expenditures in manufacturing by approximately 5 per cent; the expansionary investment funds policy in the 1962 recession seems to have increased private investment on building construction in manufacturing by approximately 15 per cent; and the fund release in 1967/68 seems to have increased machine investments by about 7 per cent. Translated into interest rate policy this would, according to the earlier-mentioned theoretical figures on the *relative* impact of interest rates on the one hand and investment taxes/investment funds on the other, indicate that every percentage point change in the long-term interest rates would have influenced investment spending in manufacturing by about 1–5 per cent in the 1955/56 boom (5 ÷ 5, or 5 ÷ 1), by about 2 per cent in the 1962 recession (15 ÷ 7 or 8) and by 1 per cent in the 1967/68 recession (7 ÷ 7 or 8). This may not be a very 'high' interest rate elasticity, but it is far from negligible.

As fluctuations in investment spending plans (*ex ante*) by a magnitude of 10–15 per cent do not seem to be unusual in many countries, our analysis would indicate that interest rate policy, as practised so far, is usually 'under-dimensioned' for achieving an efficient stabilisation of private investment expenditures. If our analysis, and the Swedish experience as reported here, are useful for *generalisations* about interest policy – in Sweden as well as in other countries – we would often need fluctuations in long-term interest rates of the order of 5–10 percentage points to stabilise private investment spending along its trend. The figure has, of course, to be adjusted downward if strong 'credit rationing' effects are connected with monetary policy. However, as is often pointed out, that would mean that the case for monetary policy, as opposed to direct controls, to influence private investment is probably somewhat weakened. This would be an additional argument in favour of investment taxes or investment funds policy, as compared with monetary policy; these types of fiscal policy actions are in fact more 'pure' forms of 'interest rate policy' than can be brought about by monetary and credit policies proper.

It has often been argued in Sweden that the effects of investment funds policy are mainly confined to the recession periods, whereas the contractive effects in the boom are small. It is true, of course, that it may be difficult to induce firms to reduce their investment expenditures in booms via appropriations to investment funds. However, by inducing firms to release funds and invest them in recessions, there will be a change in the timing of investment, which will more or less automatically reduce it in the booms. Such effects may occur either because firms speed up investment expenditures in a recession because of an investment funds release, or because firms postpone projects in a boom to take advantage of an expected release in the next recession.[9] An investment in a boom, rather than in a recession, will have an opportunity cost, owing to the accelerated depreciation achieved by making appropriation to the investment funds in a boom and postponing the project to the next recession. These opportunity costs can be strengthened by certain special arrangements. An example is the specific tax concessions given in 1960/61 to firms that paid 100 per cent of their deposition to investment funds to the blocked account in the Central Bank – a policy that resulted in a strong increase in deposition to investment funds. Through these special arrangements firms can, in principle, be offered such favourable concessions when postponing investment expenditures to recessions that they do in fact cut down their investment expenditures during booms.

It is also of interest to note that the investment funds system will increase the profitability of investment over the cycle as a whole, and hence increase the general level of investment over the cycle.

Like interest rate policy, both investment taxation and in-

[9] The existence of a 'speeding-up' effect is empirically fairly well established [37].

vestment funds policy may be classified as rather *general* types of economic policy. Private firms are allowed to decide for themselves what type of investment they want to make; the government mainly influences the cost of choosing one timing rather than another. However, both methods can, if desired, easily be used in a selective way, by gearing the actions to particular types of investment, sectors and geographical areas. In Sweden, this possibility has been used by exempting investment in housebuilding and public investment from investment taxes (except for the selective investment tax, which covered investments by municipalities) for the reason that these sectors are regulated by other measures, mainly direct control and government credit. However, with regard to the private sector, the main releases of investment funds in 1958/59, 1962/63 and 1967/68 were general, hence without much intended discrimination between firms and regions. The fund release in the recession of 1971 was *formally* selective in the sense that individual permission was required, and that the terms were not quite as favourable as in the case of general releases (there was no 10 per cent extra deduction from profits as with general releases). However, everyone applying for a release seems to have received the required permission.

There has, however, been a tendency to use 'selective' investment funds releases during the late sixties and early seventies as a part of location policy. If this tendency goes on, it may to some extent reduce the usefulness of investment funds policy as a stabilisation policy tool. There has also been a differentiation with respect to construction and machinery. In 1961 the policy was used selectively between branches by a specific release for the pulp industry, which had a recession in that period. There have also been some other minor selective releases of this type. And the 25 per cent tax on investment in the service sector in 1967/68 and 1970/71 was designed to discriminate in favour of investment in the industrial sector – evidently to help restore balance in the current account. As the tax was not deductible for taxation purposes, it became in fact prohibitive, except for investors who could obtain dispensation after special application. This made the tax actually equivalent to a physical building regulation in the form of a licensing system. Thus, the measure was in reality a partial building regulation 'masked' as a selective tax.

A difference between investment taxes and investment funds, on the one hand, and interest rate policy on the other, is that the former methods do not generate the same type of 'undesirable' side effects as does interest rate policy. For instance, the market value of the outstanding stock of bonds will not be disturbed in the same way as in the case of substantial interest rate changes. (In other connections this fall in market values of bonds has been regarded as 'desirable', as it gives a negative 'wealth effect' on demand for commodities and supply of private credit; an example is the American availability theory.) Moreover, no immediate problems will arise of changes in the cost of government debt, and of changes in the distribution of income and wealth between debtors and creditors. The fact that such side effects can largely be avoided is important, as these effects in many countries have constituted basic arguments against a powerful monetary policy.[10] However, an income redistribution to firms is, of course, an unavoidable consequence of the investment funds system, as well as of other methods to strengthen investment incentives in a profit-oriented economy.

One of the reasons for relying more on investment funds policy than on general investment taxes in recent years seems to be that the authorities have believed that investment funds policy provides a closer control of the timing of investment. It is rather easy for the labour market authorities, which administer the releases, to make sure that investments are in fact made during the period of release; this is especially so

[10] Investment taxes and investment funds policy also have some credit market effects. A payment of investment taxes reduces deposits and liquid assets of the banking system (in Sweden the Treasury keeps its balances in the Central Bank rather than in the commercial banks). Similarly, there was a tightening of the credit market when industrial firms in 1960/61 were induced by certain types of incentives to make 100 per cent of their appropriations to investment funds as deposits on blocked accounts in the Central Bank. The reduction in deposits and liquid assets of the commercial banking system which then occurred was equivalent to the effects of considerable open market sales. However, such credit market effects are not an intrinsic part of investment taxes and investment funds policy; the effects on the commercial banking system may be removed, if desired, by open market operations.

for investment in buildings. The investment funds policy has also been closely synchronised with the Swedish system of building start permits, practised for seasonal adjustment reasons and administrated by the labour market authorities. The timing of individual investment projects can in that way be easily adjusted according to local labour market conditions. In this connection a close co-operation between firms and local market authorities has been established.

Moreover, as stressed by Wickman ([248], pp. 8–13) and Eliasson ([39], pp. 131–5), the easiness of administration of investment funds makes the system very flexible, so that the implementation can be changed rapidly as new information about the economic situation is obtained. Time lags in the policy can for this reason be kept relatively short. Investment taxes, on the other hand, have to be decided in advance for a certain period; in practice they have applied to the whole country and for a whole calendar year. These administrative advantages of investment funds explain why it was possible in the 1962/63 recession to get a good timing of the effects. However, it is quite possible that an administrative system for investment taxes could be constructed so that those administrative advantages could be incorporated in that system also.

Obviously, the system of 'payments to' and 'release from' blocked accounts in the Central Bank is not a necessary part of the purpose of the investment funds policy. About the same effect could *in principle* be achieved by a system of accelerated depreciation confined to recessions, or simply by investment subsidies in recessions and investment taxes in booms provided the decision and effect lags can be cut as efficiently as in the Swedish investment funds system.

An obvious problem with investment funds policy is that the system favours firms with high *past* profits. In comparison, variations in investment taxes and general investment subsidies have a more 'neutral' effect on firms with different past profit records. In this sense investment funds policy imparts a 'conservative' bias on the allocation of resources among firms, compared with general investment taxes and interest rate policy. Moreover, the investment funds system is 'discontinuous': the funds are either released or not. The system would be a more flexible tool if the level of subsidies could be varied *continuously* so that there were, for instance, larger subsidies in deep recessions than in slight recessions. For instance, the extra deduction, at 10 per cent, could be varied depending on the depth of a recession. Now the only way to make a *small* fund release is to make it *selective*. This is presumably one of the reasons why the releases in recent years have been more selective than earlier. Moreover, it may be easier to achieve a reduction of private investment in booms by an investment tax than by investment funds policy. All these problems can in principle easily be avoided if instead of investment funds policy, general investment taxes and investment subsidies are used, provided the previously mentioned administrative advantages of the investment funds system can be 'transplanted' to a system of general investment taxes and investment subsidies.

8 Contemporary Problems in Stabilisation Policy

What are the most important problems in stabilisation policy in Sweden today? It is obvious that the classical dilemma of reconciling full employment and price stability is still with us. A number of specific aspects of this problem – some old, others new – have been highlighted in Sweden in recent years, including deficiencies in demand management, for instance those related to time lags and conflicts of goals in stabilisation policy, both between different dimensions of the stabilisation target and between the stabilisation target and other targets of economic policy such as growth and the distribution of income; the role of the tax system in the process of cost inflation; and problems connected with labour mobility policy as a means of fighting inflation. Other recent experiences have been inflationary 'hangovers' in recessions, from previous booms, and the related issue of so-called 'stagflation'; the consequences for economic policy of the attempts by labour unions to pursue a so-called 'solidaric wage policy'; complications for stabilisation policy of widely different rates of productivity increase in various sectors of the economy; problems related to the choice between 'general' and 'selective' tools in stabilisation policy; and the difficulties connected with the interdependence between different national economies in an increasingly internationalised world economy, with related conflicts between internal and external balance. All these problems are closely related to the difficulties of reconciling price stability, full employment and equilibrium in the balance of payments.

It may be worth while to comment upon these problems from the point of view of Swedish experience and discussions. As a starting point for the analysis, let us briefly sketch various factors behind the inflationary process in Sweden.

COST COMPONENTS BEHIND CHANGES IN CONSUMER
GOODS PRICES

Inflation seems to be both a long-run (trend) phenomenon for the postwar world – possibly with an inflationary bias built into the mixed economies – and a short-run problem connected with the business cycle, resulting in cyclical variations in the yearly rate of inflation.

A first rough classification of factors behind changes in the consumer goods price index in Sweden may be obtained by a rather mechanical classification of various cost components behind the yearly changes in the consumer goods price index. Such a calculation has been presented by Lars Lindberger (Table 8:A).

A classification of this type, of course, only scratches the surface of the causes of inflation. However, it might be a useful starting point for the discussion, if it is remembered that a complicated dynamic process with strongly interdependent relationships lies behind the development. The classification is based on the assumption that indirect taxes are completely shifted on to prices, that politically regulated prices (mainly in housing and agriculture) are effectively determined by the authorities, and that domestic prices of commodities in international trade follow import and export prices. ('Indirect' effects of these various cost-increasing impulses are not considered in the table.)

The table suggests that increases in indirect taxes have been an important price-raising factor throughout the sixties (see also Chart 1:4, p. 14). The other specified cost-increasing factors have usually played a rather small role; a large 'rest factor' exists. Part of this residual may reflect the effects on prices of excess demand for commodities. However, in the case of Sweden we would not expect this influence to be dominating, as domestic excess demand partly tends to 'spill over' on to imports, with only limited effects on domestic prices, in particular for commodities (as opposed to services). It is more likely that the residual reflects the effects on prices of wage increases in excess of the productivity increase. Moreover, the dramatic increase in world market prices in 1973 and 1974 had a very strong direct effect on the Swedish price level.

It is important to make clear the limitations in this 'mechan-

Table 8:A

Changes in consumer goods prices 1960–71, broken down by 'cost components' (Dec.–Dec.)*

	1959/1960	1960/1961	1961/1962	1962/1963	1963/1964	1964/1965	1965/1966	1966/1967	1967/1968	1968/1969	1969/1970	1970/1971
Increase in consumer goods price index (%)	3·9	2·2	5·0	3·4	3·8	6·2	4·7	3·1	2·0	4·6	7·0	7·5
of which refers to:												
Changes in indirect taxes (%)	2·9	—	1·8	0·6	0·2	2·5	0·7	1·1	0·5	0·1	1·4	3·2
Change in internationally determined prices (%)	−0·3	0·5	−0·2	0·7	0·8	—	—	−0·2	—	0·6	1·7	0·7
Change in agriculture prices (%)	0·2	—	0·9	0·7	0·3	0·3	—	0·1	0·2	0·5	—	0·5
Change in prices of dwellings (%)	0·5	0·3	—	0·3	0·6	1·1	0·7	0·5	0·4	2·0	0·6	0·3
Change in various public fees (%)	0·1	0·1	0·3	0·1	0·3	0·1	0·5	0·4	0·1	0·3	0·3	0·8
Trend deviation in prices of fresh food products (%)	−0·3	0·2	−0·1	−0·2	—	0·4	—	−0·1	—	0·3	0·3	0·1
Remainder (%)	0·8	1·1	2·3	1·2	1·6	1·8	2·8	1·3	0·8	1·0	2·7	1·9

Source: [81], p. 67 and [267].

* During 1972, 1973 and 1974, the rate of increase in consumer goods prices was 5·7, 8·0 and 9·0 per cent, respectively (the last figure being preliminary), with internationally determined prices becoming a more and more important component.

ical' classification of cost components behind the changes in the consumer goods price index, interpreted as a 'causal' analysis of the driving forces behind price changes. For instance, the observation that changes in indirect taxes during a particular year 'account' for 2 percentage points of the increase in consumer goods prices does not necessarily mean that the price index would have increased 2 per cent less without this rise in indirect taxes. The tax increase may have reduced an excess demand for commodities, or labour, and hence prevented a demand–pull price and/or wage increase. Moreover, the analysis neglects possible changes in profit margins. And it does not give explicit information of the role of monetary factors behind aggregate demand and the price increases. Similarly, the classifications are too aggregated to reveal the important interrelations between various sectors of the economy, such as the difference in the rate of productivity increase between different sectors of the economy and its relation to wage formation and the development of prices on international markets.

Several of those factors will be discussed below.

PROBLEMS IN DEMAND MANAGEMENT

The effects on prices, both via excess demand for goods and, indirectly, via excess demand for labour, may at least partly be regarded as the result of deficiencies in demand management policy by the authorities. That the rate of price change is related to the excess demand situation for goods and/or labour is suggested by the 'spurts' in inflation at the peak of (and immediately after) every boom, when obvious tendencies to excess demand have prevailed both in the commodity and in the labour markets. The existence of such excess demand situations during booms can be readily seen from the occurrence of deficits in the current balance, and from a high vacancy level for labour, in the case of the goods and the labour markets, respectively. That deficiencies in demand management are partly responsible for this is suggested by the earlier discussed delays in restrictive policy action during the upswings (1959, 1964, 1969), when demand management policy has been far from perfect. Unfortunately, we lack quantitative information as to how large a part of the domestic price increases can be attributed to deficiencies in demand management.

An important complication during the postwar period for demand management policy in an economy such as the Swedish one is that the business fluctuations most of the time take place within a very narrow band between 'full' and 'overfull' employment. This means that, when an upswing starts, full capacity utilisation is reached very rapidly, maybe within about twelve months after the start of the upswing. Thus, there is very little time for the authorities to take restrictive action before full capacity utilisation is reached. If such action is not taken in time, it is very difficult to stop effectively the wage and cost spiral that may already have started.

In fact, the rate of inflation as a rule continues at a 'boom-level-speed' for a while into the subsequent recession (see page 52). One reason is that it takes time before previous price increases have penetrated the entire input–output system, another that inflationary expectations might be accentuated during particularly inflationary booms (such as in 1950/51 and 1969/70), and that it may take a long time to squeeze these expectations out of the system. These are probably two of the main explanations for the tendency of price changes to lag behind the business cycle. When output falls during the following recession we may therefore experience unemployment and a slowing down of the rate of output increase hand in hand with inflation, and possibly also stagnating investment – what has recently been baptised 'stagflation'. Moreover, in an economy that operates in 'a narrow band' between full employment and a minor slack, the business cycle situation is often rather split, with excess demand in some markets existing simultaneously with excess supply in others. This is, of course, one of the rationales for experiments with selective management of demand, or actions to increase factor mobility.

NEGLECT OF COST SIDE?

Whereas stabilisation policy immediately after the war (in the period 1945–50) concentrated on cost considerations, i.e. on the supply side of the commodity markets, the policy later on dealt mainly with demand aspects, in the usual Keynesian manner. One example of the neglect of cost considerations in the policy of the last decade is the gradual increase in taxes on sales of goods and on factor (labour) inputs even in situations where the main problem, such as in 1962 and 1971, seems to have been cost inflation rather than demand inflation.

The statistics in Table 8:A suggest that the continuous increase in indirect taxes during the sixties has contributed (in the 'mechanical' sense discussed above) considerably to the increase in the consumer goods price index – on the average about one-quarter of the yearly price increases. The role of indirect taxes for the increase in consumer goods prices is also indicated by the fact that the so-called *net* price index for consumers' goods has increased by an annual rate of 3·2 per cent, as compared with 4·3 per cent for the index of market prices of consumer goods. See also Chart 1:4.

It might also be argued that another example of the neglect of cost consideration is the absence of attempts to pursue a so-called 'incomes policy', i.e. to influence the bargaining process directly. Incomes policy has, so to speak, been delegated to the labour market organisations, which particularly since the middle of the fifties have been engaged in highly centralised bargaining on a country-wide basis.[1] It must be admitted, however, that it is hard to find *any* democratic system that has succeeded with incomes policy during any period of length. There has so far (1972) been a generally accepted idea in Swedish economic policy discussions that the government should not intervene in wage formation, but that the organisations should be left to manage these problems on their own. This position has as a rule also been energetically advocated by the organisations themselves. Only in the dramatic wage bargains of 1971 did the government take a step in the direction of intervening in the bargaining process in the private sector – by making wage settlements in the public sector lead the bargaining process by declaring that it was in line with government policies that low income groups should have the highest percentage wage increases, and that the final outcome of the bargaining process

[1] On the labour side there are four main organisations – two large and two rather small. The large ones are the Confederation of Trade Unions (LO) and the Central Organisation for Salaried Employees (TCO). The small ones are an organisation for professional salary earners with an academic education (SACO) and an organisation for certain higher officers in the government sector (SR). The employer side is completely dominated by the Employers' Federation (SAF) and the government. See Holmberg [73].

ought to wind up in a wage increase quite close to the proposals of the arbitration committee set up by the government. All these actions tended to push the average rate of wage increase *higher* than without government intervention (see S. Nycander [174]). Thus an *inflationary* 'incomes policy' seems to have been pursued during this period. Perhaps more importantly, the government cut income tax rates in 1973 with the *expressed* hope that employees would then be willing to accept smaller wage increases than otherwise. As this policy probably was a success, a *da capo* is planned for 1974.

One basic argument in favour of the generally accepted 'hands-off' standpoint in wage formation is that the bargaining process in Sweden, which is very centralised, has a very good record with respect to peace in the labour market. Open conflicts have been very rare, and wildcat strikes have been practically non-existent (with the exception of some highly publicised events in the autumn of 1969 and the spring of 1970). It is generally believed that the organisations would not feel the same responsibility for their actions if the government intervened in the bargaining process; it is also often argued that it would be difficult to gain support among union members for a policy of wage restraint if union leaders were not co-responsible for wages. However, as we know, the rather centralised bargaining system in Sweden has not been able to avoid a rather rapid cost inflation.

As already mentioned, the principle of non-intervention in wage formation has been challenged by some economists, such as Hansen and Östlind. Some years ago Svennilson too suggested that the government should, to some extent, intervene in the bargaining process [220]. Like Hansen, Svennilson wanted to use the government's power over the income distribution to induce wage earners to follow a less inflationary wage policy. However, whereas Hansen wanted to 'bribe' wage earners to accept wage increases in line with the wishes of the authorities, Svennilson's proposal was designed to remove the alleged wage-raising effects of progressive taxation. More specifically, he suggested a combination of reduced tax progressivism (lower marginal tax rates) and smaller wage differentials (before tax). These two actions should be co-ordinated in such a way that the distribution of disposable income is unaffected (or possibly even becomes more equal than at present). If an agreement to this effect were made between the government and the organisations, Svennilson argued, the competition for wage increases would be reduced and the rate of wage inflation dampened. An additional advantage, in Svennilson's opinion, would be that disincentives connected with the tax system would be reduced.

Though interesting in principle, this proposal raises several problems. First of all, the incomes of employers and professional groups are determined outside the system of collective bargaining and would be difficult to include in Svennilson's system. Secondly, as the system requires that wages be reduced relatively more for qualified than for unqualified employees, wage costs would fall for the first group relative to the second. As a consequence, demand for qualified labour would increase at the expense of unqualified labour, with tendencies for the initial wage differentials to be restored after some time – particularly through wage drift.

It would seem that Svennilson's proposal rests on the assumption that the progressive part of the income tax is shifted by 100 per cent to wages, and that a reduction of the progressivism could be reshifted back on lower wage differentials. In other words, it is assumed that employees not only *try* to get 100 per cent compensation for progressive taxation, but actually succeed. This would occur either if the demand curve for the relevant type of labour is completely inelastic, or if there is excess demand for it to begin with. This might be a realistic approximation for certain types of labour with small substitutability ('specialists'), such as in part of the public sector and among consultants, and possibly among some business executives. The assumption seems less realistic for other types of employees in the private sectors. Moreover, with respect to the problem of disincentives of progressive taxation, it is not clear how incentives to work can be raised by a reduction in tax rates that is balanced by a fall of the same size in wage rates, the reward for work on the margin being unchanged.[2]

[2] There is a possibility, however, that people not only react to the reward for work, but also 'protest' against high tax rates by reducing the work effort. In the latter case we may say that their 'revealed preferences' between work and leisure are affected by taxation.

Svennilson wanted to dampen the alleged inflationary effects of attempts by the authorities to change the distribution of income. However, it has also been suggested in the debate that the attempt by the authorities to reallocate resources from the private to the public sector has inflationary effects. The idea is that labour market organisations have tried to 'retaliate' not only against *progressive* taxation but against tax increases in general. This is another case where fiscal policy has been criticised for focussing mainly on demand aspects. The basic idea seems to be as follows.

In principle, it is quite possible to eliminate the demand effects on the economy of an expansion in the public sector by raising taxes, provided these are raised more than expenditure (the marginal propensity to spend in the private sector being less than unity). In a society with a labour market dominated by organisations, however, unions can try to retaliate, if they are not satisfied with the increase in private consumption that is left after political decisions on public expenditure (and private investment).

As an illustration of such attempts by organisations to 'retaliate', it has been pointed out that wage increases often have not been consistent with the political decisions about expenditure on goods and services – a point stressed by Erik Dahmén in particular ([30]; [31]).

The issue is further complicated by the fact that unions and other organisations to a large extent have acted as pressure groups for higher public spending, housebuilding and to some extent also industrial investment. According to Dahmén there seems to be a kind of 'inconsistency' in the behaviour of the labour organisations as political pressure groups on the one hand, and as organisations participating in wage negotiations on the other, presumably because of the struggle over income shares; no conceivable redistribution of income at the expense of capital owners could remove this inconsistency.

These joint attempts by the public and private sectors to obtain more than one hundred per cent of national income is, of course, one way of describing the permanent tendency to cost inflation. However, as the fraction of national income going to private consumption has fallen steadily, the government has obviously to a great extent succeeded in its attempts to reallocate resources from private consumption to the public sector, though possibly at the cost of inflation. Almost 10 percentage points of GNP have been moved from private consumption to the public sector in the postwar period (from 65 to 55 per cent of GNP). Thus, it seems that, even if labour market organisations to some extent would have succeeded in shifting higher taxation on to *nominal wages*, the shifting has evidently not succeeded in *real terms*; the public sector, rather than the household sector, has managed to sustain its spending plans in real terms.

As the wage share of national income has risen during the first half of the sixties the employees seem, however, to have succeeded to some extent in their attempts to change the income distribution to the disadvantage of profits – though in *favour* of the public sector rather than of the employees themselves. Moreover, even if the *total* group of wage earners would fail to move the income distribution in its favour, it is hardly a sign of inconsistent behaviour from the point of view of a *specific* group of wage earners if it tries to push for considerably higher wages at the same time as it is a pressure group for public spending – in fact, trying to gain at the cost of other groups (mainly other wage earners) in society.

An interesting example of attempts by unions to retaliate against taxation is the policy of academic–professional unions (SACO) who have tried to bargain on the basis of income *after tax*, in the sense that they want to protect their 'take-home' salaries, in real terms, adjusted for both price and tax increases. Another example of a conflict between union policy and public policy is that all labour unions have, in fact, demanded compensation for price increases owing to higher regulated prices for agricultural products, even though the unions politically have mainly supported the agricultural policy. They also seem to include indirect taxes in the price index when they define their 'real wages'. In fact, during 1973–4 *all* unions have partly bargained for real after-tax incomes.

In conclusion, even if increased taxation is *necessary* to eliminate the demand effects of higher government spending in a full-employment society, it may not be *sufficient* to prevent increased government spending from having inflationary effects through the income formation process. Instead of demand inflation we would, because of the reaction of organisations, be confronted with cost inflation.

It is also possible that an increase in taxes, undertaken as an anti-inflationary measure, will in fact be interpreted by some politicians as an indicator of 'room' for reductions in other taxes or increases in government spending. This has led people such as Dahmén to question the assumption in fiscal theory that the government can raise taxes without increasing expenditure too, possibly after a time lag ([30]; [31]).

Erik Lundberg has tried to formalise the cost inflation tendencies created by attempts on the part of labour unions to compensate themselves both for taxes and price increases. The background was that, as earlier mentioned (chapter 4, pp. 73-4), wage earners during the Korean inflation apparently tried to get compensation not only for the price increase that had already occurred, but also for the price and tax increases that they expected as a result of their own wage increase.

To highlight this problem Lundberg constructed what he called a 'wage multiplier', expressing how much larger than an initial (autonomous) price rise the wage rise must be in order to provide 'full compensation' (after tax) for both initial and induced price increases ([130], pp. 291-5). Denoting the marginal and average tax rate by t_m and t_a respectively, and the ratio between the induced (relative) price increase and the (relative) autonomous wage increase by k, Lundberg's wage multiplier was written:

$$\frac{1}{\dfrac{1-t_m}{1-t_a} - k}.$$

For instance, if $t_m = 0.3$, $t_a = 0.2$ and $k = 0.5$, the wage multiplier becomes about 2.7 – fairly realistic figures for t_m and t_a for a 'typical' employee in the early fifties in Sweden. (The value of k is more open to discussion.) In the early seventies, with figures approximately $t_m = 0.6$ and $t_a = 0.35$, the wage multiplier becomes as high as 8.7 (still assuming $k = 0.5$). In fact, when the ratio of the marginal to the average tax rate is nearly 2 (0.6/0.35) – the ratio might be called the 'tax elasticity' – a 1.63 per cent increase in income before tax is needed for every percentage increase in income after tax, even *disregarding* price increases as a result of wage increases (i.e. when $k = 0$).

If income-dependent transfer payments are considered, the marginal 'tax' rate may in the early seventies be as high as 0·9 *for certain groups*, whereas the average may be as low as 0·25; the 'tax elasticity' then will be as high as 3·6, and the wage multiplier no less than 7·5 in the least 'explosive' case (when $k = 0$).

Thus, in the early seventies, wage earners may need a wage increase several times a previous increase in prices to compensate themselves for inflation. In fact, in the case of wage increases in excess of the rate of productivity increase, the effects on prices would be expected to be greater than half the percentage of the wage increase (i.e. k may be greater than 0·5 in this case). Then there may be no new equilibrium value at all, and hence it may in fact be impossible to compensate wage earners for a price rise. The result would only be that a larger and larger fraction of real national income would be transferred to the public authorities by way of marginal taxes on the wage sum. This could mean that wage earners, in the context of the highly progressive tax system in Sweden, could get higher real disposable income by *limiting* the wage increase. (In fact, wage earners could, theoretically, maximise their total real disposable income by accepting a *reduction* in wages, and hence 'cheating' the government of tax revenues. However, this outcome of lower wages presupposes a collusion between different employers' unions, as well as a revaluation of the exchange rate so that domestic prices fall for internationally traded products.)

A tax system of this type may create rather explosive cost inflation effects if income earners are concerned with their income *after* rather than before tax. Thus, even though the progressive tax system is a built-in stabiliser on *the demand side* of the economy, it might be a built-in *de*stabiliser on *the cost side*, by stimulating employees to push for wage increases to compensate for an automatic increase in the tax burden when increased real income and inflation move people up to higher tax brackets. (To limit these built-in *de*stabilising effects on the cost side, the non-socialist opposition has suggested index-regulated tax rates, so that the real value of taxes is not automatically influenced by the rate of inflation.)

FULL EMPLOYMENT VERSUS PRICE STABILITY
REVISITED

There are at least two mechanisms that may create a conflict between full employment and price stability.

One mechanism is when 'autonomous' cost increases occur, owing to higher wages by way of bargaining agreements, higher import prices, etc. The well-known dilemma in this case is that the government either has to accept an increase in aggregate demand in money terms in proportion to the cost increase, in order to guarantee full employment, or has to try to fight the inflationary effects of the cost increase by cutting aggregate demand, with unemployment tendencies as the result. In the first case full employment is sustained at the cost of inflation; in the second case unemployment has to be accepted as a byproduct of the attempts to fight inflation. The dilemma is further complicated by inter-temporal relations between inflation and employment. If we accept considerable inflation today, there may be increased unemployment tomorrow owing to problems arising for exports and for the input-competing industries (at given exchange rates).

Another mechanism that may create a conflict between full employment and stable prices is, of course, the Phillips curve relation, i.e. the tendency for wage increases to accelerate at lower levels of unemployment – 'endogenous' wage increases. In Sweden wage changes, in particular 'wage drift', seem in fact to be quite sensitive to the labour market situation, in particular if this is measured as the relation (for instance the difference) between the number of vacancies and the number of unemployed, rather than just the number of unemployed (or the unemployment rate) ([66]; [81]).

Chart 8:1 presents an attempt to estimate the empirical relationship between the labour market situation and the rate of wage increase – subdivided on negotiated wage increase (by way of bargaining) and wage drift (wage increases in excess of the bargaining agreement).[3]

The basic assumption behind the diagram is that the rate

[3] According to available estimates, about half of the increase in wages during the sixties in manufacturing (as well as in building) – amounting to about 8–10 per cent per year – is classified as the immediate result of wage negotiations, whereas the rest is classified as 'wage drift'.

of wage increase is a (positive) function of excess demand for labour, measured by the difference between the number of vacancies (V) and the number of unemployed (U). The analysis gives a reasonably good statistical fit, in particular for wage drift. It is quite likely that the function for wage drift is more stable over time than the function for negotiated wage change. (The chart refers to workers in manufacturing, a strategic group in wage formation in Sweden ([38]; [81]; [82]). See also T. Backelin [14].)

A more conventional Phillips-curve approach – with the relationship between the unemployment rate and the rate of wage change – is presented in Chart 8:2, in spite of the fact that the statistical fit is quite poor in this case. A reason is that the unemployment statistics are becoming increasingly difficult to interpret because of all the various interventions in the labour market by the Labour Market Board, for instance by retraining, public works and protected activities. The great increase in the entry of women to the labour market in recent years – about 200,000 new women in four years – has also 'blown up' the unemployment figures.

Somewhat surprisingly, studies about wage formation in Sweden do not indicate any systematic influence of previous price changes on the *yearly* rate of wage increase, except possibly after periods of exceptionally strong price increases, such as in connection with the 'Korean inflation' in the early fifties [82]. A possible explanation might be that the yearly rate of change in market prices (for consumer goods as well as for the GNP-deflator) has been fairly even during the last two decades, at least up to 1970; i.e. the price variable has not fluctuated enough to give a significant influence on the year-by-year variations in the rate of wage change. This might mean that possible influences of the price variable – for instance by way of the effects on price expectations – are 'integrated' in the wage formation curves, in the sense that the *level* of the curves reflects, *inter alia*, the rate of expected price changes during the period under consideration. More specifically, it is quite likely that the wage-formation curves (in Charts 8:1 and 8:2) would have been somewhat lower if the rate of price change during the period had been zero per cent instead of 4 per cent; how much lower we do not know.

During a typical boom in Sweden the number of vacancies has as a rule been about twice the number of registered unemployed; i.e., $V = 2U$, a situation characterised by 'more jobs than men'. Generally speaking, we may say that the excess demand in such a situation $(V - U)$ is then of the order of 20,000–30,000 persons (Chart D in Appendix). Historically this labour market situation has implied an unemployment rate of a little more than 1 per cent, *according to Labour Market Board statistics*. According to the wage formation function in Chart 8:1, this labour market situation would, on the average, result in a wage cost increase of 10–11 per cent on a yearly basis (see also Phillips curve, Chart 8:2).

In recessions the number of vacancies has usually been about the same as, or slightly lower than, the number of unemployed; in general $(V - U)$ is then approximately 0 or possibly about – 10,000 (Chart D in Appendix). According to Chart 8:1 this would, on the average, result in a rate of wage increase of about 5–7 per cent. Unemployment, as measured by Labour Market Board statistics, has then usually been of the magnitude of 2–2·5 per cent.

As the rate of (labour) productivity increase is at most 4 per cent on the average for the economy as a whole, and the target for the labour market in Sweden has been to maintain a situation of 'more jobs than men' (implying historically an unemployment rate, as measured by Labour Market Board statistics, of approximately 1·5 per cent), there seems indeed to be a fundamental conflict between full employment and stable wage costs per unit of output.

As has been observed from many countries, however, 'wage formation functions' of this type are not very stable over time, though functions with $(V - U)$ as the basic explanatory variable presumably are somewhat more stable than functions of the simple Phillips curve-type with only U as explanatory variable. One reason, in the case of Sweden, is that there seems to be a positive long-term trend in the figures for both V and U; this trend is much weaker for the difference $(V - U)$. One reason for this trend is the emergence of a more heterogeneous

CHART 8:1   Labour market situation and wage increase, industrial workers (all labour costs included: estimations of data for the period 1956–70)

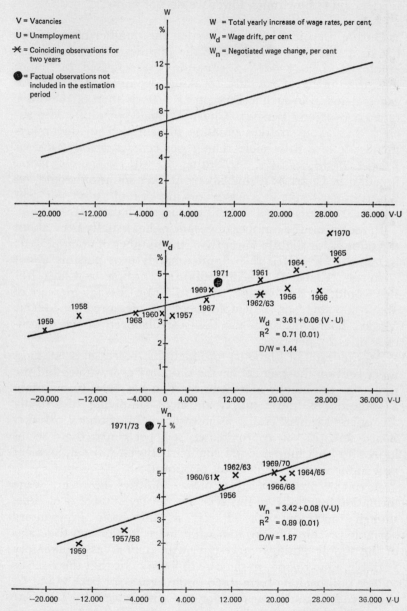

Source: L. Jacobsson and A. Lindbeck [81] and National Institute of Economic Research

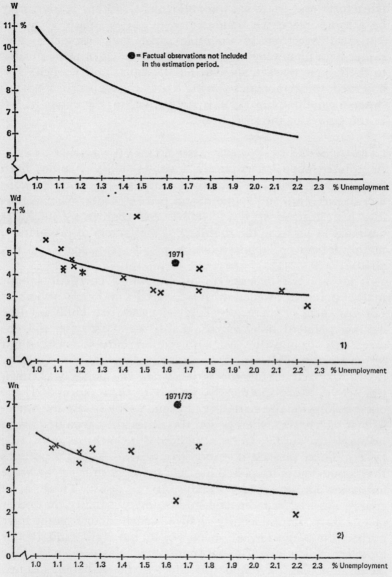

CHART 8 : 2   Phillips Curve for Sweden : workers in manufacturing
(based on data 1955–70)

● = Factual observations not included
in the estimation period.

1) Weighted unemployment rate periods t and t–1
2) Average unemployment rate 2nd quarter period t and 4th quarter period t–1

Source: L. Jacobsson and A. Lindbeck [81] and National Institute of
Economic Research.

labour market because of the rapid rate of structural change (structural and frictional unemployment). Other reasons may be a more aggressive 'solidaric wage policy', more complete statistical coverage of unemployment and vacancies, and rather high unemployment rates for a number of new entrants to the labour market, such as handicapped and women. The observed wage increases during 1971–4 have been *above* the 'wage-formation' curves; it is suggestive to talk about a *shift* in the curves in the seventies.

LABOUR MARKET POLICY AND DEMAND MANAGEMENT

As pointed out earlier, public 'incomes policy' has not been frequently tried in Sweden as a method to deal with the conflict between full employment and price stability. The authorities have instead tried to resolve this conflict by measures designed to increase the mobility of the factors of production, mainly labour – 'labour mobility policy' (see chapter 4, pp. 70–81).

What are the experiences of the rather energetic labour market policy in Sweden during the sixties and early seventies? For instance, is there any evidence that the Phillips curve has been shifted downwards? If this were the case, the observations around the wage formation curves would differ systematically between the sixties, when labour mobility policy was active, and the fifties, when the policy was much less active. More specifically, we would then expect that the observations for the sixties would tend to be below the wage-formation curves, whereas for the fifties they would tend to be above the curves. In reality, there is no such pattern ([14]; [122]). Thus, this test does not give support to the hypothesis that labour mobility policy has succeeded in shifting the wage formation curve (or the Phillips curve) down. There is, of course, as in all econometric studies, the possibility that other factors have simultaneously changed; such factors might have pushed the wage formation curves to the right, and labour mobility policy may have counteracted this tendency. One factor that may have had this effect is the earlier mentioned acceleration in the rate of structural change in the Swedish economy during the sixties. For instance, the number of firms closing down was about three times as high during the sixties as earlier (see chap. 11, pp. 219–27). It is also possible that it is difficult to obtain a smoothly functioning labour market in a society where the housing market is very imperfect, largely owing to the excess demand, and the distortions of relative rents in different houses, which are created by the system of rent control in Sweden.

The labour market policy during the sixties developed very much along the lines that had been suggested by Gösta Rehn. Were also the remaining parts of his programme realised: solidaric wage policy, squeezed profits and the removal of excess demand for labour by a restrictive general economic policy?

A solidaric wage policy has no doubt been followed, though wage differentials (*ex post*) between different sectors have not fallen very much – at least not up to 1971 (Chart C, Appendix). Moreover, profits have no doubt been squeezed (see chapter 10), as production costs (such as labour costs per unit of output) have risen somewhat more rapidly than world market prices. The increase in indirect taxes on commodities (the value-added tax) as well as on labour (a 4 per cent labour tax and social security fees on labour costs) has probably also contributed to squeeze profits, as it is unlikely that wage earners have carried one hundred per cent of these taxes and fees. It is also *possible* that the solidaric wage policy has contributed to the squeeze of profits, as the policy may have stimulated wage drift for high-wage groups.

It is open to debate to what extent these developments are the result of *deliberate* policies, and hence an application of the Rehn recommendations. However, what has *not* been achieved by Rehn's programme is a removal of excess demand for labour during booms; if excess demand for labour is measured as the number of vacancies minus the number of unemployed $V - U$), excess demand for labour would seem to have been about the same during the booms of the sixties as during the booms of the fifties (Chart D in Appendix).

THE EFO-EFFECT

The import price index for Sweden has risen since 1952 by about 2 per cent per year, and the export price index by 1·5 per cent. Consequently, changes in internationally determined prices account for rather little of yearly price changes in the 'mechanical' analysis in Table 8A of 'cost–push components' behind inflation. However, the connection between the development of international prices and the domestic price level is nevertheless an important link in the domestic inflationary process. The reason is that a stable price level in an open economy such as Sweden would require a *fall*, year by year, in domestic prices for internationally traded commodities to compensate for the price increases in sectors without international competition (mainly the service sector), where the rate of productivity increase is very slow. These complications for stabilisation policy in an open economy are well brought out by the Norwegian 'Aukrust model' and the Swedish 'EFO-Report' [38], written by Gösta Edgren, Karl-Olof Faxén and Clas-Erik Odhner.

The characteristic feature of these models is that the economy is divided into two sectors, one with foreign competition – the so-called C-sector (competitive sector) – and one without much foreign competition – the S-sector (shielded sector). The C-sector consists mainly of the commodity-producing parts of the economy, and it accounts for about one-third of GNP in Sweden. The S-sector consists mainly of services and construction and accounts for the remaining two-thirds of GNP. An important problem now, highlighted by the EFO-model, is that the rate of increase in productivity is much faster in the C-sector than in the S-sector, and that prices in the C-sector follow rather closely the world market trend. The mechanism is most easily illustrated by a numerical example.

Suppose that prices on international markets, and hence in the C-sector, tend to rise by 2 per cent per year, and that the rate of increase in labour productivity in this sector is 7 per cent (quite realistic figures during the sixties for Sweden). This means that the 'room' for wage increase, without cutting into the profit share in the sector, is 9 per cent. Suppose also that firms in the C-sector accept (or are 'forced' to accept) a wage increase of this size – by way of bargaining and wage drift. In a full-employment economy the firms in the S-sector too have to accept a wage increase of this size in order to keep their labour force and to avoid labour conflicts. However, in this sector the rate of productivity increase is considerably lower, say about 2 per cent per year. This means that the rate of price increase in the S-sector would be expected to be about 7 per cent per year $(9-2)$.

Hence, we will wind up with a price increase of 2 per cent in the C-sector and 7 per cent in the S-sector. Applying the relevant weights for the relative size of the two sectors, the average price level for the economy will rise by $5\frac{1}{3}$ per cent per year (rather close to the rate of change of the GNP deflator during the sixties). This indicates the difficulties involved in keeping a stable price level in a country with fixed exchange rates, with many prices tied to international prices, and with a different rate of productivity increase in the various sectors of the economy – particularly if international prices rise rapidly.

Several important policy conclusions follow from this model. First of all, the model suggests that it is not possible to bring about general price stability by keeping the average rate of wage increase in line with the yearly rate of increase in average productivity for the economy as a whole. Prices would rise in the S-sector, and there is no reason why they would automatically fall correspondingly in the C-sector (at fixed exchange rates).

If the rate of wage increase would follow the average rate of increase in labour productivity for the economy as a whole – in our example $3\frac{1}{3}$ per cent – there would still be a price rise in both sectors: in the C-sector by 2 per cent and in the S-sector by $1\frac{1}{3}$ per cent, or as a weighted average $1\frac{5}{9}$ per cent. However, this rather modest rate of price increase would not be stable, as profits in this case would rise rapidly in the C-sector; this would increase the demand for labour and stimulate a rate of wage increase in excess of the assumed $3\frac{1}{3}$ per cent.

To get a stable price level for the economy as a whole, it would in fact be necessary for the Swedish krona to appreciate every year sufficiently for domestic prices of internationally traded commodities to fall. This yearly appreciation has to be large enough to compensate for the rising prices in the S-sector. For instance, if the wage increase in our example is $3\frac{1}{3}$ per cent, corresponding to the average rate of productivity increase in the economy, a stable general price level would require that prices *fall* by $2\frac{2}{3}$ per cent per year in the C-sector, which presupposes a yearly appreciation of the Swedish krona by about this size *plus* the price rise in international markets. (This general argument by the EFO-Report was in fact to a large extent developed already in 1957 by Bent Hansen [60].) However, such an appreciation may not be consistent with the targets for the balance of payments. For instance, if there is a deficit in the balance of payments which the authorities are not willing to eliminate by capital imports, the balance of payments target might require a devaluation, whereas the price target may require an appreciation – an obvious 'dilemma case' for stabilisation policy. A solution suggested by Erik Lundberg might be to start by a devaluation, in order to correct the balance of payments, but to try in *future* to counteract inflationary tendencies by continuous appreciations of the currency ([141], ch. 10).

Another important policy implication of the EFO-model is that the rate of inflation goes *up* if the difference in the rate of productivity increase between the C-sector and the S-sector is enlarged. The rate of inflation is in this type of model simply determined (*a*) by the *difference* in the productivity trends in the two sectors, and (*b*) by the international price trend for the C-sector.

It is important not to interpret the model in a too 'deterministic' way. There is no absolute obstacle to the labour unions' pushing wage rates *faster* than the indicated 'room' for wage increases. In fact, whereas the 'room' for wage increase, as defined here, has risen by about 9 per cent in recent years (1960–71), wages have risen by about 9·5–10 per cent per year, with the result that profits have been squeezed. In countries where the rate of wage increase has been even faster, as compared with the 'room' for wage increase as defined here, devaluations have been necessary – in the UK, France, Denmark, Finland, etc. And in countries where the rate of wage increase has expanded more slowly than has the 'room' for wage increase, balance-of-payment surpluses have emerged, followed by pressures for revaluation – West Germany, Switzerland, Japan, etc.

The Aukrust and EFO-models clearly demonstrate the difficulties – not to say impossibilities – of achieving stable prices in an open economy at fixed exchange rates. Moreover, it shows how these difficulties are *accentuated* if the rate of productivity increase accelerates in the commodity-producing sector (at given productivity increase in the service sector). As the model has no *explicit* assumptions about monetary policy, it may be classified as a variant on 'structural' theories for inflation, built on demand–supply considerations. Aggregate demand in money terms, as well as the supply of credit and financial assets (including money), is assumed to adjust to the cost increases – to guarantee full employment.

INTERNATIONAL COMPLICATIONS

The strong dependence of the Swedish economy on international markets creates a number of complications for domestic stabilisation policy ([41]; [121]). Maybe some of the most important ones can be classified under the following five headings:

(1) price influence from abroad;
(2) volume fluctuations transmitted from the world market;
(3) conflict between internal and external balance;
(4) international factor mobility, mainly for credit and capital;
(5) international interdependency of policies.

The first problem has already been discussed in connection with the EFO-model. And the second was emphasised when the cyclical patterns of the Swedish economy were discussed in chapter 4.

The conflict between internal and external balance is illustrated by the tendency for the current balance to deteriorate at the peak of each boom, with a deficit of approximately 1 per cent of GNP in the current balance on these occasions. This conflict has been an important explanation for the continued restrictive demand management policy at least in three recession periods – 1958, 1967/68 and 1971/72.

The conflict between internal and external balance is emphasised by the internationalisation of credit and capital markets during the last decades. It has sometimes been regarded as necessary to keep rather high interest rates for balance-of-payments purposes, in spite of a domestic recession – mainly in 1967 and 1971. In fact, as in several other countries, interest rate policies have been tied more and more to balance-of-payments considerations, and less to internal economic conditions.

The international influence on the Swedish economy, in particular on the manufacturing sector, may be illustrated by a few figures on the degree of integration of the Swedish economy with the outside world (Table 8:B). Exports are about 23 per cent of GNP, and exports of the manufacturing sector are no less than 76 per cent of value added (the contribution to GDP) of this sector. If the import-content of manufacturing exports is deducted the figure falls to about 57 per cent. Employment in the operations by Swedish firms abroad

Table 8:B
Internationalisation of the Swedish Economy (per cent)

	1950	1970
Total exports/GNP	22	23
Manufacturing exports/GDP in manufacturing	58	76
Manufacturing exports/gross output in manufacturing	25	33
Import content of manufacturing exports	15	25
Manufacturing export *minus* import content/GDP in manufacturing	49	57
Manufacturing investment abroad/domestic manufacturing investment	10	15
Swedish production abroad/total Swedish exports		50

is about one-third of the employment in the manufacturing sector in Sweden. Another expression of the importance of Swedish operations in manufacturing abroad is the fact that the production value of Swedish firms abroad is about 50 per cent of the total Swedish export value. At the same time, about 7 per cent of the labour force in Sweden consists of foreigners; the corresponding figure for workers in manufacturing is 13 per cent.

Today – in the early 1970s – Sweden has perhaps the most multinational industry in the world (defined as production operations abroad relative to the size of the domestic economy), as is indicated by the international character of firms such as SKF, LM Ericsson, ASEA, Swedish Match Company, Alfa-Laval, Atlas Copco, Volvo, Gränges, Electrolux, Sandvik, Salén, Broström, etc.

TO REDUCE THE DISADVANTAGES OF INFLATION AND UNEMPLOYMENT

If it should prove impossible to resolve the conflict between full employment and price stability, an alternative strategy is of course to try to reduce the disadvantages connected with unemployment and inflation. In the case of unemployment, Erik Lundberg has asked whether the unemployed in a modern welfare state could not get so much compensation that there would be no severe drawback to being unemployed for short periods from time to time, an idea reminiscent of Galbraith's way of looking at unemployment some years ago ([44], ch. 21). Lundberg has suggested that the conventional unemployment concept should perhaps be replaced by the concept of 'adult education and retraining', unemployment compensation payments being rebaptised 'fellowships'. By allowing a slightly higher statistical unemployment of this 'fellowship' kind it might, according to Lundberg, be possible for the authorities to cut off expansionary tendencies somewhat earlier in boom periods than has been the case so far. Thus, Lundberg seems to be consistent over time in his belief in the necessity of reducing the employment level somewhat to achieve price stability – though in his new proposals without raising the level of 'conventional unemployment'.

And if it proves impossible in practice to eliminate inflation, would it then not make sense instead to remove some of the disadvantages connected with inflation? One interesting proposal, for that purpose, is to introduce index-regulated loans, i.e. loans the nominal value of which are continuously and automatically adjusted after a price index to keep the real interest rate independent of the rate of inflation. The arguments for such a reform vary, however. Some people seem to regard indexed loans as a way of *raising* the real interest rate, thereby giving savers compensation for inflation. Others, such as Tord Palander and Guy Arvidsson, have seen indexed loans mainly as a way of reducing the real-value risks on loans. Hence, in the latter case the argument for indexed loans is to provide households and firms with assets free both of default risk and real value risk.

Tord Palander, in a pioneering work on indexed loans ([191], [192]), has analysed some of the consequences for monetary policy of a 'dual market' for securities consisting of both indexed loans and conventional loans in money terms.[4] A government committee on indexed loans, with Guy Arvidsson as a member, has argued that the allocation of resources would improve if indexed loans were introduced, owing to more uniform expectations about the real interest rate and smaller risks, which would minimise the need for diversification of assets to hedge against inflation ([8], [10], [11]).

To remove the effects of inflation completely on the distribution of income and the allocation of resources, it would be necessary to move over to a completely index-regulated economy, where incomes, taxes, money holdings and regulated and negotiated prices are index-regulated. To solve the problem of the balance of payments, it would also be necessary to have flexible exchange rates, such as floating rates. In this type of society, also, the general price level would 'float'.

Even these rather substantial institutional changes would not remove all problems with inflation. It is quite likely that the information content for the consumer would be reduced, as the consumer in an economy with rapidly rising prices may lose his means of comparison for relative prices: when informed about the present price of one particular commodity, the individual will have great difficulties in judging if this price is high or low as compared with prices of other commodities, the prices of which he learned long ago (when the price level was different): rapid fluctuating and partly unexpected inflation may seriously distort the information content of the price system – the 'measuring rod' is distorted.

[4] Palander [191] also suggested that the authorities can influence commodity price expectations by changing the difference between the interest rates in these two markets by open market operations. The idea is, of course, that the difference between the rates would reflect people's price expectations. This may be true for an economy without a public sector, or with a *given* stock of government assets (hence without open market operations). But it is difficult to see how a change in the rate differential, brought about by a change in the number of government assets outstanding, could influence expectations about the future rate of inflation in an unambiguous way. Moreover, as Arvidsson has pointed out, if the government, as suggested by Palander, eliminates the interest rate differential, the government would, as long as expectations about price increases dominate, have to buy ordinary bonds and sell purchasing power bonds, which would be an exceedingly poor bargain for the government sector (Arvidsson [8], pp. 146–51).

9 Long-Term Planning

THE LONG-TERM REPORTS

In Sweden, as in several other western European countries, public documents on long-term tendencies of the economy have been presented regularly during the postwar period ([268]–[273]). Six such documents, called long-term reports, have been published (usually by specially appointed committees), the first appearing in 1948 in connection with the Marshall Plan. The director of these reports was Ingvar Svennilson, with the exception of the last two (published in 1966 and 1971) which were produced by a division of the Ministry of Finance, headed by Erik Höök. As the reports deal mainly with five-year periods, they could perhaps be more accurately described as 'medium-term economic reports'.

The long-term reports in Sweden may be regarded mainly as forecasts, with some discussions on economic policy alternatives, rather than plans.[1] They deal with the development of the basic sectors of the Swedish economy during the forthcoming five-year period and are based on detailed inquiries and discussions with representatives of firms and organisations in the private and public sectors. Thus, a considerable exchange of information between representatives of the various sectors of the economy takes place during the course of the work on the report – before it is published. On the basis of this information, the long-term committee tries to construct consistent forecasts for the economy or to discuss the inconsistencies remaining in the various plans, which have to be resolved either by the market mechanism or by government economic policy. The

---

[1] For a presentation of the general approach in Swedish long-term reports see I. Svennilson ([217]–[219]).

forecasts are to some extent hypothetical, in the sense that statements about the future course of the economy are made *if* certain specified events occur (for instance for exports and productivity). Perhaps we could talk about 'projections' rather than forecasts.

The inconsistency tests have mainly been concerned with macroeconomic equilibrium conditions in terms of national accounts (equilibrium between aggregate demand and production, between exports and imports or between the current foreign balance and the foreign capital balance) as well as balance in the labour market. The tests were rather fragmentary in the early reports, but became slightly more explicit and comprehensive in later ones, partly owing to the use of simple aggregate production functions (or at least capital/output and labour/output ratios) and, to some extent, input–output tables. With the help of Börje Kragh's earlier mentioned studies of trends concerning financial surpluses and deficits in various sectors, it has also been possible to study the consistency of the trends in real and financial sectors of the economy respectively, i.e. the consistency between investment and saving plans on the one hand and the need for financing, liquidity, borrowing and lending on the other.

The authors have stressed that the figures should be continously revised in the light of new information – a kind of 'rolling' forecasting. Actions in the short-run have to be regarded, to quote Svennilson, 'as the first step in a *strategy*, which includes different long-run alternatives of acting' ([221], p. 165). Thereby a flexibility in the planning is supposed to be achieved: 'we should not make our valuations norms for future generations' ([221], p. 171). The reports can perhaps be characterised as a modest type of 'indicative planning'. However, contrary to the *early* French plans, no fixed production targets have been formulated in the reports, and no attempts have been made to force the private sector to conform to the figures in the reports. In fact, the government as a rule has not even adopted the reports as official government policy. The documents may be regarded mainly as a method of transmitting information about activities in various sectors of the economy, whereby information obtained from markets is amplified. It is also widely believed that the publication of the reports creates confidence in the growth process, and facilitates a sustained growth of the economy.[2]

Besides transmitting information about plans and problems, and making consistency tests, the committees have to varying degrees discussed medium-term policy problems, and sometimes also made economic policy recommendations on the basis of certain value judgements. Sometimes these value judgements seem to be based on the subjective values of the committee members themselves, sometimes on what the committee believes are the dominating political valuations of society. These recommendations have above all dealt with the 'desirable' saving ratio for the economy and with the allocation of resources among very broad expenditure categories, such as private consumption, public consumption, private investment, public investment and the current balance in the balance of payments. Furthermore, the volume of housebuilding has often been a target of recommendations, and to some extent also certain components of the public sector, such as road-building.

In certain other countries, such as the UK, France and Norway, the long-term reports have been more of official government programmes than has been the case in Sweden. This holds maybe in particular for the French reports.

The French long-term reports have usually been described in the literature as much more interventionist than corresponding reports in other western European countries. One reason for this is presumably that the early reports in France (immediately after the Second World War) established fixed

---

[2] Compare the following passage by Svennilson:

It has not been part of the Swedish planning process to go back to the various economic units [after collecting data] and negotiate a revision of their plans according to the integrated national perspective. This would be regarded as an unsound intervention in the competitive system. Firms and sectors are expected to adjust to the market development that actually follows, guided by the information they receive in the published national projection. . . . The national projection creates an 'image' of economic growth that has a backing in Government policy. This 'image' will stimulate industry to plan for its long-term expansion and make it possible to do it more realistically. In this way national projections may contribute to create a better balanced economic growth ([217], pp. 195–6).

production targets for certain sectors, which the authorities during this period to some extent tried to achieve – by direct regulations, subsidies, credit controls, and 'open mouth operations'. Another reason for this opinion of the French long-term reports is, in my judgement, that both French and foreign authors writing about 'French planning' have given an exaggerated picture of the centralist and interventionist character of this planning. This holds in particular, I believe, for the sixties, when the planning system changed as the production targets for separate sectors practically disappeared, at the same time as the direct regulations to a large extent were removed as permanent factors of the policy. It is nowadays rather unclear to what extent the supply of credit in France is connected with the forecasts and plans of the French long-term reports. (On the other hand, it seems to be rather common that credit institutes in France often point out that a certain decision conforms well with the forecasts and recommendations of the reports – if this happens to be the case.)

In general, it can presumably be said that the emphasis in French economic planning during the sixties shifted from the private to the public sector. In the private sector, the plan figures became less and less binding, whereas planning became more elaborate for the public sector. The results of the operation of the market mechanism have instead been more and more accepted. The less detailed intervention in the private sector is probably connected with, *inter alia*, the increased importance of foreign competition for this sector in France, which to a large extent complicates attempts to fulfil central targets for production volumes. Along with this development, there has also been increased emphasis on short-term planning problems, i.e. stabilisation policy, as has for a long time been the case in northern European countries, such as Sweden.

It might be worth while to try to pinpoint the main differences between long-term planning in France and in Sweden, in order to provide a benchmark for Swedish long-term 'planning':

(1) The French reports give a comprehensive concise overall presentation of the development plans in the public

sector, which is not the case to the same extent in the Swedish reports.

(2) A more powerful and geographically concentrated location policy is outlined in France (with support for a number of fairly large cities, of around half a million inhabitants, at least for the future).

(3) The State has, to a much larger extent than in Sweden, made joint ventures with private firms, combined with credit supply and subsidies, in certain limited fields (steel, shipbuilding, the data industry).

(4) There probably has been, mainly earlier, some central regulation of the credit supply within the manufacturing sector in France.

Perhaps it can also be said that the Swedish long-term reports differ from the French ones by not *pretending* to be more than they really are – forecasts and numerical examples of macro relations, a discussion of problems of macroeconomic balance and of the consistency between plans, and a discussion, to some extent combined with recommendations, concerning economic policies.

THE OPTIMUM SAVINGS RATIO

As a rule, the long-term committees in Sweden have found that investment plans (or 'requirements') are much larger than expected (*ex ante*) saving with an unchanged economic policy. This has usually led the committees to argue for a higher investment ratio in the economy and heavier taxation of private consumption. In the first three long-term reports – 1948, 1950 and 1955 – the argument for a higher saving ratio was not explicitly tied to the question of the growth rate of the economy. The main argument was instead to bring about macroeconomic and sector *equilibrium* via an increase in the output capacity in certain sectors. In particular, the purpose of the increased capacity was to restore equilibrium in the balance of payments (the 1948 report) and equilibrium between demand and supply in certain capital-intensive sectors where equilibrium pricing was not accepted – mainly housing and the public sector (the 1950 and 1955 reports).

Not until the 1959 report did the growth rate of the economy as a whole come to the forefront of interest. The growth problem was then largely analysed as a problem of inter-temporal allocation of aggregate consumption, i.e. as a problem of achieving an optimum time profile of aggregate consumption. On this approach, not only the conventional investment ratio but also the volume of resources devoted to education and technological research and development came into focus – ideas well in line with the international discussion of growth at that time. Ingvar Svennilson, in particular, underlined the importance of these factors for economic growth. ([214]–[216], [219].)

This stress on the educational and technological factors is one of the reasons why the 1959 report, in contrast with the earlier ones, did not argue for a further increase in the investment ratio. However, the committee also seemed to be somewhat doubtful whether it was reasonable, from the point of view of social values, for the present generation to give up additional consumption opportunities for the sake of future generations, when the latter would anyway be very well off compared with the present generation. As Ragnar Bentzel asked provocatively in a memorandum [19] to the 1959 report: 'What are the motives for such a redistribution of consumption? Would not this be to take from the poor and give to the rich?'

In the international theoretical literature of recent years on the optimum saving ratio, the problem has usually been formulated as a question of maximising aggregate consumption within a finite, or infinite, horizon (with time discount), or as the problem of reaching a saturation level of wants ('bliss') within a minimum of time, or sometimes of finding what has been called a 'golden age' path for consumption.

Bentzel has tried to find a more operational approach to the problem by making the optimum saving ratio of the economy a function of the expected remaining lifetime, and hence the age distribution, of the population. The basic idea is that only young, and possibly middle-aged, people have anything to gain from an acceleration of the growth rate achieved by a reduction in the present consumption ratio. For elderly people, only investment projects with a short 'payback' period will be worth while. Bentzel therefore suggested that the optimum saving ratio for the economy can be determined if we simulate a hypothetical voting procedure among the entire population (including children), where everybody is assumed to vote in accordance with his self-interest as a consumer (during his expected remaining lifetime). His vote then will depend on the length of his expected remaining life, i.e., statistically, for a large group of people, approximately on what age group they belong to. The more people who belong to higher age groups, the lower will be the savings ratio calculated by this hypothetical 'voting procedure'.

In practice, it will not be necessary to perform actual voting. The outcome of the hypothetical voting could be calculated in advance, based on the stated assumptions, by knowing the age distribution of the population and the remaining life expectancy in each age group, as well as the empirical relationship between capital accumulation and growth. On the basis of statistical figures for Sweden, Bentzel derives from this type of model an optimum *net* saving ratio of about 12–14 per cent, i.e. slightly lower than the factual ratio in Sweden.

Though both simple and ingenious, Bentzel's analysis of course poses a number of problems. In particular, the political leaders may have quite different evaluations of the desirable consumption profile over time than that obtained from Bentzel's hypothetical 'voting procedure', based on assumed individual preferences.[3]

To clarify the issue further, let us assume that all investment projects can be ordered according to falling social rates of return. For a given investment project to be worth while to an old person, a very high rate of return is required, as otherwise future income increases would not, during his remaining lifetime, add up to a value larger than the investment cost. Now, it is easy to determine the relationship between the length of the remaining lifetime of a person and the lowest rate of return that is necessary to compensate him for the reduction in disposable income that is required today

[3] Another limitation in Bentzel's anlysis is that he implies a rather special type of time preference for the individual – the discount factor being unity for each period during the lifetime of the individual, and zero after that. (Thus, the individual is assumed to evaluate consumption equally regardless of which year during his lifetime a certain volume of consumption can be expected to take place.)

(and in the near future) to finance the project. On this basis we can determine the median value of the lowest rate of return required by members of the population; it is equal to the lowest rate required by people in the age groups representing the median age of the population. (For that half of the population which is younger, a lower rate of return is required and for the other, older half, a higher rate.) With the help of an aggregate production function for the economy, Bentzel finally determined the optimum saving ratio for the economy, consistent with this rate of return.

Bentzel used a Cobb–Douglas production function of the following form (for a stationary population):

$$q = Ce^{at} \times k(t)^b$$

where k is the capital stock per unit of labour input, and q the production volume per unit of labour input; $a = 0.02$, and $b = 0.25$.

On this basis Bentzel finds the following relationship between the remaining lifetime (x), the lowest acceptable rate of return (r) and the optimum saving ratio (s):

For $x = 20$, $r = 6.6\%$ and $s = 10\%$
For $x = 25$, $r = 5.6\%$ and $s = 12\%$
For $x = 30$, $r = 5.0\%$ and $s = 14\%$

It should be observed that s refers to *net* saving ratio.

Thus, let us assume that the median age of population is 40 and that the expected remaining lifetime for an individual in this age group is 30 $(x = 30)$. Then the lowest rate of return that is acceptable to a majority of the population is 5.0 per cent, corresponding to a net saving ratio for the economy of 14 per cent, i.e. about (or slightly lower than) the factual ratio at that time in Sweden.

CRITERIA FOR ALLOCATION POLICY

Measured in 1971 prices, GNP in Sweden rose from 14,600 billion dollars in 1946 to 37,900 billion dollars in 1971, i.e. an increase of 160 per cent or 3.9 per cent per year. The allocation of resources changed substantially during this period. For instance, the investment ratio (gross investment relative to

GNP), quite in line with the recommendations of the long-term reports, rose from about 18 per cent in 1950–5 to 23 per cent in 1965–70, rather a 'normal' figure for European OECD countries. This increase occurred at the expense of private consumption, which during this period fell from about 66 to 54 per cent of GNP, a lower figure than that for any other OECD country except Japan (the western European OECD average being 60 per cent).

At the same time resources were shifted from the private to the public sector. At present, public consumption constitutes about 29 per cent of total consumption (compared with 18 per cent in 1950)[4] and public investment about 37 per cent of total investment (as compared with 29 per cent in 1950). As housebuilding takes an additional 21 per cent of total investment resources, the private sector has the responsibility for about 42 per cent of the investment activity in the economy, slightly more than the public sector (excluding housebuilding). The shift of resources to public services is illustrated also by the fact that in 1970 about 17 per cent of the total number of statistically measured labour-hours is devoted to 'public services', as compared with about 7 per cent in 1950. (For a schematic picture of the role of the public sector in Sweden, see Table 1:α in chapter 1.)

The long-term development of broad aggregates of GNP (in constant prices) is indicated in Charts 9:1–9:3. As can be seen from these diagrams, both public investment and public consumption have expanded much more rapidly than GNP (except during the first part of the sixties). Public investment has also increased faster than private investment (except for the period 1955–65). And public consumption has increased faster than private consumption (except for the first half of the sixties, when both public and private consumption developed somewhat slower than GNP).

The relatively weak development of private investment during the fifties (up to 1958) may be an important explanation for the slow rate of economic growth of GNP during that period. Similarly, the acceleration of the rate of expansion of

---

[4] This is actually an underestimate of the volume of public consumption, in the sense that capital costs are not accurately included in the measures of public consumption.

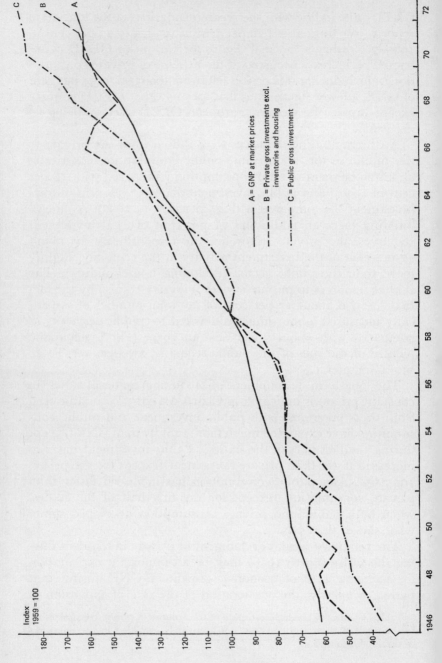

CHART 9:1 Development of private and public investment, and GNP (index 1959 = 100, 1968 prices)

Index
1959 = 100

A = GNP at market prices
B = Private gross investments excl.
    inventories and housing
C = Public gross investment

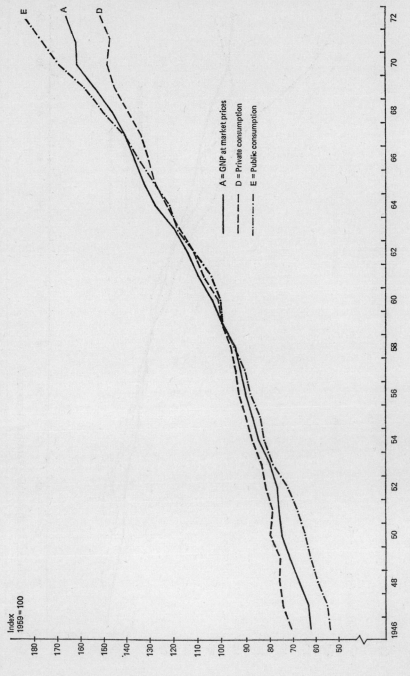

Index
1959 = 100

E

A

D

A = GNP at market prices
D = Private consumption
E = Public consumption

180
170
160
150
140
130
120
110
100
90
80
70
60
50

1946   48   50   52   54   56   58   60   62   64   66   68   70   72

Source: Central Bureau of Statistics: National Accounts.

CHART 9:3   Development of housing and exports, relative to GNP (index 1959 = 100, 1968 prices)

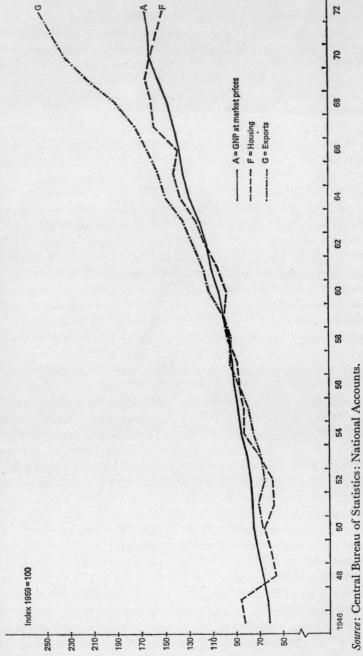

Index 1959 = 100

A = GNP at market prices
F = Housing
G = Exports

Source: Central Bureau of Statistics: National Accounts.

private investment during the period 1958–66 may be an explanation for the rather rapid growth rate of the economy during the sixties. (In the case of investment in manufacturing, there were *two* great investment spurts during this period – 1958–61 and 1965–66 (see Chart 1:6). Will the rather slow rate of growth of private investment, including investment in manufacturing, during the period 1966–72 result in a slow growth rate during the early seventies? It would seem so.

These differences in the rate of growth of private investment can presumably be explained to a large extent by the economic policy during the various periods. In the fifties, private investments were curtailed drastically during the booms, while restrictive action during the early sixties was directed more towards private consumption, for example through the continuous increase of indirect taxes on private consumption from 10 per cent in 1959 to about 18 per cent in 1970. At the end of the sixties, private investments were again curtailed by a very restrictive monetary policy in the booms – implemented partly for balance-of-payments reasons – and by a negative trend in private profits. (Uncertainty about Sweden's relations to EEC might also have dampened investment in the manufacturing sector.)

A schematic picture of the expansion of the public sector relative to GNP during different periods may be given by calculating an '*ex post* elasticity' of public consumption and investment relative to GNP (Table 9:A). The calculations give the ratio between the rate of increase in public consumption (and investment respectively) and GNP. During both the periods 1951–60 and 1961–70 the elasticity was about 1·55 for public investment; thus, public investment rose about 55 per cent more rapidly than GNP during both decades. For public consumption the corresponding figures are about 15 per cent more rapidly for both periods. (The differences between five-year periods have been substantial, however, in the case of public consumption.[5])

Another way of expressing the expansion of the public sector in Sweden is to point out that public spending on goods and services during the period 1950–70 expanded by 5·1 per cent per year (in real terms), as compared with 3·9 per cent for

[5] Figures calculated on the basis of regression lines.

Table 9:A

Ex post 'elasticities' for public expenditures with respect to GNP

	Public consumption		Public investment	
	current prices	constant prices	current prices	constant prices
1951–55	1·66	1·35	1·90	1·92
1956–60	1·08	0·96	1·36	1·89
1951–60	1·28	1·16	1·26	1·54
1961–65	1·28	0·94	1·33	1·63
1966–70	1·37	1·29	1·33	1·54
1961–70	1·40	1·16	1·25	1·58

Figures estimated on the basis of regression lines for the various periods. The elasticity (e) is then solved out from the equation $X = aY^e$, where X is public consumption or public investment and Y is GNP.

GNP. For OECD countries in general the corresponding figures are 3·8 per cent for public spending on goods and services and 4·7 per cent for GNP [121].

The discussion of the problem of the allocation of resources in Sweden has to a large extent been concerned with aggregate variables such as the growth rate of GNP, total availability of labour and capital, the investment ratio, the (*ex ante*) saving ratio, the balance of payments, etc. This characterisation holds also for the long-term reports, which broadly speaking may be described as short-run national budgets extended to a five-year basis. Problems of the optimum allocation of resources have been discussed very sparingly, except for the 'consistency test' earlier mentioned, the usual advocacy of a higher investment ratio and certain attempts to establish priorities between the public sector, the private sector and housebuilding.

However, sometimes more detailed recommendations were made in the long-term reports. Thus, on some occasions priority was advocated for investment in housing and public services, such as schools and hospitals (in the 1950 and 1955 reports); sometimes for investment in manufacturing (in the 1947, 1959, 1965 and 1970 reports). Priority for the manufacturing sector was particularly emphasised in situations where either economic growth, as in the 1959 report, or balance-of-payments problems (at unchanged exchange rates), as in the

1970 report, were at the centre of interest in the general economic policy discussion. In certain instances priority was advocated for investment in the commodity-producing sectors (in the 1948 and 1959 reports), and on some occasions it was recommended for the service sector, such as department stores and distribution in general (the 1955 report). A general pattern seems to be that a sector that had been discriminated against in one report was often favoured in some of the subsequent reports (except private consumption, which has never been very much favoured), reflecting a 'priority cycle' in Swedish economic policy.

A reason for this rather modest treatment of allocation problems is of course that it is difficult to find reasonable criteria for detailed recommendations in an economy characterised by fairly free international trade and adherence to the principle of 'consumer sovereignty'. Practically no attempts have been made to evaluate the allocation of resources arrived at via the market forces.[6]

A particular difficulty for detailed recommendations regarding intervention in the allocation of resources is that quite different price systems exist in different sectors of the economy. This means that it is very difficult to use market data either on profitability or on excess demand to draw conclusions about 'investment requirements' in various sectors. If, as has usually been the case in the long-term reports, investment requirements are measured by the excess demand in various sectors, the investment 'needs' will naturally always appear to be particularly large, not to say insatiable, in areas where the price is fixed at zero or very far below the equilibrium level. When this method of measuring investment requirements is

[6] An exception is a study by Lars Werin [244] by an activity model à la Koopmans. Werin's study is an attempt to find an optimum allocation of resources for Sweden with the help of an activity model with fixed input–output coefficients for variable factors, and with a given capital stock in each sector. The optimum position, according to this study, was surprisingly close to the actual allocation in Sweden, in the sense that the possible reallocation gain would be only about one half of one per cent of GNP. Presumably one reason for the result is that the input–output coefficient was taken from the actual production process in Sweden, which means that these coefficients were in fact assumed to be the optimum ones *within* each sector.

used, the housing sector and large parts of the public sector will necessarily seem to be undersupplied with resources compared with other sectors, where equilibrium prices prevail.

These problems might not be so difficult if it could be argued that consumer prices in these sectors are simply an expression of the valuation by the authorities of these commodities, compared with other commodities. In this case it would be rational to move resources, corresponding to the stimulated demand, to sectors with low prices. However, this is a dubious way of looking at the problem, as will be obvious if we ask how the low prices have come about in the different sectors. For instance, the high consumer prices for agricultural products cannot be interpreted as a low official valuation of food consumption; these prices are instead 'unintended' effects of the present system of income support for farmers. And in the housing field, with existing rent control, the relative price of housing is simply a result of the rate of inflation; the more rapid the inflation, the lower will be the price of housing compared with other commodities. Without inflation it is even possible that, with the present stock of dwellings, there would not be any excess demand for housing at all. Moreover, if the demand for housing, stimulated by rent control, is regarded as an expression of the authorities' valuation of housing consumption, compared with consumption of other commodities, rather inconsistent valuations have been applied on the demand and the supply side; the authorities have hardly been prepared to move enough resources into the housing field to satisfy the demand stimulated by housing policy. The tendencies to equilibrium in the market for newly built apartment houses in the early seventies, still with excess demand for the earlier produced stock, depends not only on a rather high level of housebuilding but also on rapidly increasing building costs. In fact, there is an excess supply of *new* apartments in 1973–4.

Not even the queues for public services such as schools and hospitals can, without a closer look, be taken as indicators that these areas are undersupplied with resources *compared with other sectors*. For in these areas, the queue method has consciously been chosen as a method of distributing the services, rather than relying on the price mechanism. This means, of course, that the existence of a queue, or its length, does not tell us whether this sector is discriminated against in the allocation of resources. If queues in certain sectors, as for schools and medical care, are regarded as a better way of distributing a commodity than relying on individual choice in a market with equilibrum prices, then queues have to be accepted as a more or less permanent phenomenon in these sectors. Consequently, it is necessary to use considerations other than the length of a queue, such as political judgement, social-profitability analysis or cost-benefit analysis, to determine the appropriate allocation of resources [118].

Thus, it is extremely difficult to find reasonable criteria for an appropriate allocation of resources in such a 'dual economy', with equilibrium prices in the private sector and controlled prices with permanent excess demand in housing and public services. Not only do we lack information about the demand curves for the various types of public services (and housing), but the demand curves in the other sectors are influenced by the price policy in the controlled sectors. Another problem in the public sector is, of course, how to find criteria and create incentives for efficiency when there is no market test of the performance of the institutions. These difficulties are, of course, particularly acute for a country, such as Sweden, which has a large sector of public services. So far however, politicians and administrators in the public sector have shown very little interest in these important issues. (Not until the very last years has a more serious research in this field started in Sweden; see for instance [251A].)

The importance of these problems is indicated by the present size of the price-controlled sectors. The bulk of public consumption falls on services for which prices are zero or extremely low (such as education, hospitals and administration), and about three-quarters of public investment goes to sectors where market pricing is not used for final output, such as research, education, defence, roads, hospitals and social work. To this we have to add the housing and agricultural sectors, where prices are controlled and where output constitutes 7·5 and 2 per cent, respectively, of GNP. However, by contrast the 'distortions' of the price system by way of tariffs have usually been quite small in Sweden (outside agriculture). Tariffs on industrial products were during the late sixties of the magnitude 5 per cent – or as measured in per cent of value added about 10 per cent ('effective tariffs').[7]

THE FUTURE OF LONG-TERM PLANNING

As should be clear from the previous section, there has hardly been any long-term planning in Sweden during the postwar period. The long-term reports may be regarded mainly as an instrument to communicate information about expectations and plans in various sectors of the economy, and even the term 'indicative planning' presumably gives too strong an impression of the elements of 'planning' in the context of the long-term reports.

It is difficult to forecast the future of these activities. The long-term reports have been criticised from several quite different – partly contradictory – points of view. One type of criticism has been to question the usefulness of presenting figures about five-year plans for firms, municipalities and the government, when we know that very few decision-units in the Swedish economy have plans for such a long period. It is therefore argued that figures about five-year plans in fact give false information. It is sometimes also argued that long-term reports should concentrate more on 'qualitative' data about firms, such as future tendencies for the technological development, the structural transformation of the production system, etc. Another, quite different, recommendation has been that the long-term reports should be developed into tools of central economic planning.

Another criticism of the long-term reports has been that long-term studies, confined mainly to five-year forecasts within the framework of national accounts, are much too narrow in scope. The architect of Swedish long-term reports himself, Ingvar Svennilson, has suggested that several alternative projections should be made for quite long periods, such as twenty-five years, and that the work should be interdisciplinary

---

[7] The idea of 'effective tariff rates', and the notion to make 'effective protection' about the same for all commodities, was launched by the Swedish Customs Tariff Commission as early as 1957 – Ingvar Svennilson and Kurt Martin Savosnick being the economists connected with the commission [264A].

rather than confined to economists ([221], pp. 168–71). More recently, it has been argued that we should have long-term reports that deal with the standard and quality of life in a broad sense of individuals – the consumption level of *specific* commodities for *specific* groups of people (for instance housing of poor people, health, working conditions, environmental qualities, etc.). Thus, it is argued that long-term reports concentrating on national account aggregates should be replaced by, or combined with, a number of concrete 'social indicators'.

Typical of these ideas is the work of the so-called 'Low-Income Investigation' [97], and a book by a new generation of economists working for the Swedish Confederation of Labour (LO) [28]. For instance, the Low-Income Committee concentrated, in their rather detailed empirical studies, on *nine* different indicators of the quality of life, and compared the levels for all nine indicators for different socio-economic subgroups in Sweden: health, nutrition, housing conditions, home environment during childhood, education, type of employment and concrete working conditions (noise, dirt, heavy work, stress, etc.), economic resources, participation in political decision-making, leisure and recreation [97].

It is still too early to express any opinions on how these new demands on the long-term reports will influence the future procedures. However, it is interesting to note how, for instance, economists connected with LO now criticise a policy that concentrates on a rapid growth of GNP – at the expense of neglecting the 'general environment' for the individual, such as *where* he works and lives – in spite of the fact that the 'solidaric wage policy' (which has so far *not* been questioned by the LO economists) to a large extent was designed precisely to speed up the rate of structural change and the growth rate of GNP, despite its effects of forcing people to move to other sectors and locations. However, it is also interesting to see how the slow growth rate during the period 1971–3 caused concern among labour unions for employment and real wages.

10 Allocation Policy

Apart from the expansion of the public sector in the field of public services (discussed in chapter 9), what have been the main government interventions in price formation and the allocation of resources in the postwar period, after the removal of most direct controls in the early fifties? First of all, there are, as in practically all countries, a number of excise taxes on a few 'luxury' commodities (such as furs and cosmetics) and certain 'unhealthy' products such as spirits and tobacco, as well as subsidies for certain cultural activities, e.g. the theatre, opera and various other arts. Secondly, as already pointed out, stabilisation policy has occasionally been used not only to dampen total investment demand, but also to discriminate against some sectors. An obvious example is the temporary 25 per cent tax on investment in office buildings and in the service sector during 1967/68 and 1970/71, designed to favour investment in other sectors. Moreover, monetary and fiscal policy tends to be discriminatory in various ways, even when this is not intended. One case in point is the rather heavy reliance on credit rationing by banks on certain occasions; another the favouring of firms with a good *past* profit record in the context of the investment funds policy.

Another, more deliberate, kind of intervention in the allocation of investment is the location policy initiated in the period 1963–5 for the purpose of stimulating industrial development in the northern parts of the country. The technique has involved government loans on favourable terms for investment expenditures, as well as direct subsidisation of investment costs; the subsidies amount to a maximum of 30 (or in exceptional cases 50) per cent of total investment costs. During the period 1963–1970 investment financed in this way accounted for about 8 per cent of total manufacturing investment in building and 4 per cent of investment in machinery in Sweden. (Seventy per cent of these investment expenditures with location policy support was made in 'The Northern Support Area'.)

The aim of the policy was to restrict, or possibly stop, the outflow of labour from the northern parts of Sweden, an outflow that had accelerated owing to the mechanisation of forestry, the rationalisation of the forest industry (wood products, paper and pulp) and by a contraction and rationalisation of farming, not least in the northern regions of the country. Another reason for this structural unemployment is, of course, the 'solidaric wage policy'. The new location policy was also partly initiated in response to the severe criticism, mainly by people in the north, of the labour-mobility policy, which facilitated the movement of labour out from the northern regions.

The official motivation for the regional development policy seems to have been a combination of two main ideas: (1) that the northern parts of the country have natural handicaps which, chiefly for social reasons, have to be compensated by subsidies; and (2) that the industrial environment shall be improved by creating 'external economies' in the north. In the latter case, the policy would try to create what might be called regional 'development blocs' (to borrow a term used by Erik Dahmén [34] in another context) of production units which stimulate and reduce costs for each other (for instance via common systems of communication, harbours, service firms, etc.) – i.e. 'external economies' in a wide sense. It would seem that the former idea has dominated practical policy so far (though the latter idea was stressed in the official documents when the policy was launched), as the support of investment expenditures in the northern regions has been dispersed over a very large number of geographical locations, which probably means that the industrial environment can hardly have changed very much for any of the locations.[1]

The regional development policy has been further supported by the investment funds policy. Such funds have been released,

[1] The pioneering works in the theory of regional economics in Sweden were made in the thirties by B. Ohlin [177] and T. Palander [189]. In the postwar period the emphasis has been more on empirical problems, such as in the works by R. Artle [4], P. Holm [71], G. Törnqvist [237], F. Kristensson [105] and Å. Andersson [2]. A number of articles on location policy by Swedish economists and geographers are published by a study group in the Department of Domestic Affairs, the ERU-Group [195].

even in periods without severe unemployment in the country as a whole (e.g. in 1965, 1969, 1970), to firms willing to invest in the northern areas. In fact, large industrial firms have been allowed to use investment funds in typical boom periods in the southern and central parts of the country, provided that some part of the funds (usually only a very small fraction) was used also in the northern areas. Such investment expenditures in the northern parts of the country accounted for about 5 per cent of total investment in manufacturing during the period 1963–1971.

From a theoretical point of view, it is interesting to note that, although labour is regarded as the abundant factor and capital, the scarce factor in the northern regions of the country, it was capital rather than labour that was chosen to be subsidised, thus stimulating capital-intensive production techniques and even the substitution of capital for labour in existing firms. This means that the employment-creating effects will be smaller than if mainly labour costs had been subsidised. However, in recent years some subsidisation of labour costs has also been introduced for new employment in the northern 'development areas'. In the late sixties and early seventies there has also been a tendency to introduce general subsidies of the labour costs for *specific* groups of labour with difficulties to be absorbed by the ordinary labour market, at prevailing wages (influenced by bargaining agreements) – in particular handicapped and elderly people.

Other types of government intervention in the allocation of resources are found in the price-controlled sectors, above all housing and agriculture. These are, in fact, the only major price-controlled areas in the private sector in Sweden (except for the temporary price-freeze during August 1970–December 1971, and the partial price controls in 1972–4) after the removal of the general price control in the middle of the fifties.

Housing policy in Sweden in the postwar period has been inspired mainly by the experiences in the thirties and by the expectations of a postwar slump. This is probably the main reason why the policy has been designed to stimulate the *demand* for housing. The two main tools have been rent control and housing subsidies – subsidies of interest costs of house-owners, as well as rent-subsidies paid directly to households (the last mentioned form above all from the late sixties).

There has been a tendency during the late sixties and early seventies to remove the *general* types of rent control. Thus, the control is completely abolished for co-operative apartments since 1969; these can be sold and bought freely in the market. However, publicly owned apartment houses still practise a rent policy that deviates from equilibrium pricing. And the removal of rent control for private apartments has been substituted by a system of central bargaining between organisations in the housing market, combined with arbitration decisions by courts. The principles to be followed by the courts are extremely vague, and it seems at the present time unlikely that rents can adjust to the equilibrium levels in the market for private apartments. Thus, it would seem that one rent control system has simply *replaced* another for private apartments.

Owing to the combination of rent control and inflation, the relative price of housing (as compared with prices for other consumer goods) has fallen by about 20 per cent since the end of the thirties, when the housing market was in equilibrium, though the housebuilding market was then probably characterised by unusually high profits. The entire fall occurred during the forties; during the sixties rents in fact rose somewhat more rapidly than prices for other consumer goods, owing mainly to increases in production costs and interest rates for newly built houses. In spite of a rather high housing production (possibly the highest in the world on a *per capita* basis), the policy resulted early in the postwar period in a huge excess demand for housing – a housing shortage. During most of the sixties the waiting period in the official queues for apartments was from four to eight years in Greater Stockholm and two to four years in medium-sized expanding towns.

Owing to the considerable rent increases in *newly built* houses during the late sixties and early seventies, the waiting periods were considerably shortened for new, particularly large, apartment houses. Some of them even became difficult to let at rents that covered (partly subsidised) production costs, at the same time as the excess demand still prevailed for the remaining part of the housing stock. Because of high rents for newly built apartments in recent years, a 'support system' has been created, where a substantial number of tenants obtain direct rent subsidies; in fact, about 50 per cent of all households with children below 16 years of age obtain such subsidies (in the early seventies).

Hence a housing market situation has emerged with tendencies to excess supply for *new* apartments, and thereby connected tendencies for housebuilding to fall, combined with excess demand for the stock of older apartments (where rents are controlled at lower levels). Thus, rent control has created a 'dual' housing market, with difficulties to keep up housebuilding, in spite of the existence of excess demand in the bulk of the housing market. A housing market with *both* a housing shortage and difficulties for new production has emerged – or rather been created by housing policy.

The main inspiration for the housing policy in Sweden in the postwar period has been the works by Alf Johansson, who has stressed the importance of demographic factors behind the demand for housing and minimised the possibility of achieving equilibrium in the market via higher rents. The official policy, following Johansson, has for thirty years maintained that the housing shortage could be removed, in the early postwar period 'within a few years', by large production of new houses, and that higher rents either could not remove the shortage, or were undesirable for various social considerations, such as the effect on the distribution of income and housing consumption. Johansson has also argued that fluctuations in rents would be detrimental to new construction, by raising costs and creating building crises from time to time. He also contended that 'high' equilibrium rents would result in a greater concentration of new construction on smaller apartments than he considered suitable from a long-run point of view.

Other economists in Sweden participated very little in the housing debate during the first fifteen years after the war. One exception was Sven Rydenfelt, who, in heated debates with Alf Johansson at the end of the forties, argued that rent control was responsible for the housing shortage and that the shortage could not be removed without higher and more flexible rents.[2] A similar attack on Swedish housing policy was made at the

---

[2] The official policy was outlined in government reports, largely written by Alf Johansson. The main document is [258]. For the discussion between Johansson and Rydenfelt see [83], [202]–[203].

beginning of the fifties by Eli Heckscher in two newspaper articles ([68], [69]).

During the sixties the interest in housing policy among economists increased. One example is an analysis of the effects of rent control by Bentzel, Lindbeck and Ståhl [21].[3] The essence of their analysis was to try to show that the goals behind rent control – such as a high volume of new construction and a reasonable distribution of income and housing consumption – could in fact be more efficiently reached *without* rent control, by the application of various taxes and subsidies to a market with equilibrium pricing. Another main point was that the housing shortage could not be removed by a high production of *new* houses; even if a balance were achieved in *new* apartments, the shortage would still be there in the earlier produced stock, where rents are considerably lower.

Bentzel–Lindbeck–Ståhl also analysed various 'non-desirable' side-effects of rent control, such as the abolition of 'consumer sovereignty' and the absence of 'market tests' of newly produced dwellings in a situation of large permanent excess demand. Thus, they argued that the lack of contact between the demand and the supply side – an effect of rent control – had made it possible too for builders (mainly municipalities and co-operative associations) to determine the *composition* of output regardless of the preference of consumers – a normal effect of a 'sellers' market' situation. It may be noticed, for instance, that 70–75 per cent of new lodgings have during the postwar period been in apartment houses, often of very impressive dimensions. However, a drastic shift of production to small owner-occupied houses occurred in 1973–4.

Bentzel–Lindbeck–Ståhl also stressed that incentives for efficiency in housing production are minimised when everything can be let regardless of cost and quality; that the stock of houses deteriorates owing to lack of incentives to make repairs, and so on. Another basic point was that the principles used to distribute housing consumption between households become rather dubious from a social point of view in a market with a permanent shortage, as housing consumption then is mainly determined on historical grounds: Those who happen to sit in a

[3] See also Lindbeck ([119] and [123]) and Ståhl [211]. For a more general and formalised analysis of housing markets see H. Dickson [35].

particular apartment are allowed to keep it at an unchanged rent no matter how highly other people without an apartment evaluate it. In fact, the usual way to get an apartment in Sweden seems, according to sketchy empirical evidence, to be through relatives, friends and employers rather than via the official queues; the black market also seems to play an important role.[4]

The rent-control policy has in recent years been defended, apart from Alf Johansson [84], by Per Holm and Bo Södersten. Per Holm [72] has stressed the same points as Alf Johansson, whereas Södersten ([222], [223]) has put emphasis on considerations of distribution of income and wealth. He has referred mainly to the capital gains which in a market without rent control accumulate for owners of earlier produced houses because of increased land values and higher building costs. It has been pointed out in the discussion, however, that there are in principle fiscal measures to counteract such capital gains.

Whereas one of the aims of rent control has been to favour consumers at the expense of producers (houseowners), the main purpose of the regulation of *agricultural prices* has been to achieve a redistribution of income from consumers to producers of agricultural products. The basic idea of the policy has been that price support policies should be used to guarantee a certain income level to farmers, whereas the efficiency of the sector should be stimulated by 'administrative' measures – loans on favourable terms, technical advice and government purchases and sales of land. Thus, an administrative process should partly replace the market mechanism for the purpose of increasing efficiency in agriculture.

The policy has undoubtedly succeeded in keeping up the incomes of farmers, by a support price that was in 1972 about 70 per cent above world market prices. However, the policy has been confronted with the same problem as in other countries: the agricultural sector has become uneconomically large and the transformation of its farm structure delayed. In twenty-five years, the average size of farms has risen by only about 6 hectares – approximately from 12 to 18 hectares – while the

---

[4] According to available empirical evidence, only about 20–25 per cent of those who have moved into apartments in the mid-sixties have obtained these via the official queues ([119], p. 66).

optimum size of farms (for grain production), according to studies by Lennart Hjelm [70], has risen from about 20–30 to about 100–200 hectares. As a comparison, the average size of farms in the United States has risen from about 65 to about 120 hectares during the same period.

However, in spite of the heavy price support, the incomes of the large number of farmers with very small holdings (2–10 hectares) have been so low in recent years, compared with incomes in other sectors, that the outflow of labour has accelerated considerably (to about 5–8 per cent per year of the agricultural labour force). Thus, it seems to be mainly the amalgamation of farms rather than the contraction of the labour force that has been delayed.

Swedish economists have long participated in the agricultural policy debate. Myrdal, in a study in the thirties [166], stressed that the difficulties of agriculture were not 'temporary', but rather were intimately connected with the transformation of the economy during a growth process: the continuous increase in productivity and the low income elasticity of demand for agricultural products. Consequently, he argued that the problems for agriculture could not be solved by subsidies alone, but that a long-term policy should be designed with the purpose of facilitating the contraction of the sector.

Agricultural policy during the first twenty years after the Second World War has been founded on the Report of the 1942 Agriculture Committee, of which Erik Lundberg and Ingvar Svennilson were members. In a special appendix to the committee report they argued that the majority of the committee were too little concerned with aspects of efficiency, price policy being completely tied to the income goal for the agricultural population [142]. Clas-Erik Odhner, economist for the Confederation of Trade Unions, in a number of books and articles has particularly pointed out that a contraction and improvement of efficiency of the agricultural sector is facilitated in a full-employment economy, and that the case for heavy subsidies is for this reason weakened in such an economy ([175], [176]). Odd Gulbrandsen and the present author in more recent contributions have again taken up these issues, both theoretically and empirically, as well as tried to estimate the macroeconomic costs of the agricultural policy, and also the minimum costs necessary to reach the production goal of agricultural policy, i.e. to guarantee the food supply in case of a breakdown in foreign trade because of a war in the outside world ([48]–[50]).

A typical suggestion in most proposals put forward by economists has been to rely more on deficiency payments and other types of transfers ('low-price line'), labour-mobility policy, retraining programmes and measures to speed up the amalgamation of farm holdings, rather than to continue the heavy reliance on price support by way of tariffs ('high-price line'), which has been characteristic of the agricultural policy pursued. For instance, it has been argued that an agricultural policy relying on a system of high *consumer* prices for agricultural products (as compared with world market prices) means an income redistribution to a considerable extent 'from the poorest consumers to most affluent farmers'.

At the same time, relative consumer prices are dramatically distorted, both between agricultural products and other commodities and between different agricultural products. A drastic distortion of producers' prices for different agricultural products (relative to world market prices) has also occurred – exemplified by tariffs of about 40 per cent for pork, 150 per cent for wheat and often several hundred per cent for sugar beet.

Through the 'new' agricultural policy established in 1967, on the suggestion of the 1960 Agriculture Committee, some changes in the direction of more reliance on aspects of efficiency were introduced. One target has been to contract the production capacity of the sector (down to 80 per cent of peacetime consumption of calories); another, to speed up the rate of consolidation of farm holdings. At the same time the previous rather firm tie between support prices and incomes has been slackened. In the price policy of the future, more importance is supposed to be attached to the production capacity and to the rate of structural change.

During the late sixties and early seventies concern about the regional distribution of people and income, and the natural environment ('an open landscape') has played an increasingly important role in the agriculture policy discussion – the 'green wave'. However, it is too early to judge whether such considerations will have much influence on the future agricultural policy, in particular in view of an increasing criticism by consumers of the rather high food prices in Sweden, as compared with other countries – in particular before the world-wide 'agriculture price explosion' in 1973.

Finally, an area in which government intervention in the allocation of resources has for a long time been advocated by economists is where severe external diseconomies exist, such as water and air pollution, noise, etc. Erik Dahmén ([32], [33]) has probably been the most energetic proponent of such intervention, recommending fees and taxes à la Pigou [193].

A rather active policy in this field started at the end of the sixties. However, the policy has relied more on direct regulations and subsidies than on taxes and fees. The regulations have consisted mainly of prohibitions of the use of certain chemicals – such as DDT – and of maximum limits on polluting activities, such as a ceiling on sulphur in oil used for burning. The subsidies have consisted mainly of government financial contributions to investments in purification devices in industries and municipalities. The methods will, no doubt, result in an improved environment; in fact, pollution of air and water by firms, households and municipalities will probably be rather small before the end of the seventies.

However, the methods chosen often imply a subsidy of specific industries. This means, no doubt, a distortion of the allocation of resources, both within Sweden and relative to other countries – as compared to alternative methods (such as fees) where the costs of anti-pollution devices were reflected in the production costs and prices of each industry. Hence, the environmental subsidies in Sweden imply a distortion of the trade pattern between Sweden and the rest of the world, if other countries leave the cost of anti-pollution devices as part of the production costs of each industry.

The reasons for the heavy reliance on regulations and subsidies – rather than fees – are many. One is simply that the authorities have not been able to see the environmental problems as an application of the theory of externalities in the context of the theory of resource allocation. Maybe regulations and subsidies also give the decision-makers in the public sector a satisfying feeling of 'power' and 'importance', which would be less pronounced if the more general and anonymous price mechanism were relied on (by fees on polluting activities). Moreover, a large fraction of the business community seems to prefer regulations, particularly if combined with subsidies, to fees. A reason is probably that many business firms believe they can obtain more favourable positions by 'bargaining' with public officials than by adjusting to general fees and taxes.

11 Income Distribution Policy and Structural Changes

Concern over the distribution of income has, from time to time, played a great role in the economic policy discussion in Sweden in the period following the Second World War. One example is the previously mentioned 'solidaric wage policy' of the Swedish Confederation of Labour (LO). Similar concern over income distribution and 'equality' has had a strong influence also on other aspects of Swedish economic policy. One outstanding example of this, of course, is the system of social insurance and other transfer payments, which now (in 1972) amount altogether to about 20 per cent of GNP. Another example is the expansion of the sector of public consumption – above all in education, health and welfare – which at present accounts for about 23 per cent of GNP. For instance, the 'explosive' expansion of the educational system is generally believed to have strong egalitarian effects on the income distribution in the long run. Whereas about 5 per cent of the population in the age group 20–24 were studying at universities in the early fifties, the corresponding figure had increased to about 20 per cent by the early seventies. The progressive tax system, of course, is also an example of a rather ambitious income distribution policy. Moreover, regional (location) policy and price regulations – mainly in housing and agriculture – have largely been motivated by considerations of income distribution.

There have probably been fewer attempts to influence the distribution of wealth within the private sector, in spite of the fact that wealth is much more unevenly distributed than income. The most important policies in the field of wealth distribution are presumably those connected with the partial 'collectivisation' of savings that has taken place during the sixties, owing mainly to the accumulation of wealth in the semi-public pension funds.

Our knowledge about the distribution of income, living standards and wealth in Sweden, and about their change over time, is still rather fragmentary. However, let us to begin with, look at two aspects of the income distribution, where some knowledge is available: (1) the 'vertical' distribution of individual income – before as well as after tax; and (2) the 'horizontal' distribution of disposable income and savings between the main sectors of the Swedish economy: households, firms and the public sector.

PERSONAL INCOME

We know, thanks to Ragnar Bentzel's studies, that a rather substantial equalisation of the vertical income distribution occurred in Sweden from the 1930s to the 1940s. Generally speaking, we may say that 9 per cent of national income was 'redistributed' from income earners above to income earners below the average income level between 1935 and 1948 [17]; these figures refer to *disposable* household income, i.e. income after taxes and transfer payments. Practically all of this equalisation was the result of a more equal distribution of 'factor incomes', i.e. incomes *before* taxes and transfer payments. It would seem that this equalisation to a large extent was the result of the removal of mass unemployment. Hence, a similar development occurred in other highly developed countries as well.

It is less certain what has happened to the vertical income distribution *during the postwar period*. If we look only at income earners who are included in the official income statistics, based on taxation figures, we get the impression that the vertical distribution of income has changed very little before taxes; it may even have become slightly more *unequal* during the course of the postwar period (1951–69) [22]. However, statistics of this type are quite misleading, as they refer only to people with an income high enough to include them in the taxation statistics. For instance, when housewives enter the labour force in greater numbers, and when old people get higher pensions and incomes, a number of people enter the income distribution statistics in the lower income brackets. Consequently, the *measured* income distribution looks more *unequal* than before, in spite of the fact that these groups might have received greater improvement than other income earners. Similar problems arise in the interpretation of income distribution statistics when the number of students with part-time work increases.

In empirical studies in connection with the 1970 Long-Term Report, an attempt was made to cope with these problems, by studying schematically the income distribution for *all* individuals over 20 years of age, regardless of whether or not their income was high enough to be included in taxation statistics [273]. Some results of such an approach are presented in the Lorenz curves in Chart 11:1.[1]

The curves indicate that there has in fact been an equalis-ation of the vertical distribution of income, including all individuals over 20, during the postwar period. However, there seems to have been no equalisation for *men* over this perod; a slight increase in the disparity would in fact seem to have occurred for this group. This observation is fairly consistent with figures over the dispersion of wages in different industries, which have remained rather unchanged since 1946; (Chart in Appendix). It may be difficult to draw any rigorous con-clusions from these figures about success or failure of 'the solidaric wage policy', as we do not know what would have happened in the absence of such a policy. However, a rather regular pattern emerges where 'wage drift' for high-income workers tends to restore original income differentials after attempts in the bargaining process to equalise wage differen-tials. It is too early to say if the unusually strong ambition to 'equalisation' in the 1971 bargaining has been more successful.

The figures suggest that an important factor behind the equalisation of income for the population as a whole, after 1951, is the increased participation of women in the labour market. In fact, the labour market participation rates for women (over 20 years of age) have increased from about 28 per cent in 1950

---

[1] A Lorenz curve shows the percentage of the income sum that is obtained by a given percentage of the individuals, ranked from low to high incomes. The Lorenz curve will coincide with the diagonal line in the chart if everybody has the same income. The closer the curve comes to the diagonal line, the more even is the distribution of income. The statistics have been supplied by Pebbe Selander and R. Spånt, Economics Depart-ment, Uppsala University [207].

CHART 11:1   Lorenz curves for vertical income distribution before tax in Sweden

A. All male and female, above 20 years of age

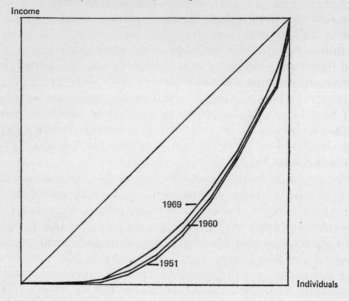

B. All men, 20–66 years of age

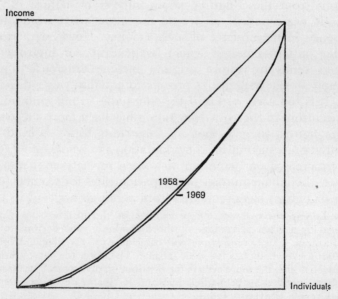

Source: Data from P. Selander and R. Spånt [207].

to about 40 per cent in 1969, according to official population statistics; (the rate has during the same period fallen somewhat for men – from 87 to 76 per cent – due mainly to the 'education explosion'). According to the (quarterly) labour force studies, the labour force participation rates for women are even higher than this – about 60 per cent in the age group 20–64. These are probably internationally very high figures for women's participation in the labour market for developed 'Western' countries.

It may be of interest to find some 'simple' summary figures for the changes in the distribution of income for the population as a whole (over 20), as reflected in the Lorenz curves. One way to express the development is to say that 3·5 per cent of the income sum (before taxes) among income earners *above* the average has been redistributed to income earners *below* the average since 1950 ([273], pp. 173–82). It is also of interest to note that 95 per cent of the dispersion of incomes in the late 1960s can be traced to the distribution of other incomes than capital income (which accounts for approximately 5 per cent of the total income sum of individuals). Thus, the inequalities in the *aggregate* distribution of income (before taxes) in Sweden seem to be connected almost entirely with the distribution of income from labour. For high income groups, for instance above 200,000 kronor, however, capital income is an important component.

The Low Income Committee has tried to pin down in more detail the various factors behind the inequalities of income. The main conclusion – well in line with the observations in the Long-Term Report – was that two factors are particularly important: the number of work-days and the profession, while factors such as age and wealth were found to be of lesser importance ([97], pp. 42–3). This, again, suggests that a successful income distribution policy must rely heavily on a 'high-employment policy', and on investment in human capital, including rehabilitation of handicapped people, as well as on compensation to persons who because of sickness and other handicaps are unable to work full time.

The distribution of income after taxes is somewhat more equal than the distribution of factor income. However, it is extremely difficult to know how taxes actually influence the distribution of after-tax income because of problems of shifting

CHART 11:2   Direct impact of taxes on income distribution of households, 1966

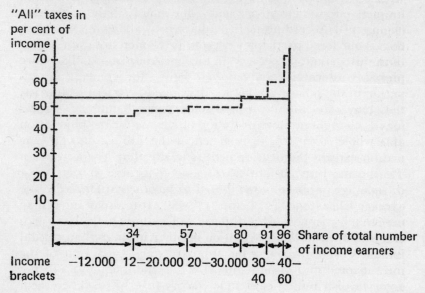

Source: M. Hellström [69A].

and incidence of taxes, and hence the effects of taxes on income before taxes. However, in Chart 11:2, constructed by Mats Hellström, the 'direct impact' of all taxes, i.e. the effects *neglecting* indirect effects by way of changes in factor income (i.e. income before taxes) is schematically calculated [69A]. The diagram shows taxes as a percentage of income in different income brackets, as well as the average tax percentage for the population as a whole (in 1966). All types of taxes are, in principle, included – income taxes and indirect taxes, as well as profit taxes – but transfer payments and public consumption are not. (The analysis of the distribution, on income brackets, of profit taxes is, however, quite doubtful.) As is seen from the diagram, the lowest income groups, with incomes below 12,000 kronor, on the average gained 8–10 per cent of their income on having a progressive tax system rather than a proportional one, with a tax rate of 54 per cent for everybody. The income classes immediately above earned somewhat less on the progressive elements, while the top-income group, with an income above 60,000 kronor, lost about 18 per cent of their income because of the progressive elements in the system. A study of the very highest income earners, with an income above for instance 150,000 kronor, would give a much stronger 'direct impact' of the progressiveness of the tax system, as people in these groups may have a total tax burden of about 80 per cent of net ('taxable') income, and hence a loss of about 25 per cent of their taxable income, because of the progressively graduated scales. Thus, while the income redistribution effects of the tax system in 1966 seem to have been fairly modest for that bulk of income earners below 30,000 kronor (i.e. for 80 per cent of income earners), the progressiveness seems to be of considerable importance for the high-income groups, particularly above the 60,000 kronor level. A piece of evidence of the importance for the income distribution of *the state income tax* alone is supplied by the *1970* Long-Term Report. The authors calculated that this particular type of tax – a rather progressive part of the tax system – redistributed 4·5 per cent of incomes above the average to income earners below the average. It should, again, be emphasised that these studies do not take into account possible shifting of progressive taxation on factor incomes.

It is likely that a study for 1971, when the tax rates became more progressive in, and slightly above, the mid-income brackets, would give a greater 'equalisation effect' of the Swedish tax system in the mid-income brackets.

The data on the distribution of transfer payments – and hence 'disposable income' – are incomplete. However, we would expect that transfer payments contribute to an equalisation of the distribution of disposable income. This is illustrated for a number of different socio-economic population groups, with varying average incomes, in Table 11:A, based on a study by Lars Söderström for the Low-Income Committee ([226A], p. 61), referring to conditions in 1967. Whereas disposable income is about 30 per cent *lower* than taxable income for full-time employees (20–67 years of age), it is about 40 per cent *higher* for people with a short working time, and nearly 90 per cent

Table 11:A

Taxable income and disposable income for various groups in 1967: average incomes and measure of inequality within groups (kronor)

Population groups[1]	Taxable income (average) (A)	Disposable income (average) (B)	Measure of inequality of taxable income[2] (C)	Measure of inequality of disposable income[2] (D)	Disposable income as percentage of taxable income (E)	Inequality of disposable income as percentage of inequality of taxable income[2] (F)
1 Full-time employees (20–67)[3]	23,700	17,000	135	89	71.7	65.9
2 Workers	15,600	12,400	182	134	79.5	73.6
3 Employees	20,100	14,800	239	157	73.6	65.7
4 Men	20,400	15,100	282	192	74.0	68.1
5 People with sickness tendencies[4]	13,800	11,900	357	205	86.2	57.4
6 People with short schooling[5]	12,300	10,300	396	274	83.7	69.2
7 Unmarried	11,200	9,300	398	276	83.0	69.3
8 All (20–67)	15,600	12,200	442	288	78.2	65.2
9 People living in big cities	16,800	13,100	473	323	78.0	68.3
10 People living in countryside	12,000	9,800	480	323	81.7	67.3
11 All (15–75)	13,900	11,100	492	325	79.9	66.1
12 People with poor liquidity[6]	7,900	7,300	516	310	92.4	60.0
13 People in families with low incomes (20–67)[7]	7,800	7,100	517	310	91.0	60.0
14 Women	7,400	7,000	653	401	94.6	61.4
15 People with short working time[8] (20–67)	3,600	5,000	973	548	138.9	56.3
16 People with incomes below lowest income tax bracket	1,800	3,400	1276	636	188.9	49.8

[1] Age group 15–75 if not otherwise stated.
[2] Theil's inequality coefficient ('redundancy').
[3] More than 2000 hours a year.
[4] Sick at least eight days a year.
[5] At most seven years of schooling.
[6] Declaring themselves unable to raise 2000 kronor (approx. $400) within one week.
[7] Less than 20,000 kronor ($4000) for married and 10,000 kronor ($2000) for unmarried.

higher than taxable income for people with taxable income below the minimum tax bracket – in fact implying a system of 'negative income tax' for these groups (column E). It is also seen from the table (column F) that about 50 per cent (100–49·8) of the inequalities of income is removed by taxes and transfer payments among people in the groups with the lowest average income, whereas about 26 per cent (100–73·6) of the inequalities are removed among workers, who are a rather representative group in terms of average income in the country, and also a rather 'homogenous' group.[2] It is also quite likely, though not completely self-evident, that public consumption is more evenly distributed on income brackets than is disposable income itself.

Moreover, it is likely that the expansion of income-related transfers during the late sixties and early seventies, in combination with the new tax scales in 1971 (somewhat modified in 1973), have further evened out the distribution of income within the middle-income brackets – 25–40,000 ($6500–9000).

Also, other government interventions in the economy have, of course, important effects on the distribution of income. The system of rent control redistributes (instantaneously) approximately 1 per cent of national income from houseowners and public authorities to tenants ([21], [123]), though the distributional effects *among* tenants is quite arbitrary. And the agricultural price regulation redistributes, instantaneously, approximately 1·5 per cent of national income ([48], pp. 91–2) from consumers to producers of agriculture products (see chapter 10).

Does the income distribution in Sweden differ substantially from other countries? International comparisons of income distribution are very difficult to make, and even more difficult to interpret, for instance because of differences in labour force participation rates between countries. However, *available* studies indicate that the vertical distribution of factor incomes, hence incomes before taxes and transfer payments, is rather similar in most north-western European countries – particularly the Scandinavian countries, the United Kingdom and Holland. About 30 per cent of incomes before tax is in most

---

[2] As measure of the income inequalities within each group, Theil's inequality coefficient (what Theil calls 'redundancy') has been used.

of these countries acquired by the richest 10 per cent of the taxpayers, and about 7–10 per cent by the richest 1 per cent. The poorest 10 per cent of the taxpayers usually seem to obtain about 1–2 per cent ([77], chapter 6; [147], Appendix 7). A schematic comparison of some countries is made in Chart 11 : 3, quoted from a study by the Economic Commission for Europe (ECE). Sweden does not seem to differ significantly, with respect to the distribution of personal incomes before taxes, from other high-income north-western European countries (except for West Germany). It is quite likely that the income distribution in Sweden is more egalitarian *after* taxes, transfer payments and public consumption than in most other north-western European countries. However, this statement is more of an 'educated guess' than a statement of statistically observed facts. The main reason for making it is the earlier mentioned high progressiveness of the tax and transfer system for middle income groups ($6000–9000).

The attempts to influence the income distribution – by way of solidaric wage policy and tax-subsidy programmes – have resulted in some obvious conflicts with other goals of economic and social policy, in particular during the late sixties and early seventies, when the ambition to equalise income increased. The marginal tax rates became rather high, about 60 per cent for quite ordinary income receivers in the bracket 25,000–40,000 kronor ($6500–9000). If the marginal effects of income-dependent transfers of various other types are added, in particular for families with children (housing subsidies and subsidies for nursery schools), then very high marginal effects arise. For instance, for a family with two children, the construction of the housing subsidies alone creates a 'marginal effect' on disposable income of about 30 per cent, making the *total* marginal effect about 90 per cent, implying that the household will be allowed to keep only 10 per cent of an increase in income before tax. In some cases the marginal effect will in fact be over 100 per cent when subsidies for nursery schools are lost as income rises. In such special cases it will pay the household to *reduce* the supply of labour, for instance by absenteeism from work, or to negotiate a *reduction* in wage rates before taxes.

For families with children, in particular, it is in fact quite difficult for them to raise disposable income significantly in

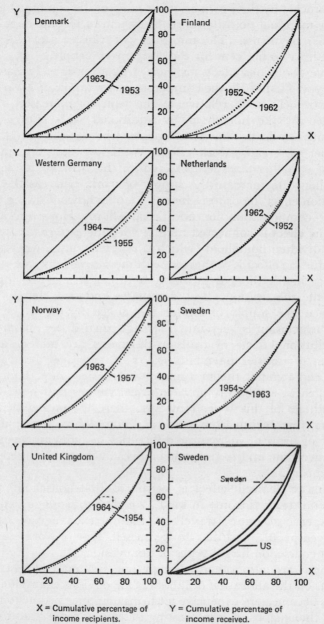

X = Cumulative percentage of income recipients.

Y = Cumulative percentage of income received.

Source: Economic Commission for Europe [77] and (for last section) P. A. Samuelson [206], chap. 6.

this bracket by their own effort because of the combined effects of the marginal tax rates and the system of income-dependent transfer payments. (The marginal tax-transfer rate will often be at least 80 per cent for these groups of people.)

Several obvious effects are caused by a tax-subsidy system of this type. First of all, the compensation for additional work will be extremely small relative to the value of increased output created by the household by additional work. On *a priori* grounds we do not know, of course, whether the net effect is smaller or greater work effort. We know that the 'income effect' of higher taxes tends to reduce the demand for leisure, and hence to increase the supply of work, whereas the 'substitution effect' tends to reduce the supply of work owing to the lower compensation for additional efforts. However, as the income effect is connected mainly with the *average* tax rate for an individual household (which is relatively low), whereas the substitution effect is connected with the *marginal* tax rate (which is very high), there is probably a rather strong presumption that the substitution effect dominates and that therefore, on balance, the supply of labour is reduced by the tax system. This conclusion is very much strengthened if the income and substitution effects of transfer payments are added, as the system of transfer payments *lowers* the average 'tax-transfer' rate and *increases* the marginal 'tax-transfer' rate. Unfortunately, there are hardly any empirical studies that have tested hypotheses of this type. However, there is some evidence of higher absenteeism from work and complaints from management of firms of increasing difficulties in inducing people to take overtime and to train themselves for more qualified work in industry.

A more clear-cut effect is, of course, that households try to concentrate on 'income in kind', which is difficult to tax, such as expense accounts, travelling, mutual exchange of services between people, and the 'do-it-yourself' type of work – as well as, of course, on illegal types of tax evasion.

There are also other, though not systematically studied, effects on the allocation of labour. One obvious example is that it has become very expensive for firms to induce people to move, or to change jobs. It is interesting to see that some sectors of the Swedish economy have obvious difficulties in recruiting labour, even in situations of rather substantial unemployment, such as in 1971–2. In particular, the manufacturing industry has great difficulty in filling vacancies. Thus, it is likely that the solidaric wage policy, in combination with the high marginal tax (and transfer) rates, has reduced the incentives for mobility of the labour force. We can also see difficulties arising for Swedish firms to employ internationally outstanding specialists; to give them a salary of, say 100,000 kronor ($22,000) *after* tax, a firm has to pay salary costs of about 500,000 kronor ($111,000) *before* tax. However, 'ingenuity' often solves the problem!

Maybe income distribution policies in Sweden, with the help of solidaric wage policy, progressive taxes and income transfers, have reached the limits for an economic system that builds on economic incentives and a free labour market. In fact, there are already signs that the political parties will compete to reduce the marginal effects of the tax system – after having in fact earlier competed in increasing the marginal effects.

INCOME DISTRIBUTION BETWEEN PRIVATE AND PUBLIC SECTOR

There has been a rather dramatic shift in the distribution of disposable income and savings between the three main sectors of the Swedish economy during the postwar period – households, firms and the public sector (Table 11:B). The share for households of total disposable income has fallen from about 75 per cent to 62 per cent, i.e. a fall of 13 percentage points, from 1950 to 1970. (This is, of course, the basic 'explanation' for the fall in private consumption from 66 to 54 per cent of GNP – by 12 percentage points.) Also, the share of total disposable income held by firms (gross savings by firms) has fallen substantially – from about 6 per cent to about 3·5 per cent, i.e. by about 2·5 percentage points. *Before* tax, interest incomes plus dividends amount in Sweden in the late sixties and early seventies to no more than about 5 per cent of net national income. 10 per cent is a more typical figure for capitalist countries.

The mirror image of the drop in the shares of households and firms is, of course, the increase in the shares of public (and semi-public) authorities – from about 20 per cent of total disposable income in 1950 to about 34·5 per cent in 1970, i.e. an increase of 15 percentage points. In these calculations,

Table 11 : B
Distribution of disposable income (per cent of total)

	1950–4	1955–9	1960–4	1965–9	1970–1	Change 1950–4 / 1965–9	Change 1950–4 / 1970–1
Households	74·2	74·0	69·5	64·5	61·9	–9·7	–12·3
Firms[1]	6·0	4·0	4·0	3·3	3·3	–2·7	–2·7
Public authorities	19·6	21·4	24·3	27·8	29·6	8·2	10·0
Social insurance institutions	0·2 } 19·8	0·6 } 22·0	2·2 } 26·5	4·4 } 32·2	5·2 } 34·8	4·2 } 12·4	5·0 } 15·0

[1] Includes only 'juridical persons', such as various types of corporations, private as well as public, and government public utilities (*affärsverk*).

CHART 11:4 Distribution of national income between households, firms and the public sector: factor income (i.e. incomes before taxes and transfer payments)

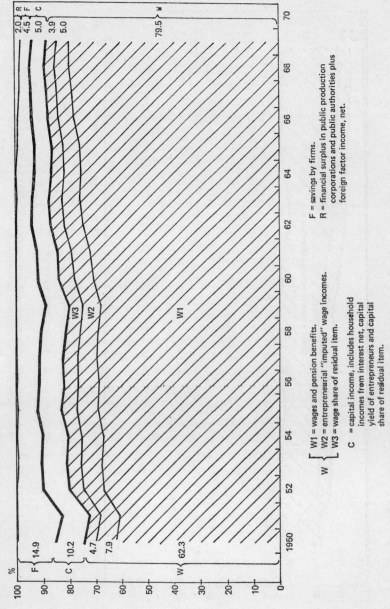

W {
W1 = wages and pension benefits.
W2 = entrepreneurial "imputed" wage incomes.
W3 = wage share of residual item.

C = capital income, includes household incomes from interest net, capital yield of entrepreneurs and capital share of residual item.

F = savings by firms.

R = financial surplus in public production corporations and public authorities plus foreign factor income, net.

Source. Central Bureau of Statistics: National Accounts.

CHART II·5   Disposable income, (direct) taxes and transfer payments

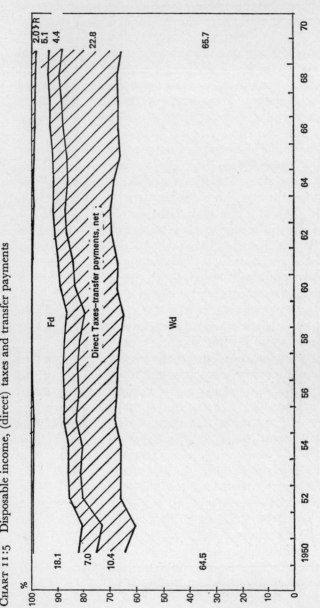

Wd = Wage earner, disposable income.

Fd = Disposable income of firms and disposable capital
income by households.

R = Financial surplus in public production corporations and public authorities plus
foreign factor income, net and foreign transfer payments, net.

Source: Central Bureau of Statistics: National Accounts. Obs.: only direct taxes are included in shaded area, indirect taxes
being classified here as part of private consumption, and hence private disposable income.

public transfer payments have been registered as disposable income for the household rather than for the public sector. (Disposable income of the public sector is defined here as public consumption, public investment and public financial saving.)

The developments are also illustrated in Charts 11:4 and 11:5. The shaded area in Chart 11:4 shows the development of wage incomes, including pensions and 'imputed' wage income of entrepreneurs. According to the chart they have increased from about 62 per cent of national income in 1950 to about 80 per cent in 1970. Capital incomes (items C and F in the chart) have fallen from about 25 per cent of national income to about 10 per cent.

Chart 11:5 shows the development of three main types of *disposable* income of the Swedish economy – wage-earner income, capital income (by firms *and* households) and the public income – hence not quite the same type of information as in Table 11:B. The shaded area there depicts direct taxes *minus* transfer payments, i.e. the incomes obtained by the public sector by direct taxes not paid back as transfer payments to the private sector. This item has, according to the chart, increased from about 17 to about 27 per cent of national income. Disposable income of wage earners has been a constant share of national income, whereas capital income has fallen considerably.

These changes in the distribution of disposable income are reflected also in the distribution ('origin') of savings and the supply of credit. The share of total gross savings by the private sector has fallen from about 70 per cent in the late fifties to 50 per cent in the early seventies. This is, of course, balanced by a corresponding increase in the share of public saving (Table 11:C; see also T. Backelin [14]). It is interesting to note that there has hardly been any increase in the *total* saving ratio (with respect to GNP) during the last decade; it was 22 per cent in the period 1960–2 (average) and 24 per cent in the period 1969–71 (average): the share of private saving of GNP has fallen as much as the share of public saving has increased. As a description of what has happened, we may say that a considerable part of saving by households and firms (roughly speaking, about one quarter-of the firms' and about half of the households' share of total saving) have been 'moved over' to public

Table 11:c
Origin of saving (per cent of total)

Saving	(1) Central government	(2) Local governments	(3) Social security system	Σ(1)–(3)	(4) Housing	(5) Private insurance funds	(6) Firms	(7) Household (excl. insurance saving)	Σ(1)–(7)
1957–60	11·5	13·7	1·3	26·5	7·0	10·1	44·1	12·3	100·0
1961–4	17·3	12·5	9·6	39·4	6·0	6·8	33·3	14·5	100·0
1965–9	13·3	17·4	17·0	47·7	6·2	8·3	30·3	7·5	100·0
Change	+1·8	+3·7	+15·7		−0·8	−1·8	−13·8	−4·8	
		+21·2					−21·2		

CHART 11:6   Household savings ratio

Defined as the difference between disposable income and private consumption,
as the share of saving of disposable income.

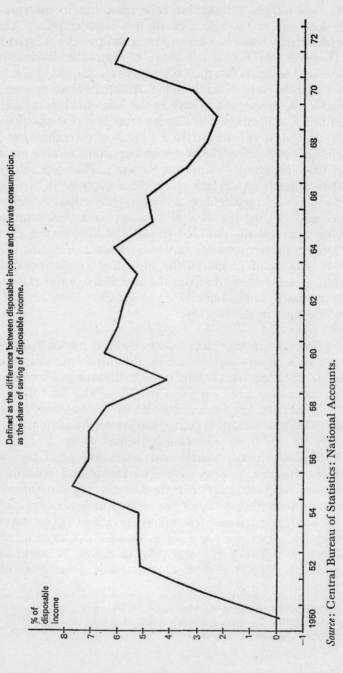

Source: Central Bureau of Statistics: National Accounts.

and semi-public authorities. It is tempting to interpret this development as the effect of the tax-transfer policy and the social security fees (to a large extent paid to the AP-system).

However, the fall in the share of disposable income of the household sector is not the only reason for the fall in the household sector's share of total saving. Another reason is a negative trend in the propensity to save by the household sector since the mid-fifties, as illustrated in Chart 11:6.[3] It is perhaps likely that this fall, too, is at least partly the result of the expansion of the social security system, whereby an important motive for saving has been removed ('rainy-day saving'). However, then it is rather difficult to explain the sudden increase in the savings ratio in 1971, in particular as the ratio has stayed at this higher level also during the period 1971–4; as a result household saving has suddenly doubled its share of total saving.

These long-term changes are also reflected in the distribution of the supply of credit in the organised credit market. The public sector's share has from the late fifties to the early seventies increased from about 10 to about 40–50 per cent of total credit supply in the market.

OWNERSHIP OF CAPITAL AND SUPPLY OF CREDIT

In Sweden, as in other countries, the distribution of capital is considerably less equal than the distribution of income. However, the statistics are even less reliable in this field than in the field of income. For instance, small wealth holdings below the level of taxable wealth (150,000 kronor per household) are very poorly covered in the taxation statistics.

The most equally distributed assets are probably owner-occupied houses, co-operative apartments and possibly bank accounts, whereas shares are the least evenly distributed type of asset. According to available figures only about 8 per cent of the adult population owns shares, i.e. about 15 per cent of the households. And ·01 per cent of owners would seem to own about 25 per cent of the total value of shares. It would appear that the distribution of shares in Sweden is rather more uneven

---

[3] It is possible that the statistics exaggerate the fall in the saving ratio of the household sector, as the coverage of consumption statistics is broader now than earlier for certain commodities. However, it is very *likely* that a fall in the ratio has in fact occurred.

than in many other highly developed countries [262].

The most important change in the distribution of wealth in Sweden during the postwar period is the relative shift of wealth from the private to the public sector. In the case of financial assets, the huge and rapidly expanding 'semi-public' pension fund (the AP-fund) has become increasingly important during the last decade. In 1971 it accounted for about 25 per cent of the stock of financial assets in the organised credit market. Some of the basic questions in relation to this fund are: What has been the incidence of pension contributions, i.e. who 'pays' for it by a reduction in real income in 'the final outcome'?; How is the credit supply influenced by growth of the fund?; and To what extent will the fund be 'deliberately' used to influence the allocation of resources and the ownership of real capital in the economy?

The incidence of the pension contributions is important both in judging the effects of the expansion of the fund on the saving ratio and on the distribution of income, savings and wealth. The more the pension contributions are shifted on to wages and/or prices, and the less the propensity of households to save declines owing to the new pension system – i.e. the poorer substitute AP-savings are to other types of saving – the greater is the probability that the new pensions system has in fact resulted in an *increase* in the propensity to save for the economy as a whole.

When looking more closely at the development of disposable income and saving ratios during the sixties, as just outlined, we find that the share of incomes and savings by households (*excluding* the accumulation of the pension funds) fell only slightly to begin with during the first half of the sixties, whereas profits fell by about the same amount later as the AP-funds increased. During the second half of the sixties, by contrast, the income share of firms was about constant, whereas the household share fell approximately by the amount of the rise in the pension funds. It is tempting to interpret this as if firms had to 'carry' the increase in pension fees to begin with (1960–5), whereas households 'carried' the burden of increased pension fees during the later period (1966–71). However, we cannot be sure that this is a correct interpretation, as we do not know for certain what would have happened with the income shares in the absence of the increase in the pension fees. For instance, the profit share of national income seems to have fallen also in several other countries during the first half of the sixties.

The effects on the supply of long-term capital appear to be more clear-cut than the effects on saving. Whereas the pensions fund lends mainly on the long-term credit market (the capital market), firms and households contribute to a large extent to the supply of short-term credit, partly via banks and other credit institutions. Thus, the AP-system can be expected to have increased the supply of funds on the *long-term* capital market. (The quantitative magnitude of this effect depends largely on the incidence of the pension contributions.)

So far, the allocation of the supply of credit does not seem to have changed *drastically* because of the pension fund, as the policy of the fund has followed about the same principles as those of private pension funds and insurance companies, with the portfolio concentrated on mortgage bonds, securities issued by local governments and bonds and similar loans to industry. Moreover, the effect on the availability of the funds of firms has been dampened somewhat by the right of firms to borrow a certain fraction of the fees they have paid into the fund. (Such loans currently constitute about 6 per cent of the assets of the pension fund.)

The composition of the flow of loans by the AP-system, as well as by other credit institutes, is illustrated in Tables 11:D and 11:E. Nearly one-third of the supply of credit on the 'organised' credit market came from the semi-public social

Table 11:D

Supply of funds from the organised credit market (net flows) (per cent of total)

	1951–5	1956–60	1961–5	1966–70
Central Bank	5·1	9·7	0·7	7·5
Commercial banks	19·4	26·6	28·2	22·4
Other banks	33·1	31·5	29·7	22·8
Private insurance institutions	26·4	23·1	12·3	10·0
Public insurance institutions	1·0	2·7	22·7	31·4
Others (residual item)	15·0	6·4	6·4	5·9
Total	100·0	100·0	100·0	100·0

Table 11:E
Sources of credit to private industry (flow) (per cent of total)

	Central Bank	Commercial banks	Other banks	Private insurance institutions	Public insurance institutions	Others (residual item)	Total
1951–5	—	-13·7	25·0	55·5	—	33·2	100·0
1956–60	—	25·0	12·5	43·2	1·1	18·2	100·0
1961–5	0·4	45·0	13·2	11·0	14·5	15·9	100·0
1966–70	0·7	26·6	15·9	13·1	34·0	9·7	100·0

security funds at the end of the sixties (Table 11:D). By the middle of the seventies the figure is expected to reach 40 per cent. It is also interesting to note that during the late sixties about one-third of the credit obtained by private firms from credit institutes was obtained from the semi-public social security funds (Table 11:E). (The AP-fund at that time allocated about one-third of its funds to production firms and a little less than half to housebuilding.) The most drastic drop in the 'market share' in the organised credit market has occurred, not very surprisingly, for private insurance institutions – from about 26 to about 10 per cent.

The AP-fund has (at least up to 1974) followed a rather 'passive' policy of portfolio management, in the sense that the rate of return on the assets has determined the allocation of funds between different kinds of private bonds. However, a debate started during the end of the sixties as to whether the AP-fund, in which the board members consist mainly of representatives of labour market organisations and government officials, should try to supply more 'risk capital', such as shares, to firms. Another question was whether the fund should try to exert power over the firms obtaining capital from the fund, and whether the board members of the fund should try to steer the capital market in certain politically determined directions. In this event it would mean that in the future the fund could be a very important centre of power in the economy.

The AP-funds could, in fact, technically be used to create something very close to a monopoly on the capital market, for bonds as well as shares – which would be a substantial movement in the direction of state capitalism, most likely of a very centralised nature. Sweden would then move in the direction of a more centralised economic system with respect to capital formation and the allocation of investment. However, it is still uncertain to what extent the AP-fund will be allocated to 'risk' capital such as shares, and just how much influence officials of labour market organisations and political leaders will want to have, or are able to get.

These tendencies for a large fraction of capital to be administrated by institutions and foundations rather than by 'private' capitalists is, of course, a pattern that is found in many highly developed countries today. Maybe we can talk about an institutionalisation of the administration of capital. For instance, in the US, various types of funds – such as insurance companies and pension funds – own about 40 per cent of the stock of marketed shares. And in Sweden 'juridical persons' – including both production enterprises and financial institutions – own nearly 50 per cent of the stock of marketed shares in the country. In fact, it is quite usual for 20–30 per cent of the shares in big Swedish corporations to be held by financial institutions such as investment companies, insurance companies, share-foundations, etc. (However, insurance companies in Sweden do not exert much power at company meetings, as they are not allowed to own more than a maximum of 5 per cent of the shares in a firm, and they do not in reality take a very active part at company meetings.)

The increased importance of the public pension funds on the Swedish long-term capital market conforms to this pattern of more 'institutionalised' administration of capital – or 'fund-capitalism'. The main difference between these types of funds and the Swedish AP-fund is, of course, the enormous size of the latter, relative to the capital market as a whole, and the ease by which the government can exert control of its operations. As an illustration, the *stock* of the AP-funds is presently about half of the GNP, and the yearly *increase* of the funds is nearly the same size as the increase in assets by the entire banking system.

PROFITS, THE FINANCING OF CAPITAL FORMATION AND STRUCTURAL CHANGE

The previously discussed shifts in the distribution of income between firms, households and the public sector should be seen in relation to the structural changes on the production side in the Swedish economy.

There has been a substantial change in the proportions between the production sectors in Sweden during the post Second World War period. Thus, the production of services has changed from 43 per cent of GNP in 1950 to 50 per cent in 1970; consequently, the commodity-producing sectors have fallen from 57 to 50 per cent of GNP. The bulk of the shift is due to the expansion of the production of public services, from 13 to 18 per cent of GNP (see also R. Bentzel [20]).

There have also been substantial shifts between the various

sectors when we look at more disaggregated data. Some of the most noticeable shifts are, of course, the fall of agriculture from 5 per cent of GNP to 2 per cent, and of forestry from 3·5 per cent to 1·7 per cent. Substantial changes have occurred also within manufacturing industry. The most dramatic changes here are presumably the fall of textiles, from 15 per cent of value added in manufacturing to 6 per cent, and the increase in engineering from 30 per cent to 42 per cent. There have also been very strong *intra*-industry changes, in the form of changes in the structure and distribution of size of firms.

All these developments are, of course, very much related to developments in international markets. They have, so far, been the product of a decentralised market adjustment without much government intervention, except in the public sector, of course, and in agriculture, where government policy has slowed down the process.

One important explanation for the acceleration of the rate of structural changes is probably that international competition has hardened considerably in recent years. In Sweden, as in several other countries, this shows up as a fall in profit margins. Among conceivable explanations for this development could be mentioned not only the continuous increase in labour costs, including various social security fees and taxes on the wage sum, but also trade liberalisation for commodities in manufacturing, a fall in transportation costs in international trade and the emergence of a number of new exporting countries in manufacturing.

Some figures may illustrate the fall in profit margins, the rate of return on capital and the solidity ('solvency') of firms. Profit margins *before* profit taxes and depreciation ('gross profits') in manufacturing, as a percentage of sales, would appear during the course of the sixties to have fallen from 10–11 per cent to 8–9 per cent. (As a percentage of total physical capital of firms, gross profits seem to have fallen from 9–10 per cent to 7–8 per cent.) The rate of return on 'owned capital' *after* profit tax and theoretically calculated depreciation seems to have fallen to a level corresponding to the bond yield, or about 6–8 per cent.[4]

By accepting a fall in owned capital in relation to borrowed

[4] For analyses of the developments of profits, and their relation to capital formation, see V. Bergström [24] and J. Södersten [225].

capital, firms have to some extent cushioned the reduction in the rate of return on owned capital – hence utilising a 'leverage effect' on this return. This effect had, of course, to be 'bought' at the cost of the solidity of the balance sheets of firms. While owned capital was about 40–45 per cent of the total capital stock in firms in the early sixties, the figure had fallen to 30–35 per cent in the early seventies. During the latter period it was not unusual for borrowed capital to be about twice the value of owned capital, while it was quite normal in the late fifties or early sixties for owned and borrowed capital to be about the same size. These developments have presumably made the firms more vulnerable to profit squeezes, and hence increased their mortality rate – through closing down of plants and mergers.

The acceleration of the rate of structural change in recent years may be illustrated by some figures. For instance, the number of mergers in Sweden increased strongly during the sixties: while mergers each year during the fifties involved firms employing less than 1 per cent of the labour force, the corresponding figure climbed to 3–5 per cent during the sixties (Chart 11:8). Partly as a result of these structural changes, wage costs per unit of output seem to have kept the relation to other western European countries – even after allowance for exchange rate changes in various countries (see Chart 11:7).

These tendencies have contributed to some new trends in the economic policy debate in Sweden in recent years. One example is the demand for subsidies to rescue, or at least extend the life of, existing firms, as well as to create new industries in areas hit by contracting industries; the new regional development policy and certain selective uses of investment funds policy are cases in point. Another example is the recent discussion on the desirability of providing government credit on favourable terms to shipbuilding, which is heavily subsidised in some other countries. A further example is a combination of releases of investment funds for industry and a selective investment tax of 25 per cent for so-called 'non-priority sectors' (office buildings, and services) in the early seventies. Thus, as compared to a subsidy of about 10–35 per cent for *some* investments in manufacturing (those financed by investment funds), there has been

CHART 11:7   Wage costs per unit of output, relative to other countries

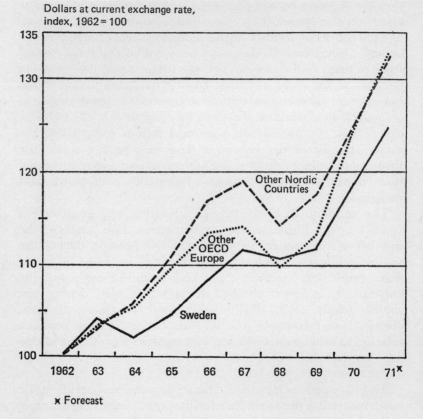

Source: OECD: Sweden, Economic Survey, April 1971.

a tax on investment in offices, distribution and service of a magnitude of 25 per cent. This means, of course, that projects in manufacturing with a rather low rate of return (without government tax subsidy intervention) in many cases will squeeze out projects with a high rate of return in other sectors. The motive behind this policy seems mainly to have been to improve the balance of payments – analogous to the motive for similar policies in some other countries, such as the United Kingdom.

Obviously, a certain deterioration in the efficiency of the

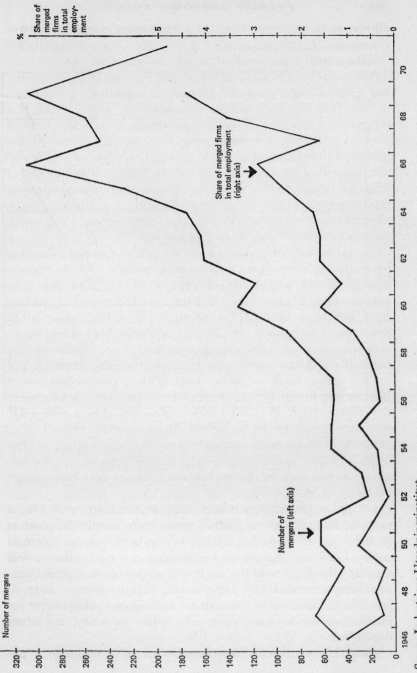

Number of mergers

320–
300–
280–
260–
240–
220–
200–
180–
160–
140–
120–
100–
80–
60–
40–
20–
0–

%

Share of
merged
firms
in total
employ-
ment

5–
4–
3–
2–
1–
0–

70   68   66   64   62   60   58   56   54   52   50   48   1946

Share of merged firms in total employment (right axis)

Number of mergers (left axis)

Source: Industriens Utredningsinstitut.

allocation of resources, then, is a price to be paid for an improvement in the balance of payments – as compared, for instance, with a policy of adjusting the exchange rate.

Thus, the acceleration of structural change in the economy has created some tendency to 'neo-mercantilism' in Swedish policy. It is still too early to say, however, whether this is a temporary phenomenon or a new trend. From the point of view of principle, it is interesting to note, however, that the period of liberalisation of trade by the reduction of tariffs and the removal of quotas may very well be followed by a period of selective subsidies. We may ask whether such a system might not lead to even more 'distortions' of national and international allocation of resources; tariffs are fairly general and open devices compared with most types of subsidy.

An interesting question is how the profit squeeze influences productivity, structural change and economic growth. On the one hand, we would expect that it would force the least efficient firms to close down and the remaining ones to increase their efficiency in order to survive and defend their profit positions. This type of mechanism is particularly likely in an economy such as the Swedish one, where an 'export-or-die' mentality is characteristic of a number of leading export firms, for the simple reason that the bulk of their production is sold internationally. If this hypothesis is correct, the productivity development would not be independent of the rate of wage increase, export prices being mainly given from abroad. This means that an incomes (or guide-post) policy, designed to keep wage increases in line with the rise in productivity, is considerably complicated, as the productivity rise in that case cannot be taken as 'given'.

On the other hand, the hypothesis of the favourable effects of a profit squeeze on productivity can hardly be correct *generally* and in an *unlimited* way. It can hold only in a certain interval of wage changes, and perhaps only for a limited period of time; the limit may be exceeded either when considerable unemployment is created because of a high domestic cost level, when investment incentives fall because of low profitability, or possibly when the firms, because of a low liquidity, cut down expenditure for research and development.

Empirical evidence in Sweden is consistent with the hypothesis that the first mentioned effect (an acceleration of the rate of productivity increase) predominates in the short run, whereas the second effect (unemployment and low levels of investment) predominates in the long run. Simultaneously with the squeeze on profit margins during the sixties, there was an extraordinary acceleration of the productivity increase in the manufacturing sector in Sweden. Labour productivity (value added per man-hour) increased by about 7 per cent during the sixties as compared with 4·5 per cent in the fifties ([273], ch. 2, p. 32). The development of total 'productivity' – output per unit of input – is for well-known reasons more difficult to measure. According to simple production function studies, 'total (net) productivity' seems to have increased as follows in various periods during the post Second World War period (yearly rate of change in per cent): 1947–55: 0·6; 1951–5: 1·3; 1956–60: 3·5; 1961–5: 4·3; 1966–9: 4·9.[5]

However, there has also during the second half of the sixties been a weak development of the *volume* of investment, an increase in unemployment and possibly also some stagnation in expenditure for research and development. Thus the Swedish experience seems to be consistent with the hypothesis that a rate of increase in wage costs resulting in a profit squeeze has the effects of: (1) speeding up the rate of productivity increase in the short run; (2) increasing the level of structural unemployment; (3) reducing, after some time, investment incentives and possibly also expenditure for research and development; and, as a consequence, (4) slowing down the rate of growth of production and the employment level in industry. Clearly, the 'sample' is small – one country! It might therefore be of interest if this hypothesis could be tested for a number of countries.

Thus, Gösta Rehn's hypothesis that a policy of squeezing profits would accelerate the rate of structural change and *in the short run* also the rate of productivity increase seems to be consistent with available evidence, though in a long-run perspective productivity may fall owing to a reduction in incentives for investment in real capital and research and

---

[5] Estimates based on a Cobb–Douglas type of production function, with 'total productivity' increase calculated as residual ([50], p. 31).

development. Similarly, the argument that many employees would experience a loss in the freedom of choosing between income and 'environment' (place to work and place to live) – a point stressed by Bent Hansen – is also illustrated by developments during the last decade. Moreover, Rehn's 'hopes' and Lundberg's 'fears' that falling profit margins would lead to a more selective and interventionist policy would also seem to be well in line with accumulated evidences – as well as the 'deformations' of the price system and the concentration of economic power to the state, which are most likely connected with those developments. Lundberg, therefore, has strong empirical support for his summary statement (in 1972) of the development: 'We [Lundberg *and* Rehn] were both right – both the hopes and the fears became good forecasts over the future development'. ([142A], p. 179.)

Questions of structural change were discussed already by the Myrdal Commission [266] and the Labour Movement Programme [3] at the end of the Second World War. After that, however, problems of stabilisation policy rapidly absorbed most of the interest, and questions of industrial structure and competition came very much in the background during the following two decades. (An exception is the anti-cartel legislation in the middle of the fifties, with its prohibition of 'producers' prices' in retailing and its intervention against 'harmful' restrictions of competition by an 'ombudsman' regarding questions of freedom of trade (*Näringsfrihetsombudsmannen*) and a special public board – Freedom of Commerce Board (*Näringsfrihetsrådet*).) A characteristic feature of 'competition policy' in Sweden is the 'case by case approach', i.e. the judgement of each individual case in order to ascertain whether or not it is actually 'harmful'.

The new interest in questions of structural change that emerged during the sixties is reflected both in the studies carried out by industry itself, for instance concerning the steel industry, and in some government initiatives, such as the new government Investment Bank (*Investeringsbanken*), a new consolidated concern for public corporations (*AB Statsföretag*) and the publicly owned Corporation for Development and Research (*Statliga Utvecklingsbolaget*). Government study committees have often been in operation regarding some contracting sectors of the economy – agriculture, textiles and forestry. Some industry studies are also pursued in the new Department of Industry and the new Industrial Board (*Industriverket*). There is also in the early seventies some increased tendencies to government investment in manufacturing (steel, for instance) and some joint ventures with private firms.

A general experience of empirical economic analysis is, of course, that 'historical trends' sooner or later – often 'sooner' – turn around. This may hold also for the previously discussed trends for profits, private saving, and the rate of structural change. In fact, profits increased dramatically in Sweden in 1973 and 1974, in connection with the 'explosive' rise in world market prices. This resulted also in an increase in corporate savings relative to public saving, at the same time as household saving doubled.

12 Summary and Concluding Remarks

How should the main features of Swedish economic policy in the postwar period be characterised? How has the general character of the policy changed? What has succeeded and what has failed? What lessons can be learned for economic theory and policy from the Swedish experience? Let us discuss these issues in a summary fashion.

SHIFTS IN ECONOMIC POLICY

Swedish economic policy has passed through many different phases since the breakthrough of deliberate counter-cyclical policy in the early thirties. The employment issue may be regarded as a *'leitmotiv'* of policy. There has been a gradual development from the sole reliance on public works, combined with some slight attempts to stimulate private consumption, in the thirties to the attempts to influence the *aggregate* volume of demand and its composition, in particular investment expenditures, in the postwar period.

The policy mix has changed considerably also during the postwar period. Immediately after the war the policy was characterised by two features in particular: (1) an expansionary monetary and fiscal policy and (2) a removal, or liberalisation, of a number of war regulations. We have seen that the immediate effects were both a considerable increase in imports, resulting in a balance-of-payments crisis in 1947, and a domestic wave of inflation.

The immediate counter-measures were a partial return to a regulated economy, import control and building regulations being important features. Moreover, price regulations and rationing were kept for a longer time than had initially been planned. A situation of 'repressed inflation' therefore became characteristic during most of the forties, after the temporary removal of certain regulations immediately after the war.

The period of 'repressed inflation' ended with the Korean War in 1950, when the public authorities did not vigorously resist the inflationary impulses coming from abroad. Thus, the period of 'repressed inflation' was followed by a period of a strong 'open inflation' – a 25 per cent increase in consumer goods prices within two years. Obviously, in order to limit domestic inflation considerably in this situation, it would have been necessary both to cut down on domestic expenditure and to undertake an appreciation of the Swedish krona.

After the Korean inflation there was a period in which there were successive removals of administrative regulations, often of a rather detailed nature, and a shift of emphasis to economic incentives, mainly by way of monetary and fiscal policies. In connection with this we can also talk about a shift from selective to more general methods of policy. One of the most important steps in this direction was the liberalisation of foreign trade, by the removal of import regulations during the first part of the fifties and the later reduction of tariffs, partly in the context of the establishment of EFTA and the GATT and Kennedy-Round agreements. Other important reforms along the same lines were the removal of price control in the middle of the fifties and the successive softening of building regulations during the course of the fifties. Instead, increased importance was given to fiscal policy and, particularly after the abolishment of the low interest rate doctrine in the middle of the fifties, to monetary policy. However, as monetary policy relied to a large extent on credit market regulations, the previous excess demand for commodities was to some extent replaced by excess demand for credit.

At the end of the fifties, particularly from the 1958 recession, there was a vigorous activation of labour market policy. This was to begin with mainly concerned with fighting unemployment, but to a larger and larger extent it has also become an ingredient in the attempts to facilitate structural change of the economy by helping the high-income sectors to expand. Labour market policy then has been nearly as active (and expensive) during booms as during recessions. Help for the labour force to change occupation and to move to other areas is still limited mainly to the unemployed, but has on a small scale been extended also to people who expect to become unemployed, or who simply want to change to a better paid job. This development of labour market policy during the postwar period has to a large extent been inspired by the programme of the Swedish Confederation of Labour (LO). In connection with tendencies to an increased regional split in the labour market situation during the sixties and a certain social and political backlash against the exodus of labour from unemployment areas and sparsely populated districts, measures to stimulate firms to move to such areas of the country – location policy – were implemented in the middle of the sixties. In the political field this issue has been pushed in particular by one of the opposition parties with a historically strong position in farm districts, the Centre Party.

Both labour market policy and location policy, in the forms in which they have in practice been implemented, must be regarded as rather selective types of policies. There is also a tendency to more improvised types of selective subsidies to private as well as public firms with employment difficulties. Fiscal and monetary policies have also, as has been shown, been pursued in a more selective way in recent years than earlier. Another example of a strongly selective policy is the favouring of investment in manufacturing at the cost of investment in the private service sector (such as distribution and office buildings) by a combination of investment fund releases and a selective investment tax during the period 1967–71. Maybe we can also say that, during the late sixties and early seventies there has been a tendency to 'go back' to the older techniques of the twenties and thirties: to rely heavily on public works programmes to fight unemployment, for example (see chapter 6, pp. 104–7).

Thus, we could perhaps talk of certain 'neo-mercantilistic' tendencies in Swedish economic policy. This does not necessarily mean a return to a regulated economy such as the one during the forties. However, there seems to be a tendency to use the incentive method in a more selective way than during the fifties. One explanation for this is probably the increased differences in the economic situation between various sectors, regions and firms, which have come to the forefront in an economy that most of the time is very close to full capacity

utilisation – a balancing act on a 'narrow band' on the border-
line between inflation and unemployment tendencies. The
neo-mercantilist tendencies also have something to do with increased international competition, and the related acceleration
of the rate of structural change of the economy during the
sixties. If the authorities have ambitions, in such a situation, to
remove remaining pockets of unemployment, general methods
of demand management might not be enough, particularly
if the authorities want to avoid pushing the economy into a
situation of overfull employment – Gösta Rehn's old problem.
The policy has also, as 'traditional' mercantilism, to a large
extent been designed to protect various sectors of the economy
against harder international competition, and to help improve
the balance of payments.

Thus, the most dramatic shifts in economic policy in the
postwar period seem to have been: (1) a shift during the fifties
from selective, administrative regulations to incentives by
general monetary and fiscal policies (approximately in line with
the recommendations by economists such as Erik Lundberg)
and (2) later during the sixties increased emphasis on selective
incentives, particularly in the context of labour market and
location policies (approximately in line with the recommendations by Gösta Rehn), but to some extent also in order to influence the structure of some branches with specific problems
– textiles, glass manufacturing, etc.

It is also of interest to note that stabilisation policy in Sweden,
more from the mid-fifties than earlier, has been concerned with
the balance-of-payments situation – especially after the deficits
in the 1965/66 and 1969/70 booms. Thus, restrictive policies
have for balance-of-payments reasons been pursued in the
recessions of 1967/68 and 1971/73, thereby aggravating the unemployment problem. In this connection, interest rate policy has
been more and more tied to the balance-of-payments situation,
as has been the case also in several other countries. And in
connection with the unusually rapid inflation during the 1969–
1970 boom, and the continuing price increases in the following recession (1971–3), the inflationary issue became, at least
temporarily, regarded as more urgent than earlier. Thus,
stabilisation policy has been confronted with a delicate three-
dimensional balancing act between unemployment, inflation

and balance-of-payments problems. If the increased awareness of income distribution problems, the 'disaggregation' of the employment target and the ambitions to influence growth are added, the issue of economic policy looks quite complicated indeed.

Has the balance-of-payments situation in Sweden during the second half of the sixties indicated a problem of 'fundamental disequilibrium' for the external balance? An analysis of labour costs (per unit of output) during the sixties in Sweden does not indicate that the cost level in Sweden has increased as compared with the dominant trading partners (Chart 11:7). The problem is rather that the strong negative trend for services and transfers on the balance of payments calls for a continuous *improvement* of the trade balance, which requires both an improvement in the competitive position *vis-à-vis* other countries and a strong expansion of the *capacity* of the export- and import-competing sectors.

The squeeze of profit margins of existing firms, which has taken place during the course of the sixties, may not be very favourable for such a rapid expansion of capacity in the export- and import-competing sectors. Thus, to keep the level of costs per unit of output *ex post* in line with development in other countries – after the least efficient firms have gone out of business – is not a satisfactory measure of the 'competitiveness' of a country. It is also necessary to look at the *capacity* level in the export- and import-competing sectors, and this presumably is highly dependent on profits and profit expectations, especially as many leading Swedish firms are international enterprises, which can shift their investment expenditures from Sweden to other countries.

Moreover, it is possible that foreign countries tend to improve their competitive position *vis-à-vis* Sweden by filling out the 'technology gap' relative to us, both by improving the quality of their products and by expanding the assortment, without any effect of this development in index series over relative production cost. This might in fact be what happened between the US and western Europe during the fifties and sixties (to the advantage of western Europe).

However, even if Sweden for these reasons has experienced a certain reduction in the competitive position of the current balance of payments as compared with the outside world, it would be a reduction from a rather strong position in the early fifties, immediately after the 1949 devaluation and the improvement in the terms of trade in connection with the Korean inflation. Moreover, the current balance improved in 1971–3.

SUCCESSES AND FAILURES

The great achievement for economic policy during the postwar period is of course connected with the removal of mass unemployment. However, this has occurred in most industrialised countries, though Sweden was, together with the UK, one of the first countries to reach a very high employment level. Certain achievements have also been reached in dampening short-run fluctuations around this high employment level. An early example is when the authorities succeeded in postponing the investment boom for private investment from the 1955/56 boom to the 1958/59 recession – even if not sufficiently to prevent a substantial recession in 1958. Two other successes for short-run stabilisation policy were the breaking of the 1960/61 boom by strong measures against private consumption, public investment and housebuilding, and the checking of the tendency towards a recession in 1962 by a broad expansion of state and private investment and housebuilding. Hence, the period 1955–1963 must, compared with other countries and with other periods for Sweden, be regarded as a rather successful period in dampening fluctuations in production and employment. This is particularly the case for the period 1960–2, even if some of the successes might have been the result of good luck rather than skill: the removal of the investment tax in 1958 and the introduction of the sales tax and pension fees in 1960 were both measures decided a long time in advance, without immediate connection with short-term stabilisation policy considerations. (However, the size of the 'outside' disturbance of the economy was very small in the slight business downturn in 1962.)

The authorities have also succeeded, along the lines of established targets, in their attempts to shift the allocation of resources from private consumption to public consumption and public investment, with the result that private consumption, as earlier mentioned, has fallen from 65 to 54 per cent of GNP during the postwar period. The redistribution of savings, wealth and credit supply from the private to the public and 'semi-public' sector during the last decade may also be regarded as a success of the policy, from the point of view of established targets. Another characteristic feature of economic policy in the postwar period has been its rather strong experimental nature. Several new economic policy tools have been tried, some with obvious success – investment taxes, investment funds and possibly labour market policy.

What has succeeded least in the economic policy? The most obvious weakness is of course the limited success in fighting inflation. As has been pointed out, Sweden has had a slightly more rapid inflation than the OECD countries in general – about the same as European OECD countries for the period *after* the 'Korean inflation' (which was particularly rapid in Sweden). The difficulties in this field are of course connected with the achievements of employment policy. Sweden has, for longer periods than most countries, been in the 'narrow band' between full and overfull employment. The lack of success is also connected with the difference in productivity increase in the sector with international competition and the 'shielded' sector, as emphasised by the EFO Report. However, another reason for the limited success in fighting inflation has been that demand-reducing actions during booms have often been considerably delayed. The policies in 1959, 1964 and 1969 are obvious examples. The stimulating actions during the previous recessions were broken off so late that the next boom was given a flying start, whereby the brakes had to be used very hard to counteract inflation and eliminate balance-of-payments problems.

In fact, the economy was stimulated more in 1959, when it had already turned upwards, than in the recession year of 1958. And the stabilisation policy in the booms of 1964/65 and 1969/70 must be regarded as obvious failures. During a strong upswing, the policy was rather passive or at least not very contractive. This holds in particular for fiscal policy. Furthermore, some minor stimulating fiscal action for location purposes was implemented in the midst of the booms. When contractive action was finally undertaken, the labour market was so strained that wage drift had already started to occur, with cost-push effects into the next recession.

At the end of both booms, in 1966 and 1970, the labour

organisations agreed on a three-year contract with rather large wage increases – in the last boom of the magnitude of 10 per cent per year (including expected wage drift) – guaranteeing several years of cost-push inflation after the previous demand inflation. The attempts in the early recession to limit inflation and balance-of-payments problems then accentuated the unemployment problems. Thus, even a rather short period of failure to counteract an inflationary boom may have effects for several years ahead, by way of the bargaining agreements and the successive penetration of cost increases through the input–output system, and possibly by the influence of previous inflation on price expectation.

All this means that a 'policy cycle' (fluctuations caused by policy itself) is intertwined with the 'pure' business cycle. We have seen that this policy cycle sometimes runs *against*, and sometimes *parallel with* the 'pure' cycle. In any case, it is obvious that the business cycles in Sweden – or in any other highly developed western society, for that matter – can no longer be explained solely by 'traditional' kinds of business cycle theories. The policy itself is part of the pattern; for instance, an analysis of time lags and conflicts of goals in stabilisation policy are crucial for an understanding of the fluctuations.

However, to get some perspective on the failures of stabilisation policy in recent years with respect to the unemployment situation, it may be instructive to look at Chart 1:2 (p. 12): the fluctuations in 'open' unemployment during the entire postwar period look trivial in relation to the size and fluctuations in unemployment before the Second World War. We might even start to wonder if the attempts to do 'fine tuning' in stabilisation policy – to remove to small fluctuations that remain in unemployment – is worth while, in view of the inconviences that are created for the economy by the stream of policy measures by the authorities – not always well timed, and often with unpredictable effects. This raises the old question of whether *minor* fluctuations in output could not be accepted if they were prevented from resulting in socially unacceptable unemployment, either by introducing greater flexibility in wages (as suggested by Bent Hansen), by 'replacing' unemployment by 'fellowships' or paid vacations (as suggested by Galbraith and Lundberg), or by speeding up labour mobility and by rehabilitation of marginal workers, such as people with handicaps or poor education (as suggested by Gösta Rehn).

The price trend should also be seen in the light of the successive shift to greater reliance on indirect taxes. During the sixties indirect taxes were raised from about 10 per cent to 18 per cent for consumer goods, pension fees from 3 to about 8 per cent (of total wage sum), and a labour tax (paid by employees) to 4 per cent. Both types of policy must have accentuated the problems of cost inflation. Thus, while the demand side was considerably neglected during the forties, when inflation was fought on the cost side, it is probably reasonable to say that the cost side has been neglected in stabilisation policy during the sixties and early seventies.

The increased complexity of economic policy in recent years, discussed above, and the related problems of conflicts of goals might be illustrated by a schematic list of the 'main' targets of economic policy in the early seventies, as compared with the early fifties. (See also Lundberg and Wibble [145A].) It is unavoidable that such a list represents rather subjective interpretations by the author. Nevertheless, they probably convey a reasonably correct *impression* of the shifts in emphasis in economic policy in recent decades.

MAIN POLICY TARGETS
Early 1950s
1. *Full employment* (not more than 1–2 per cent unemployment according to Labour Market Board Statistics), without much disaggregation on various subgroups of the labour force, except the ambition to reduce the very high unemployment figures for building workers.
2. *Price stability* (interpreted rather rigorously before the Korean War, less rigorously afterwards).
3. *Balance-of-payments equilibrium*, probably without much capital imports or capital exports.

Early 1970s
1. *Full employment for a great number of specific groups*, such as women, elderly, handicapped and people living in depressed areas.
2. Ambitions to influence the *distribution of population on*

geographical regions of the country (target implied in location policy).

3. *No faster inflation than other developed countries* (i.e. no more than about 3–5 per cent per year *before* 1973) for consumer goods prices (excluding indirect taxes?)
4. About the same *growth rate* as in other developed countries (i.e. no less than 3–5 per cent per year).
5. A falling, or at least not rising, *profit share* of national income – up until 1973, when a profit increase was *welcomed*!
6. A reduction in the inequality of the *vertical income distribution*, before as well as after taxes/transfer payments.
7. *A surplus* (of about 1 per cent of GNP) *on the current balance of payments*, to finance aid to underdeveloped countries.
8. A retardation of *the rate of structural change of the economy*.
9. *Environmental considerations*, concerning the natural environment and the physical environment created by men (cities, etc.), as well as working conditions in factories, etc.

The most dramatic of the shifts in emphasis has probably occurred for the employment target. Nowadays the emphasis is not so much on the average *unemployment* rate, but rather on the *employment* opportunities for various groups of people who were not earlier included in the statistical measures of the 'labour force' – housewives, the handicapped, the elderly, etc. More and more emphasis has also been placed in recent years on the *quality* of working conditions and on the rehabilitation of the people who have been hurt by bad working conditions.

It should be no surprise that this complicated set of policy targets has created serious problems for economic policy in recent years, by increasing risks of serious conflicts of goals. Moreover, international influence has made it more difficult to reach domestic targets independent of the outside world, partly because some measures of economic policy (such as tariffs and interest rates) are increasingly difficult for the government to use independently of other countries.

A further explanation of the tendency towards cost inflation is probably the interaction between taxation and wage formation. To the extent that labour market organisations try to compensate themselves for tax increases, to protect their real income after tax, the rapid rise in taxes during the sixties might have contributed to the cost inflation. The highly progressive tax-subsidy system may also, as earlier (chapter 8) explained, function as a built-in *de*stabiliser on wage formation. Obviously, the 'incomes policy problem' in Sweden has not been solved – in fact, it has only recently been tackled.

An important question raised by the Swedish experience is how much taxes, social insurance and squeezes of profits that an economic system based on economic incentives can withstand. Up to the mid-sixties, with taxes amounting to more than 40 per cent of GNP it was still difficult to argue that incentives had been destroyed to any noticeable extent. It is *possible* that some severe incentive problems have emerged later on. Some of the signs are a slower rate of private investment, a fall in the establishment of new firms, difficulties to fill vacancies even during unemployment periods, a higher level of absenteeism, tendencies by firms to invest more abroad, in particular in research departments, etc. At present we do not know the *quantitative* importance of these problems. It is therefore still an open question to what extent those incentive problems are responsible for the slower growth rate in Sweden in the early seventies, and the increase in unemployment connected with it.

Lessons for Economic Theory and Policy

Swedish economic policy experiences suggest a number of lessons both for the theory of economic policy and for economic theory in general.

For *the theory of economic policy* both positive and negative lessons may be learned. Among the positive ones it should first of all be mentioned that short-run counter-cyclical actions have proved definitely possible on several occasions, in the case both of fiscal and of monetary policy (provided the effect lag of monetary policy is not very long – say, not more than two years). For instance, it would seem possible to even out the fluctuations in private fixed investment considerably over the cycle if very strong measures, such as rather high investment taxes and investment subsidies, are used. The Swedish experiences also indicate that it is possible to move public investment and housebuilding counter-cyclically to exports and private investment, by a system of a 'shelf' of ready projects in this field.

However, there are also a number of negative lessons. One is that stabilisation policy actions very often tend to be much delayed. Moreover, politicians sometimes tend to decide about fiscal policy changes for future periods far ahead of the forecasting possibilities. For instance, increases in indirect taxes have on several occasions been proposed by the government about one year ahead of the suggested implementation (for instance in 1968, 1970 and 1972).

Another negative experience is that very few of the available instruments are in fact used for stabilisation purposes. For instance, income tax rates, social security fees and the labour tax have hardly been used as tools of counter-cyclical policies. One reason is that the complexity of targets in recent years has partly paralysed stabilisation policy. Of particular importance here are the conflicts (real or conceived) with income distribution considerations. For instance, proportional reductions in income or consumption taxes, to fight unemployment, have been ruled out by the argument that people in higher income brackets would get a greater tax increase (in absolute terms) than people in lower income groups – in spite of the fact that *increases* in indirect taxes are also often said to be particularly unfavourable to low income groups. And suggestions to stimulate investment by lower production costs – for growth and balance-of-payments reasons – have been turned down with the argument that an income redistribution in favour of profits cannot be accepted. The authorities have also turned down suggestions of reductions in the tax on wage costs (*arbetsgivaravgift*) during an unemployment period (1971–3) – partly because this removal would raise profits. However, in reality the importance of these notions is difficult to separate from other considerations, such as short-term conflicts between full employment, 'price stability' and equilibrium in the balance of payments – and short-term party politics.

Moreover, attempts to stabilise inventory investments do not seem to have been successful. The inventory cycle looks quite 'undisturbed' by economic policy actions, such as monetary policy and investment funds policy; in fact, the rules in the latter system give only very small incentives to investment in inventories. *Very strong* doses of taxes or subsidies (or of interest rate changes) would presumably be necessary for a stabilisation of inventory investment.

It has also proved difficult to cut off the expansionary actions, undertaken during a recession, early during the ensuing upswing. Consequently, the expansionary action during a recession easily accentuates the next boom.

Another disappointing lesson is that there is hardly any evidence that the energetic programmes for labour mobility and retraining the labour force have in fact reduced the inflationary propensity of the labour market (at a given level of unemployment); thus, there is no real evidence that these policies have actually contributed to shifting the Phillips curve downwards, possibly (partly at least) because other factors have tended to push the Phillips curve in the opposite direction.

Several conclusions are suggested also by the monetary experiences. One conclusion, and a trivial one, is that a restrictive monetary policy is very difficult to pursue without interest rate flexibility. It has also been demonstrated how attempts on the part of the authorities to restrain the supply of credit by credit-rationing techniques, i.e. by creating market imperfections in the credit market, tend to increase the volume of credit transactions outside the 'organised' credit market. There is also much evidence that very heavy interest rate changes are necessary to stabilise private fixed investment along the trend – maybe fluctuations by 8–10 percentage points.

Another important lesson of monetary policy is that the reliance on the control of the availability of liquidity and credit, rather than on directly influencing the profitability of investment, is confronted with several problems and limitations. One example is that during recessions firms take the opportunity to invest in financial capital rather than physical capital, i.e. to increase their liquidity, whereby they become rather immune to restrictive credit and liquidity-limiting actions by the authorities during ensuing booms. One conclusion seems to be that an efficient monetary (credit) policy designed to influence private fixed investment cannot rely solely on credit and liquidity control; it must influence, vigorously, the relative profitability of investing in booms as compared with recessions – by heavy interest rate fluctuations or tax-subsidy programmes. This point is obviously of relevance also for the monetary controversy, whether monetary (credit) policy exerts its (main) effects by way of interest rates or by way of the supply of liquid assets, such as money.

Another rather obvious conclusion to be drawn from stabilisation policy experiences in Sweden is that the policy easily has strong, 'non-planned' effects on the allocation of resources in the economy. That credit rationing easily results in deviations in the allocation of new investment from what would be required to maximise the rate of return on aggregate investment is, of course, to be expected. Empirical evidence also indicates that a credit policy, which relies heavily on credit rationing, has a very different impact on firms of different size, with the strongest effects on small- and medium-sized firms (except the *very* small ones with less than ten employees). Moreover, the investment funds system favours old-established firms, with previously accumulated investment funds. As the Swedish tax system is very unfavourable towards firms with concentrated ownership (family firms) – owing to wealth and inheritance taxation – we can presumably safely conclude that economic policy in Sweden is not well disposed towards new and small firms. Sketchy empirical evidence also suggests that the entry of new firms has dropped dramatically during the last decade.[1]

More generally, the experiences of credit rationing illustrate a rather general principle of economic theory and policy: the difficulties and problems connected with price controls. Rather similar conclusions may be drawn from other areas of price control – with drastic illustrations of the realism of simple 'textbook' economic theory. The experiences of rent control are an illustration of the effects of keeping a price *below* the equilibrium level: excess demand, resulting in queues and black markets; arbitrariness in the distribution of the commodity; lack of incentives among producers to discipline costs; loss of freedom of choice for the individual consumer; lack of influence on production from the demand side (a loss of 'consumer sovereignty'); arbitrary relative prices for different types of products within the regulated product area, etc. Similarly, the experiences of price support for agriculture illustrate the difficulties that emerge when political prices are kept *above* the equilibrium level: excess supply forcing the authorities to build

[1] A more comprehensive study on the entry of new firms is presently being undertaken at the Institute on Industrial Social Research (IUI).

up a complicated system of market regulations to sustain the politically determined price, including dumping of products on the world market; a slowing down in the rate of structural change in the sector; arbitrary relative prices inside the protected sector, with related loss of efficiency, etc.

Also, the attempts on the part of the labour market organisations to control wages highlight the problems typical for systems of price control; it would seem that a wage structure has developed, which has resulted in excess demand (vacancies) in some parts of the labour market (skilled workers mainly in expanding regions) simultaneously with excess supply (unemployment) in other parts (white-collar employees, including people with a short academic training, and unskilled workers, particularly in contracting regions). It is also possible that the attempts of the organisations in recent years to push up wages, particularly for low-wage groups, have contributed both to 'structural unemployment' and to an acceleration of the rate of wage drift for other groups, and have hence speeded up the rate of cost inflation. Thus the increase in structural unemployment in Sweden in recent years, and the tendency towards excess demand for skilled blue-collar workers simultaneously with excess supply of unqualified white- and blue-collar workers, is partly a result of the inflexible wage policy of labour unions, including the so-called 'solidaric wage policy'. Such a policy also, as pointed out in particular by Bent Hansen, to some extent eliminates the freedom of the individual to choose between on one hand income and on the other hand working and living conditions (chapter 3, pp. 44–6).

Another important point raised by the economic policy experiences in Sweden is to question the habit in economic theory of treating the actions of politicians as 'exogenous variables' and to limit the analysis largely to the *effects* on the economy of 'exogenous' shifts in the actions of politicians. The economists can, of course, in a model *assume* that the government can counteract an inflationary boom by increasing tax rates or reducing expenditures. But suppose that politicians in reality tend regularly to use the increased budget surplus to expand expenditures again (before the boom is over). Should the economists then go on recommending tax increases to fight inflationary booms?

And suppose that increased government spending during recessions is regularly cut off only very late in the forthcoming booms. Is it then not necessary to weigh the employment-creating effects during the recession against the inflationary effects in the forthcoming boom (and possibly the more severe unemployment problems during a *forthcoming* recession)? Perhaps politicians in many countries behave quite as 'regularly' as do for instance consumers or private investors. If so, maybe we should treat the politicians as 'endogenous' rather than 'exogenous' variables when we build business cycle models to explain the cycle, or when forecasting the future?

Some additional examples may further clarify the point. We may, as theoreticians, analyse the theoretical possibilities of replacing a devaluation of the currency by general (proportional) taxes on imports combined with general (equi-proportional) subsidies of exports. But dare we recommend such actions when we invariably find in the real world that politicians practically always make such taxes and subsidies strongly selective with protectionist consequences? Or we may point out in theoretical analyses that 'perfect' price regulations might force monopolies to a policy more in line with static allocative efficiency. But when we look at the practice of price regulations we see in fact that completely different principles are actually followed by the politicians and administrators. In the case of agricultural price support, a usual principle seems to be to make the price support for each product proportional to the comparative *disadvantage* for the product under consideration (in Sweden with the smallest support for pork and the highest for sugar beet).

Thus, perhaps the economist must treat politicians to some extent as an endogenous variable – 'endogenous politicians' – in forecasting, in analysing the effects of policies and in making policy recommendations.

The Swedish experience also suggests a number of lessons for *general economic theory*. One of the most trivial ones is, of course, that domestic trends and fluctuations within an open economy are closely tied to developments in the world markets. This holds both for the short-term fluctuations in volume components and for the price trend – for a country with a fixed exchange rate. Of greater theoretical interest is the specific complication for domestic anti-inflationary policy which follows from the difference in the rate of productivity increase in different sectors, such as the rapid rate of productivity increase in commodity-producing sectors with international competition, as compared with the service sectors (with relatively small international competition) – problems emphasised by the EFO-model.

Another important lesson is the role of money in an economy where business fluctuations are caused by 'exogenous' shifts in export demand. In an economy of this type the time path of the quantity of money will follow the general pattern suggested by 'modern' quantity theorists, in spite of the fact that fluctuations in national income are easily explained by the exogenous shifts in exports demand rather than by the changes in the quantity of money. This conclusion is, of course, no denial of the fact that the effects on the economy of these exogenous shocks would have been modified in various respects if monetary–fiscal policy had been different, i.e. if the credit volume and the quantity of money had developed differently over the cycle.

Of theoretical interest are also the time lags between various variables during the cycle (as outlined in chapter 4); exports lead inventory investment and fixed private investment, and production leads labour input and unemployment. This results in a systematic productivity cycle, with labour productivity rising in booms and falling in recessions, a pattern that is observed in several countries [226]. Of interest, too, is how sensitive wage drift in Sweden seems to be to the labour market situation, and how employees with rather 'inflexible' wage categories therefore lag behind other groups. This would seem to be one explanation of why it takes quite a long time after a boom before the rate of aggregate wage and price increase levels off substantially, with the rate of price increase levelling off about one to one-and-a-half years after the peak of the boom. Another experience that is apparently shared by many countries is that the current foreign balance deteriorates at the peak of each boom, when domestic excess demand for commodities and factors 'spills over' into imports at the same time as exports level off owing to lack of capacity. This kind of capacity effect on the trade balance is, as a matter of fact, integrated in some modern econometric models for 'high employment economies'.

Some theoretical reflections are natural also on the basis of the development of profits. It would seem that the short- and medium-trend of profits depends largely on the difference in the development of international prices (for products of importance for foreign trade for the country in question) and domestic labour costs per unit of output. For short-run behaviour of profits, capacity utilisation seems to be of very great importance for profits. Other hypotheses suggested by the Swedish experience are that a squeeze of profits, to begin with, results in an acceleration in the increase in productivity, as firms are forced to remove 'organisational slack', and as part of the 'tail' of the least efficient firms disappears. The experience is also consistent with the hypothesis that in a longer-run perspective a profit squeeze results in the volume of investment being slowed down, and that expenditure on research and development is also curtailed, creating perhaps later problems for the employment level and the balance of payments.

CAPITALISM OR SOCIALISM?

Looking in retrospect at the development of economic policy in Sweden in the postwar period, we may ask if the ambition embodied in the Labour Movement programme from 1944, 'to give the economy a new organisation and to reshape society in a socialist direction' has actually been realised. Or, instead, has the winner been the more 'liberalistic' idea expressed in the same programme, namely, that the private enterprise system 'can in future be allowed to function in about the same way as before the war', provided it functions efficiently?

Obviously, there has in certain respects been a development in a liberal direction: direct controls have gradually been removed; even fewer nationalisations than proposed in the Labour Movement Programme have been carried out. Moreover, the ambition of society to conduct and co-ordinate investment activity and control foreign trade has been rather modest. Markets, competition and free trade have dominated.

Also, the attempts to increase the mobility of the factors of production, mainly labour, may be regarded as a way of making the free enterprise market system work more smoothly, rather than trying to overthrow the system. This ambition has, in fact, been explicitly formulated in a programme for structural policy presented by the economists of the Confederation of Trade Unions: 'Our assumption is, thus, that a development as free as possible – free not only from detailed government controls but also from elements of rigidity inherent in the system – favours the expansive powers and leads to the best economic result' ([204], p. 64).

No doubt, ideas of this type have had a strong influence on Swedish economic policy in the postwar period. However, there are also tendencies that might as well be called 'socialist', such as the rapid expansion of the public sector in the service field, the gradual 'nationalisation' of income through higher tax rates and transfer payments, including the rather elaborate social security system, and government intervention through monetary, fiscal, labour market and location policies to promote stability and growth. The collectivisation of saving – by way of public and collective saving in the pension funds – is another example of the increased importance of the public sector, in this case as an administrator of wealth and supplier of credit. The increased activities to protect the environment, and the new 'mercantilist' tendencies by way of some selective subsidies, could also be put under the heading of 'increased state intervention'. Some 'new' *suggestions* have also been put forward in recent years, with rather interventionist – 'corporativist' or 'etatist' – implications for the economic system: purchases by the AP-fund of shares in private firms, the creation of 'branch funds' for different industrial branches and the establishment of a specific council for investment problems, with representation from industry employees and the government [3A]. The decision by Parliament that two representatives for the employees should be members of the boards in all firms with more than one hundred employees is more difficult to classify 'ideologically'. It is interesting to note that several of these issues have been pushed in particular by the LO, rather than by the government. (The possibilities that these developments will continuously move the economic system in Sweden towards a more centralised and regulated economy have been discussed by several authors in recent years [1].)

The activities of the public sector that are nowadays of the greatest 'importance' in Sweden are presumably: (1) the large volume of public consumption (23 per cent of GNP, compared to 13–16 per cent for most western European countries); (2) the attempts to redistribute income (transfer payments, including the social security system, amount to 20 per cent of GNP, a rather high figure for western Europe); (3) the relatively high direct taxes, particularly on households (taxes and other public incomes amount to about 51 per cent of GNP as compared with about 35–40 per cent for most other countries in western Europe); (4) the rate of public savings and public credit supply (collective saving, including the semi-public pension funds, in the early 1970s account for about 45 per cent of total gross saving, and collective credit supply to 40 per cent of total credit supply in the 'organised' credit market); (5) the public 'infrastructure', such as railways, the postal system, telephones and also electric power (60 per cent of production of energy); (6) the housing market (about one-third of the stock of apartments are owned either by co-operatives or by municipalities); and finally (7) the attempts by the government to influence the private sector by various types of economic policy measures, mainly of a stabilising nature, such as fiscal, monetary and labour market policies.

How should a 'mixed economy' of this type be classified by such traditional ideological terms as capitalism, liberalism, socialism, etc.? The main point to be made on this 'ideological issue' is that it is anachronistic to use such terms as 'capitalism' and 'socialism' to characterise modern economic policy in a 'mixed economy' of the Swedish type, with an interventionistic economic policy and a large sector for government services alongside strong private domination on the production side and great autonomy for individual households and firms.

For instance, it does not seem to make much sense to argue whether or not strong government intervention to remove elements of rigidity in various markets constitutes liberalism and socialism. And it is not self-evident either how to classify the 'neo-mercantilist' tendencies, or even to know whether they are temporary or if they signal a new long-term trend.

All these ambiguities illustrate the point that questions about 'economic systems' are *multi-dimensional*, rather than one-dimensional problems. The dichotomy capitalism–socialism, or liberalism–socialism, has in realistic analyses to be replaced by a *number* of dichotomies, such as decentralisation versus centralisation in the decision process; market systems versus administrative processes as methods to allocate resources; private versus collective ownership; equilibrium pricing versus rationing as methods to distribute commodities; economic incentives versus orders; competition versus monopoly, internationalisation versus autarchy; etc. All these aspects on economic systems cannot, without an enormous loss of information, be mapped into a one-dimensional issue such as capitalism versus socialism.

APPENDIX A Real GNP *per capita* 1862–1970: yearly rates of change

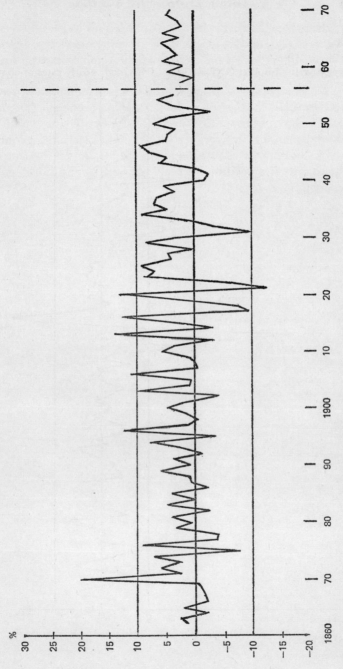

Source: Chart 1:1. There is a break in the statistical series in 1955/56.

APPENDIX B   Implicit GNP-deflator 1862–1970: yearly rates of change

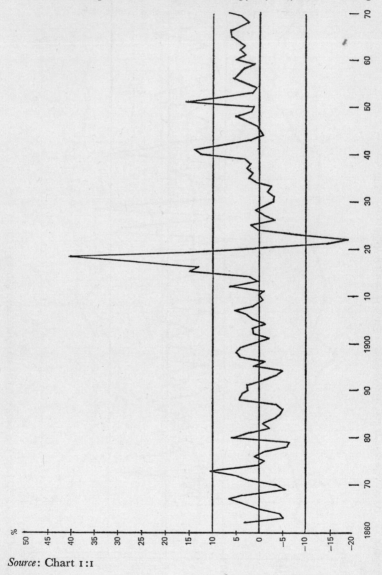

Source: Chart 1:1

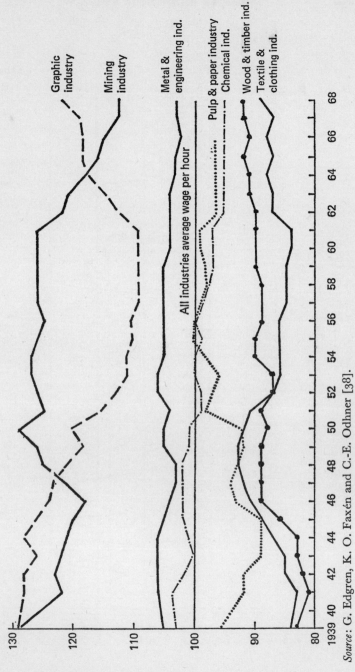

APPENDIX C Relative wage levels in different industries during the period 1939–68

Index

Graphic industry

Mining industry

Metal & engineering ind.

All industries average wage per hour

Pulp & paper industry
Chemical ind.

Wood & timber ind.

Textile & clothing ind.

130

120

110

100

90

80

1939 40   42   44   46   48   50   52   54   56   58   60   62   64   66   68

Source: G. Edgren, K. O. Faxén and C.-E. Odhner [38].

APPENDIX D   Unemployment (U), vacancies (V), and shortage of labour (VS), 1949–70 (second and fourth quarter)

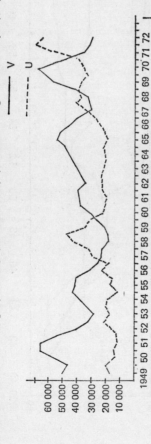

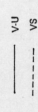

Source: L. Jacobson and A. Lindbeck [82] and National Institute of Economic Research.

References

[1] G. ALBINSSON et al., Blandekonomi på villovägar? (Stockholm, 1972).

[2] Å. ANDERSSON, 'Näringspolitiken och de regionala strukturproblemen', in [224] pp. 231–56.

[3] Arbetarrörelsens efterkrigsprogram. De 27 punkterna med motivering (Stockholm, 1944).

[3A] Arbete, Miljö, Demokrati, Rapport till socialdemokratiska partikongressen 1972, mimeo (Stockholm, 1972).

[4] R. ARTLE, Studies in the Structure of the Stockholm Economy (Stockholm, 1959).

[5] G. ARVIDSSON, 'Kreditpolitiken och utvecklingen på kreditmarknaden', Meddelanden från Konjunkturinstitutet, hösten 1952, series A:22, (Stockholm, 1952) pp. 77–96.

[6] G. ARVIDSSON, 'En enkät rörande verkningarna av investeringsavgiften, kreditåtstramningen och räntehöjningen på den svenska industrins investeringar 1955', Ekonomisk tidskrift, 58 (1956) 40–60.

[7] G. ARVIDSSON, 'Om varaktighetens betydelse för investeringars räntekänslighet', Ekonomisk tidskrift, 59 (1957) 11–36.

[8] G. ARVIDSSON, 'Om indexlån', Ekonomisk tidskrift, 60 (1958) 123–51.

[9] G. ARVIDSSON, Bostadsfinansiering och kreditpolitik (Stockholm, 1958).

[10] G. ARVIDSSON, 'Bidrag till indexlånens teori I och II', Ekonomisk tidskrift, 61 (1959) 34–42, 59–81.

[11] G. ARVIDSSON, 'Reflections on Index Loans', Skandinaviska Banken Quarterly Review, 40 (1959) 1–14.

[12] G. ARVIDSSON, 'Några randanmärkningar till Keynes' investeringsteori', Ekonomisk tidskrift, 62 (1960) 9–27.

[13] G. ARVIDSSON, Bidrag till teorin för verkningarna av räntevariationer, (Lund, 1961).

[14] T. BACKELIN, 'Inkomstbildning och ekonomisk politik', in [141] pp. 227–54.

[15] G. BAGGE, Arbetslönens reglering genom sammanslutningar (Stockholm, 1917).

[16] R. BELLMAN, Dynamic Programming (Princeton, 1957).

[17] R. BENTZEL, Inkomstfördelningen i Sverige (Stockholm, 1952).

[18] R. BENTZEL, 'Produktivitetsproblem i den penning- och lönepolitiska diskussionen i vårt land', Ekonomisk tidskrift, 58 (1956) 219–36.

[19] R. BENTZEL, 'Avvägningen mellan konsumtion och investering', 1959 års långtidsutredning, material 105 (1961).

[20] R. BENTZEL, 'Tillväxt och strukturomvandling under efterkrigstiden', in [224] pp. 82–120.

[21] R. Bentzel, A. Lindbeck and I. Ståhl, *Bostadsbristen. En studie av prisbildningen på bostadsmarknaden* (Stockholm, 1963).

[22] V. Bergström, 'Inkomstfördelningen under efterkrigstiden', in L. E. Eriksson and M. Hellström, *Välståndsklyftor och standardhöjning* (Stockholm, 1967) pp. 11–33.

[23] V. Bergström, *Den ekonomiska politiken i Sverige och dess verkningar* (Stockholm, 1969).

[24] V. Bergström, 'Industriell utveckling, industrins kapitalbildning och finanspolitiken', in [141] pp. 282–321.

[25] W. H. Beveridge, *Unemployment. A Problem of Industry* (London, 1909).

[26] E. Browaldh, News Report, *Svenska Dagbladet* (1 October 1948).

[27] E. C. Brown, 'Fiscal Policy in the 'Thirties: A Reappraisal', *American Economic Review*, 46 (1956) 857–79.

[28] Å. Burstedt et al., *Social Goals in National Planning* (Stockholm, 1972).

[29] E. Dahmén, 'Banklikviditet och kreditmarknad', *Ekonomisk tidskrift*, 54 (1952) 129–46.

[30] E. Dahmén, *Kapitalbildningsproblemet, Några samhällsekonomiska synpunkter* (Uppsala, 1959).

[31] E. Dahmén, 'Skärpt prisövervakning under inflation', *Svensk handel*, 22, No. 5 (1966) 5–6.

[32] E. Dahmén, 'Planerar vi för den ekonomiska utveckling på längre sikt som vi verkligen vill ha?', *Svensk ekonomisk tillväxt – en problemanalys* (Stockholm: Finansdepartementet, 1966) pp. 17–28.

[33] E. Dahmén, *Sätt pris på miljön* (Stockholm, 1970).

[34] E. Dahmén, *Entrepreneurial Activity and the Development of Swedish Industry, 1919–1939* (Homewood, Illinois, 1970) (Sweden, 1950).

[35] H. Dickson, *Bostadsmarknaden i USA och Sverige* (Stockholm, 1949).

[36] J. S. Duesenberry, *Business Cycles and Economic Growth* (New York, 1958).

[37] H. Edenhammar and S.-E. Johansson, *Investeringsfonders lönsamhet* (Stockholm, 1968).

[38] G. Edgren, K. O. Faxén and C.-E. Odhner, *Lönebildning och samhällsekonomi*, 'EFO Report' (Stockholm, 1970).

[39] G. Eliasson, *Investment Funds in Operation* (Stockholm, 1965).

[40] G. Eliasson, *Kreditmarknaden och industrins investeringar* (Stockholm, 1967).

[41] G. Eliasson, *Diagnos på 70-talat* (Katrineholm, 1971).

[42] Å. Elmér, *Folkpensioneringen i Sverige* (Lund, 1960).

[43] Å. Elmér, *Svensk socialpolitik* (Stockholm, 1969).

[44] J. K. Galbraith, *The Affluent Society* (London, 1958).
R. R. Glauber, see J. R. Meyer

[45] S. Grassman, 'The Balance of Payments Residual', *Skandinaviska Banken Quarterly Review*, 48 (1967) 43–50.

[46] S. Grassman, *Valutareserven och utrikeshandelns finansiella struktur*, SOU 1971:32 (Stockholm, 1971).

[47] S. Grassman, 'Sveriges finansielle status', *Skandinaviska Enskilda Banken Quarterly Review*, 4 (1972).

[48] O. GULBRANDSEN and A. LINDBECK, *Jordbrukspolitikens mål och medel* (Stockholm, 1966).

[49] O. GULBRANDSEN and A. LINDBECK, 'Swedish Agricultural Policy in an International Perspective', *Skandinaviska Banken Quarterly Review*, 47 (1966) 95–107.

[50] O. GULBRANDSEN and A. LINDBECK, *The Economics of the Agriculture Sector* (Stockholm, 1972) (Sweden 1969).

[51] T. GÅRDLUND, 'Inflationen – en politisk fråga', in *Recept mot inflation* (Stockholm: Finansdepartementet, 1957) pp. 9–29.

[52] D. HAMMARSKJÖLD, *Konjunkturspridningen. En teoretisk och historisk undersökning*, SOU 1933:29 (Stockholm, 1933).

[53] D. HAMMARSKJÖLD, '*P.M. angående principerna för budgetens balansering*', in Bihang D., *Kungl. Maj:ts proposition nr 1 år 1946* (Stockholm, 1946).

[54] D. HAMMARSKJÖLD, 'Reflexioner kring ett ränteproblem', *Ekonomisk tidskrift*, 48 (1946) 241–53.

[55] D. HAMMARSKJÖLD, 'Replik till Bent Hansen', *Ekonomisk tidskrift*, 49 (1947) 60–5.

[56] B. HANSEN, 'Hammarskjölds Renteproblem', *Ekonomisk tidskrift*, 49 (1947) 38–59.

[57] B. HANSEN, *A Study in the Theory of Inflation* (London, 1951).

[58] B. HANSEN, 'Kreditrestriktionerna och konjunkturpolitiken', *Ekonomisk Revy*, 13 (1956) 526–38.

[59] B. HANSEN, *The Economic Theory of Fiscal Policy* (London, 1958) (Sweden 1955).

[60] B. HANSEN, 'Den yttre och den inre inflationen', in *Recept mot inflation*, Finansdepartementet (Stockholm, 1957) pp. 30–53.

[61] B. HANSEN, 'Statsbudgetens verkningar', *Ekonomisk tidskrift*, 61 (1959) 128–45.

[62] B. HANSEN, 'Löner och priser', *Nationalekonomiska föreningens förhandlingar* (1961) 97–113.

[63] B. HANSEN, 'Abetsmarknad och inflation', *Ekonomen*, 37, No. 12 (1961) 1–7.

[64] B. HANSEN, *Foreign Trade Credits and Exchange Reserves* (Amsterdam, 1961).

[65] B. HANSEN, assisted by W. W. SNYDER, *Fiscal Policy in Seven Countries 1955–1965* (Paris: OECD, 1969).

[66] B. HANSEN, 'Excess Demand, Unemployment, Vacancies and Wages', *Quarterly Journal of Economics*, LXXXIV (1970) 1–23.

[67] B. HANSEN and G. REHN, 'On Wage-Drift. A Problem of Money-Wage Dynamics', in *25 Economic Essays in Honour of Erik Lindahl*, (Stockholm, 1956) pp. 87–138.

[68] E. HECKSCHER, 'Recept på bostadsbrist', *Dagens Nyheter* (22 November 1952).

[69] E. HECKSCHER, 'Recept på bostadtillgång', *Dagens Nyheter* (26 November 1952).

[69A] M. HELLSTRÖM, *Ett försök att uppskatta den totala progressiviteten i det svenska skattesystemet 1966* (Stockholm, 1967).

[70] L. HJELM, *Det svenska lantbrukets effektiviseringsvägar*, SOU 1963:66 (Stockholm, 1963).

[71] P. HOLM, *Lokala samhällskostnader vid industrilokalisering*, SOU 1963:62 (Stockholm, 1963) pp. 263–342.

[72] P. HOLM, 'Bostadsmarknaden i ett expanderande samhälle', in *Konsumtionsmönster på bostadsmarknaden*, SOU 1964:3 (Stockholm, 1964) pp. 69–148.

[73] P. HOLMBERG, *Arbete och löner i Sverige* (Stockholm, 1963).

[74] P. HOLMBERG, 'Svensk socialpolitik – nuläge och tendenser', in [224] pp. 272–309.

[75] E. M. HOOVER, 'Some Institutional Factors in Business Investment Decisions', *The American Economic Review*, XLIV (1954) 201–13.

[76] G. HULTCRANTZ, 'Prognos och "verklighet" ', in [141] pp. 104–63.

[77] *Incomes in Post-War Europe*, E/ECE/613/Add. 1, (Geneva: United Nations, 1967).

[78] G. INGHE and M.-B. INGHE, *Den ofärdiga välfärden* (Stockholm, 1968).

[79] L. JACOBSSON, *'Industriinvesteringarnas beroende av kreditopolitiken'*, mimeo (Stockholm: Konjunkturinstitutet, 1971).

[80] L. JACOBSSON, *An Econometric Model of Sweden* (Stockholm, 1972).

[81] L. JACOBSSON and A. LINDBECK, 'Labor Market Conditions and Inflation – Swedish Experiences 1955–67', *The Swedish Journal of Economics*, 1 (1969).

[82] L. JACOBSSON and A. LINDBECK, 'On the Transmission Mechanism of Wage Change', *The Swedish Journal of Economics*, 3 (1971).

[83] A. JOHANSSON, 'Bostadsbristens orsaker', *Balans*, 1 (1949) 121–7.

[84] A. JOHANSSON, 'Bostadsbrist och hyresreglering', *Att bo*, 13 (1963) 54–67.

[85] S.-E. JOHANSSON, 'An Appraisal of the Swedish System of Investment Reserves', *The International Journal of Accounting*, 1 (1965) 85–92. See also EDENHAMMAR

[86] S.-E. JOHANSSON, 'Beskattning och kapitalbildning', *Nationalekonomiska föreningens förhandlingar*, häfte 2 (1970) 41–69.

[87] Ö. JOHANSSON, *The Gross Domestic Product of Sweden and its Composition 1861–1955* (Stockholm, 1967).

[88] K. G. JUNGENFELT, *Löneandelen och den ekonomiska utvecklingen* (Stockholm, 1966).

[89] L. JÖRBERG, *Growth and Fluctuations of Swedish Industry 1869–1912* (Stockholm, 1961).

[90] L. JÖRBERG, 'Svensk ekonomi under 100 år', in [224] pp. 17–50.

[91] E. KARLSSON, 'Kreditmarknadsmatriser för åren 1955-60', Bilaga 5, SOU 1962:11 (Stockholm, 1962).

[92] J. M. KEYNES, *How to Pay for the War* (London, 1940).

[93] J. M. KEYNES, *A Treatise on Money* (London, 1930).

[94] H. KJELLMAN and D. NORDLING, *'Industrins finansiering 1955–1975'*, mimeo (Stockholm: Sveriges Industriförbund, 1971).

[95] L. KLEIN, *Economic Fluctuations in the United States 1921–1941* (New York, 1950).

[96] K. KOCK, *Kreditmarknad och räntepolitik 1924–1958* (Stockholm, 1962).

[97] 'Kompendium om Låginkomstutredningen', mimeo (Stockholm: Arbetsgruppen för låginkomstfrågor, 1971).

[98] B. KRAGH, 'Sparande, köpkraftsöverksott och likviditet', *Ekonomisk tidskrift*, 47 (1945) 34–45.

[99] B. KRAGH, *Prisbildningen på kreditmarknaden* (Uppsala, 1951).

[100] B. KRAGH, 'Inkomstbildningen, det finansiella sparandet och utvecklingen på kreditmarknaden', in *Svensk Ekonomi 1960–1965*, SOU 1962:10, Appendix B (Stockholm, 1962) pp. 181–211.

[101] B. KRAGH, *Konjunkturbedömning* (Stockholm, 1964).

[102] B. KRAGH, *Finansiella långtidsperspektiv*, SOU 1967:6 (Stockholm, 1967).

[103] B. KRAGH, 'Stabiliseringspolitik och samhällsekonomisk balans', in [224] pp. 121–56.

[104] B. KRAGH, *Nationalekonomi 3*, TRU (Stockholm, 1971).

[105] F. KRISTENSSON, *Människor, företag och regioner* (Stockholm, 1967).

[106] S. KUZNETS, 'Quantitative Aspects of the Economic Growth of Nations, I. Levels and Variability of Rates of Growth', *Economic Development and Cultural Change*, 5, No. 1 (1956–7).

[107] S. KUZNETS, *Economic Growth of Nations* (Cambridge, Mass., 1971).

[108] K.-G. LANDGREN, *Economics in Modern Sweden* (Washington, 1957).

[109] K.-G. LANDGREN, *Den nya ekonomin i Sverige. J. M. Keynes, E. Wigforss, B. Ohlin och utvecklingen 1927–39* (Stockholm, 1960).

[110] L. LEWIN, *Planhushållningsdebatten* (Uppsala, 1967).

[111] E. LINDAHL, *Studies in the Theory of Money and Capital* (London, 1939).

[112] E. LINDAHL, *Spelet om penningvärdet* (Stockholm, 1957).

[113] E. LINDAHL, 'Några riktlinjer för penningvärdets stabilisering', *Recept mot inflation* (Stockholm: Finansdepartementet, 1957) pp. 54–71.

[114] A. LINDBECK, 'Finanspolitikens ekonomiska teori', *Tiden*, 47 (1955) 463–71.

[115] A. LINDBECK, *Statsbudgetens verkningar på konjunkturutvecklingen*, SOU 1956:48 (Stockholm, 1956).

[116] A. LINDBECK, *The 'New' Theory of Credit Control in the United State* (Stockholm, 1959).

[117] A. LINDBECK, *A Study in Monetary Analysis* (Stockholm, 1963).

[118] A. LINDBECK, 'Prissystemet i långtidsplaneringen', *Svensk ekonomisk tillväxt – en problemanalys* (Stockholm: Finansdepartementet, 1966) pp. 73–112.

[119] A. LINDBECK, 'Rent Control as an Instrument of Housing Policy', in *The Economic Problems of Housing*, ed. A. A. Nevitt (New York, 1967) pp. 53–72.

[120] A. LINDBECK, *Montetary–Fiscal Analysis and General Equilibrium*, Yrjö Jahnsson Lectures (Helsinki, 1967).

[120A] A. LINDBECK, 'Theories and Problems in Swedish Economic Policy in the Post-War Period', *The American Economic Review* (June 1968), Suppl.

[121] A. LINDBECK, 'Vart är vår ekonomi på väg? Nationella och internationella aspekter', *Vårt ekonomiska läge 1972* (Stockholm, 1972).

[122] A. LINDBECK, 'Is Stabilization Policy Possible – Time Lags and Conflicts of Goals', *Essays in Honour of Richard Musgrave* to be published.

[123] A. LINDBECK, *Bostadsmarknad och hyreskontroll* (Stockholm, 1972).

[123A] A. LINDBECK and N. LUNDGREN, 'Nationalstaten i en internationaliserad världsekonomi', *Nationalekonomiska föreningens förhandlingar*, häfte 4 (1971) 105–51. *See also* BENTZEL, JACOBSSON, GULBRANDSEN.

[124] L. LINDBERGER, 'PM rörande byggnadsregleringens verkningssätt', Bilaga A, *Generella metoder och fysiska kontroller inom investeringsverksamheten*, SOU 1953:6 (Stockholm, 1953) pp. 115–59.

[125] L. LINDBERGER, *Investeringsverksamhet och sparande*, SOU 1956:10 (Stockholm, 1956).

[126] B. LINDSTRÖM, *'Utlandstransaktionerna och konjunkturen – Svenska erfarenheter under Bretton Woods-perioden'*, (mimeo Stockholm: EFI, 1972).

[126A] E. LUNDBERG, *Studies in the Theory of Economic Expansion* (Stockholm, 1937).

[127] E. LUNDBERG, 'Kommentar till B. Kraghs artikel om sparande, köpkraftsöverskott och likviditet', *Ekonomisk tidskrift*, 47 (1945) 46–8.

[128] E. LUNDBERG, 'Inflationsanalys och ekonomisk teori', *Ekonomisk tidskrift*, 50 (1948) 143–70.

[129] E. LUNDBERG, 'Lönepolitik under full sysselsättning', *Ekonomisk tidskrift*, 52 (1950) 43–61 (Engl. edn in [236]).

[130] E. LUNDBERG, *Business Cycles and Economic Policy* (London, 1957) (Swed. edn 1953).

[131] E. LUNDBERG, *Produktivitet och räntabilitet* (Stockholm, 1961).

[132] E. LUNDBERG, 'The Possibilities of Monetary Policy', *Skandinaviska Banken Quarterly Review*, 42 (1961) 99–108.

[133] E. LUNDBERG, 'Economic Stability and Monetary Policy, *Skandinaviska Banken Quarterly Review*, 43 (1962) 9–18.

[134] E. LUNDBERG, 'What do we know about the Efficacy of Monetary Policy?', *Skandinaviska Banken Quarterly Review*, 43 (1962) 107–16.

[135] E. LUNDBERG, 'Varför har Sverige inga allvarliga valutaproblem?', *Fagersta Forum*, 18, No. 1 (1963) 1–11.

[136] E. LUNDBERG, 'Störningar i tillväxtprocessen', *Svensk ekonomisk tillväxt – en problemanalys* (Stockholm: Finansdepartementet, 1966) pp. 133–68.

[137] E. LUNDBERG, 'Några frågetecken till dagens konjunkturpolitik', *Industriförbundets tidskrift*, No. 4 (1966) 198–203.

[138] E. LUNDBERG, *Instability and Economic Growth* (New Haven, Conn., 1968).

[139] E. LUNDBERG, 'Efterkrigstidens ekonomisk-politiska problem', in [141] pp. 11–38.

[140] E. LUNDBERG, 'Problemorientering inför 70-talet', in [141] pp. 361–89.

[141] E. LUNDBERG et al., *Svensk finanspolitik i teori och praktik* (Stockholm, 1971).

[142] E. LUNDBERG and I. SVENNILSON, 'Målsättningen för jordbrukspolitiken', särskilt yttrande 1 till *Riktlinjer för den framtida jordbrukspolitiken*, SOU 1946:46 (Stockholm, 1946).

[142A] E. Lundberg, 'Några möjliga och omöjliga framtidsperspektiv', in G. Albinsson *et al.*, *Blandekonomi på villovägar?* (Stockholm, 1972) pp. 172–91.

[143] E. LUNDBERG and B. SENNEBY, 'The Dilemma of the New Monetary Policy in Sweden', *Skandinaviska Banken Quarterly Review*, 37 (1956) 79–88.

[144] E. LUNDBERG and B. SENNEBY, 'Views on an Effective Credit Policy', *Skandinaviska Banken Quarterly Review*, 38 (1957) 6–14.

[145] E. LUNDBERG and J. JÄRV, 'The Balance of Payments and Economic Growth', *Skandinaviska Banken Quarterly Review*, 47 (1966) 1–7.

[145A] E. LUNDBERG and ANN WIBBLE, '"Nymerkantilism" och selektiv ekonomisk politik', in *Ekonomisk politik i förvandling*, ed. E. Lundberg (Stockholm, 1970). *See also* KRAGH and REHN.

[146] L. LUNDBERG, *Kapitalbildningen i Sverige 1961–1965* (Stockholm, 1969).

[147] H. LYDALL, *The Structure of Earnings* (Oxford, 1963).

[148] A. MADDISON, *Economic Growth in the West* (New York, 1964).

[149] J. MARSCHAK, 'Money and the Theory of Assets', *Econometrica*, 6 (1938) 311–25.

[150] L. MATTHIESSEN, 'Finanspolitiken som stabiliseringspolitiskt instrument', in [141] pp. 164–226.

[151] L. MATTHIESSEN, *Investment Funds, Growth and the Effective Tax Rate*, Stockholm Economic Studies, Pamphlet Series (Stockholm, 1972).

[152] R. MEIDNER, 'Lönepolitikens dilemma vid full sysselsättning', *Tiden*, 40 (1948) 464–71 (Engl. edn in [236]).

[153] R. MEIDNER, *Svensk arbetsmarknad vid full sysselsättning* (Stockholm, 1954).

[154] R. MEIDNER, 'Arbetsmarknadspolitikens målsättningar', in *Samhälle i omvandling* (Stockholm, 1967) pp. 101–14.

[155] R. MEIDNER and R. ANDERSSON, '*The Overall Impact of an Active Labor Market Policy in Sweden*', mimeo (Stockholm, 1971).

[156] B. METELIUS, *Utlandstransaktionerna och den svenska ekonomin*, SOU 1955:13 (Stockholm, 1955).

[157] J. R. MEYER and E. KUH, *The Investment Decision* (Cambridge, Mass., 1957).

[158] J. R. MEYER and R. R. GLAUBER, *Investment Decisions, Economic Forecasting and Public Policy* (Boston, 1964).

[159] *Modern Swedish Labour Market Policy* (Stockholm: National Labour Market Board, 1966).

[160] F. MODIGLIANI and M. H. MILLER, 'The Cost of Capital, Corporation Finance and the Theory of Investment', *The American Economic Review*, 48 (1958) 261–97.

[161] A. MONTGOMERY, 'Björnen i porslinsbutiken', *Svenska Dagbladet* (24 May 1948).

[162] A. MONTGOMERY, *Nationalekonomiska föreningens förhandlingar* (1948) 24–6, and (1949) 13–14, 25.

[163] R. A. MUNDELL, 'The Appropriate Use of Monetary and Fiscal Policy for Internal and External Stability', *International Monetary Fund, Staff Papers*, 9 (1962) 70–9.

[164] R. MUSGRAVE, 'On Measuring Fiscal Performance', *The Review of Economics and Statistics*, XLVI (1964) 213–20.

[164A] JOHAN MYHRMAN, '*Penningmängd, bankutlåning och penningpolitikens verkningar*', mimeo (Stockholm: Stockholm University, 1969).

[165] G. MYRDAL, *Prisbildningsproblemet och föränderligheten* (Stockholm, 1927).

[166] G. MYRDAL, *Jordbrukspolitiken under omläggning* (Stockholm, 1938).

[167] G. MYRDAL, *Monetary Equilibrium* (London, 1939).

[168] G. MYRDAL, 'PM angående verkningarna på den ekonomiska konjunkturutvecklingen i Sverige av olika åtgärder inom den offentliga hushållningens område', *Bilaga III, Kungl. Maj:ts Proposition No. 1* (1933).

[169] G. MYRDAL, *Finanspolitikens ekonomiska verkningar*, SOU 1934:1 (Stockholm, 1934).

[170] G. MYRDAL, 'Höga skatter och låga räntor', *Studier i ekonomi och historia*, tillägnade Eli F. Heckscher (Uppsala, 1944) pp. 160–9.

[171] G. MYRDAL, *Varning för fredsoptimism* (Stockholm, 1944).

[172] G. MYRDAL, 'Utvecklingen mot planhushållning I och II', *Tiden*, 43 (1951) 71–84, 134–50.

[173] G. MYRDAL, 'Blir inflation oundviklig i en demokrati av den svenska typen?', *Samhälle i omvandling* (Stockholm, 1967) pp. 127–52.

[174] S. NYCANDER, *Kurs på kollision. Inblick i avtalsrörelsen 1970–71* (Stockholm, 1972).

[175] C.-E. ODHNER, *Jordbruket vid full sysselsättning* (Stockholm, 1953).

[176] C.-E. ODHNER, *Nytt grepp på jordbrukspolitiken* (Stockholm, 1966).

[177] B. OHLIN, *Interregional and International Trade* (Cambridge, Mass., 1933).

[178] B. OHLIN, *Penningpolitik, offentliga arbeten, subventioner och tullar som medel mot arbetslöshet*, Arbetslöshetsutredningens betänkande II, bil. 4, SOU 1934:12 (Stockholm, 1934).

[179] B. OHLIN, *Fri eller dirigerad ekonomi?* (Stockholm, 1936).

[180] B. OHLIN, 'Some Notes on the Stockholm Theory of Savings and Investment', I and II, *Economic Journal*, XLVII (1937) 53–69, 221–40.

[181] B. OHLIN, 'Alternative Theories of the Rate of Interest', *Economic Journal*, XLVII (1937) 423–7.

[182] B. OHLIN, *Kapitalmarknad och räntepolitik* (Stockholm, 1941).

[183] B. OHLIN, 'Stockholmsskolan kontra kvantitetsteorin. En analys av variationer i penningmängd, likviditet, köpkraft och prisutveckling', *Ekonomisk tidskrift*, 45 (1943) 27–46.

[184] B. OHLIN, 'Socialismen och Europas rekonstruktion', *Stockholms-Tidningen* (5 August 1949).

[185] B. OHLIN, *The Problem of Employment Stabilization* (New York, 1949).

[186] B. OHLIN, *Obekväma fakta* (Stockholm, 1971).

[187] I. OHLSSON, *On National Accounting* (Uppsala, 1953).

[188] L. OHLSSON, *Utrikeshandeln och den ekonomiska tillväxten 1871–1966* (Stockholm, 1969).

[189] T. PALANDER, *Beiträge zur Standortstheorie* (Uppsala, 1935).

[190] T. PALANDER, 'On the Concepts and Methods of the "Stockholm

School" ', *International Economic Papers*, 3 (1953) 5–57 (Swed. edn *Ekonomisk Tidskrift* 1941).

[191] T. PALANDER, *Värdebeständighet. Ett problem vid sparande, livförsäkringar och pensioner* (Stockholm, 1957).

[192] T. PALANDER, *Om ovisshet, värderingsenheter, riskvärdering och förväntningsspridning* (Stockholm, 1957).

[193] A. C. PIGOU, *The Economics of Welfare* (London, 1913).

[194] T. PUU, *The Effects of Monetary and Fiscal Policy* (Uppsala, 1965).

[195] *Regioner att leva i*, Essays published by *ERU*, Expertgruppen för regional utredningsverksamhet (Stockholm, 1972).

[196] G. REHN, 'Ekonomisk politik vid full sysselsättning', *Tiden*, 40 (1948) 135–42 (Engl. edn in [236]).

[197] G. REHN, 'Lönepolitiken och fullsyselsättningen', *Ekonomisk tidskrift*, 52 (1950) 62–7 (Engl. edn in [236]).

[198] G. REHN and E. LUNDBERG, 'Employment and Welfare: Some Swedish Issues', *Industrial Relations*, 2 (1963) 1–14. See also HANSEN.

[199] O. RENCK, *Investeringsbedömning i några svenska företag* (Stockholm, 1967).

[200] K. RUDBERG and C. ÖHMAN, '*Investeringsfonderna – 1967 års frisläpp*', mimeo (Stockholm: Konjunkturinstitutet, 1971).

[201] S. RYDENFELT, 'Bostadsnödens orsaker', *Balans*, 1 (1949) 75–85.

[202] S. RYDENFELT, 'Bostadsnödens orsaker. Replik till Alf Johansson', *Balans*, 1 (1949) 230–3.

[203] S. RYDENFELT, 'Kan vi bygga oss ur bostadskrisen?', *Balans*, 2 (1950) 257–65.

[204] *Samordnad näringspolitik* (Stockholm: LO, 1961).

[205] P. A. SAMUELSON, *Foundations of Economic Analysis* (Cambridge, Mass., 1948).

[206] P. A. SAMUELSON, *Economics* (New York, 1970).

[207] P. SELANDER and R. SPÅNT, '*Inkomstfördelningens utveckling i Sverige 1951–1966*', mimeo (Uppsala: Uppsala University, 1969).
B. SENNEBY, *see* E. LUNDBERG.

[208] P. SILENSTAM, *Arbetskraftsutbudets utveckling i Sverige 1870–1965* (Stockholm, 1970).

[209] A. SMITHIES, 'The Behavior of Money National Income under Inflationary Conditions', *The Quarterly Journal of Economics*, LVII (1942) 113–28.

[210] O. STEIGER, *Studien zur Entstehung der neuen Wirtschaftslehre in Schweden* (Berlin, 1971).

[211] I. STÅHL, 'Some Aspects of a Mixed Housing Market', in *The Economic Problems of Housing*, ed. A. A. Nevitt (New York, 1967) pp. 73–84.

[212] I. STÅHL, 'Allokeringsproblem i den offentliga sektorn', in [224] pp. 157–98.

[213] I. SVENNILSON, *Ekonomisk Planering. Teoretiska studier* (Uppsala, 1938).

[214] I. SVENNILSON, 'Samhällsekonomiska synpunkter på utbildning', *Ekonomisk tidskrift*, 63 (1961) 1–23.

[215] I. SVENNILSON, 'Framstegstakt och samhällspolitik', *Nationalekono-miska föreningens förhandlingar* (1962) 29–45.

[216] I. SVENNILSON, 'Vårt lönebildningssystem', *Nationalekonomiska förenin-gens förhandlingar* (1965) 64–71.

[217] I. SVENNILSON, 'Planning in a Market Economy', *Weltwirtschaftliches Archiv* (1965) 184–201.

[218] I. SVENNILSON, 'Swedish Long-Term Planning – The Fifth Round', *Skandinaviska Banken Quarterly Review*, 47 (1966) 37–43.

[219] I. SVENNILSON, 'Framstegstakt vid ekonomisk balans', *Svensk ekonomisk tillväxt – en problemanalys* (Stockholm: Finansdepartementet, 1966) 169–90.

[220] I. SVENNILSON, 'Den framtida lönepolitiken' (address to the TCO Conference, November 1966).

[221] I. SVENNILSON, 'Behovet av planering på lång sikt', *Samhälle i omvandling* (Stockholm, 1967) pp. 163–71. *See also* E. LUNDBERG.

[222] B. SÖDERSTEN, 'Bostadsbristen och de tre räntorna', *Tiden*, 55 (1963) 292–301.

[223] B. SÖDERSTEN, 'Bostadsförsörjning och bostadspolitik under efterkrigs-tiden', in [224] 199–230.

[224] B. SÖDERSTEN (ed.), *Svensk ekonomi* (Stockholm, 1970).

[225] J. SÖDERSTEN, 'Företagsbeskattning och resursfördelning', in [224] 322–59.

[226] H. SÖDERSTRÖM, 'Cyclical Fluctuations in Labor Productivity and Capacity Utilization Reconsidered', *The Swedish Journal of Economics*, 74 (1972) 220–37.

[226A] L. SÖDERSTRÖM, *Den svenska köpkraftsfördelningen 1967*, SOU 1971:39 (Stockholm, 1971).

[227] B. THALBERG, 'Om renteendringers virkninger for "langsiktige" og "kortsiktige" investeringer', *Ekonomisk tidskrift*, 59 (1957) 1–10.

[228] B. THALBERG, 'The Market for Investment Goods. An Analysis where Time of Delivery Enters Explicitly', *The Review of Economic Studies*, 27 (1960) 99–108.

[229] B. THALBERG, *A Keynesian Model Extended by Explicit Demand and Supply Functions for Investment Goods* (Stockholm, 1964).

[230] B. THALBERG, *A Trade Cycle Analysis* (Lund, 1966).

[231] L.-E. THUNHOLM, *Svenskt kreditväsen* (Stockholm, 1949).

[232] L.-E. THUNHOLM, 'Inflationen och penningpolitiken', *Svenska Dagbladet* (19 March 1951).

[233] L.-E. THUNHOLM, 'Vad innebär en restriktiv penningpolitik?', *Svenska Dagbladet* (20 March 1951).

[234] L.-E. THUNHOLM, 'Penningpolitiken som investeringsregulator', *Betänkande angående generella metoder och fysiska kontroller inom in-vesteringspolitiken*, SOU 1953:6 (Stockholm, 1953) pp. 160–200.

[235] *Trade Unions and Full Employment* (Stockholm: LO 1953) (Swed. edn 1951).

[236] R. TURVEY (ed.), *Wages Policy under Full Employment* (London, 1952).

[237] G. TÖRNQVIST, *Studier i industrilokalisering*, SOU 1963:49 (Stockholm, 1963).

[238] B. ÜSTÜNEL, *Economic Growth in Sweden, Japan and Turkey: A Comparison of Success and Failure*, Institute for International Economic Studies, Seminar Paper No. 16, mimeo (Stockholm: University of Stockholm, 1972).

[239] J. WALLENBERG, Interview, *Dagens Nyheter* (17 September 1947).

[240] J. WALLENBERG, *Nationalekonomiska föreningens förhandlingar* (1948) 19-24, 35; (1949) 15-17, 23-4; and (1950) 25-6.

[241] C. WELINDER, 'Utkast till en institutionalistisk ränteteori', *Ekonomisk tidskrift*, 44 (1942) 23-40.

[242] C. WELINDER, *Socialpolitikens ekonomiska verkningar*, SOU 1945:14 (Stockholm, 1945).

[243] C. WELINDER, 'Budgetpolitiken inför kravet på samhällsekonomisk balans', *Ekonomisk tidskrift*, 48 (1946) 79-99.

[244] L. WERIN, *A Study of Production, Trade and Allocation of Resources* (Stockholm, 1965).

[245] E. WESTERLIND and R. BECKMAN, *Sveriges ekonomi* (Stockholm, 1971).

[246] A. WIBBLE, 'Selektiv och generell ekonomisk politik', in [141] 39-75. *See also* E. LUNDBERG.

[247] K. WICKMAN, *'Preliminär redogörelse för vissa resultat av en undersökning rörande verkningarna av olika ekonomisk-politiska åtgärder på industrins fasta investeringar 1955-1956'*, mimeo (Stockholm, 1957).

[248] K. WICKMAN, *The Swedish Investment Reserve System. An Instrument of Contra Cyclical Policy* (Stockholm: The Swedish Institute, 1964).

[249] K. WICKSELL, 'Valutaspörsmålet i de skandinaviska länderna', *Ekonomisk tidskrift*, 27 (1925) 205-22.

[250] E. WIGFORSS, 'Den nya ekonomiska politiken', *Ekonomisk tidskrift*, 62 (1960) 185-94.

[251] O. VIRIN, 'Konjunkturbarometerdata som konjunkturindikatorer', *Konjunkturbarometern*, mimeo, Konjunkturinstitutet (17 January 1972).

[251A] B.-C. YSANDER, *Förvaltningsekonomiska problem* (Stockholm, 1972).

[252] R. ZENKER, 'Den offentliga sektorns tillväxt', in [141] 76-103.

[253] K. ÅMARK, *Kristidspolitik och kristidshushållning i Sverige under och efter andra världskriget*, Del 1, SOU 1952:49, 50 (Stockholm, 1952).

[254] Y. ÅBERG, *Produktion och produktivitet i Sverige 1861-1965* (Stockholm, 1969).
C. ÖHMAN, *see* K. RUDBERG.

[255] A. ÖSTLIND, 'Kan arbetsmarknaden göras mindre inflationistisk?', *Recept mot inflation* (Stockholm: Finansdepartementet, 1957) 114-33.

OFFICIAL DOCUMENTS

[256] *Balanserad regional utveckling*, ERU, SOU 1970:3, 1970:14, 1970:15 (Stockholm, 1970).

[257] *Bankutskottets utlåtande* nr 6 (Stockholm, 1948).

[258] *Bostadssociala utredningen*, SOU 1945:63 (Stockholm, 1945).

[259] *Generella metoder och fysiska kontroller inom investeringspolitiken*, SOU 1953:6 (Stockholm, 1953).

[260] *Indexlån*, SOU 1964:1 and 1964:2 (Stockholm, 1964).

[261] *Inkomstutveckling och köpkraftsöverskott under krigsåren*, Meddelanden från Konjunkturinstitutet, Ser. B:2 (Stockholm, 1943).

[262] *Koncentrationsutredningen*, SOU 1966:21, 1968:3, 1968:5, 1968:6, 1968:7, 1969:36, 1970:30 (Stockholm).

[263] *Konkurrensbegränsning I-II*, SOU 1951:27–28 (Stockholm, 1951).

[264] *Mål och medel i stabiliseringspolitiken*, SOU 1961:42 (Stockholm, 1961).

[264A] *Revision of the Swedish Customs Tariff* (Stockholm, 1957).

[265] *Om riksbankens sedelutgivningsrätt och därmed sammanhängande penningpolitiska frågor*, SOU 1955:43 (Stockholm, 1955).

[266] *Utredningar angående ekonomisk efterkrigsplanering*, Framställningar och utlåtanden från kommissionen för ekonomisk efterkrigsplanering 1, SOU 1944:57 (Stockholm, 1944); and 4, SOU 1945:36 (Stockholm, 1945).

REPORTS ON BUSINESS CONJUNCTURES

[267] *Konjunkturläget–Nationalbudget* published periodically by the National Institute of Economic Research (Stockholm) and the Treasury Department.

LONG-TERM REPORTS

[268] *Svenskt långtidsprogram 1947–1952/53*, SOU 1948:45 (Stockholm, 1948).

[269] *Ekonomiskt långtidsprogram, 1951–1955*, SOU 1951:30 (Stockholm, 1951).

[270] *Balanserad expansion*, SOU 1956:53 (Stockholm, 1956).

[271] *Svensk ekonomi 1960–1965*, SOU 1962:10–11 (Stockholm, 1962).

[272] *Svensk ekonomi 1966–1970 med utblick mot 1980*, SOU 1966:1 (Stockholm, 1966).

[273] *Svensk ekonomi 1971–1975 med utblick mot 1990*, SOU 1970:71 (Stockholm, 1970).

N.B. SOU =*Statens offentliga utredningar* (Official Investigations by the State).

Index

Agriculture Policy, 190–3, 203–4
Åkerman, J., 27
Allocation policy
  criteria for, 178–82
  description of, 172–8, 184–94
Andersson, Å., 185
Artle, R., 185
Arvidsson, G., 96–7, 119–20, 124,
  130, 163–4
Aukrust model, 158, 160
Automatic stabilisers and
  destabilisers, 147–50
Availability theory of credit
  and money, 95–6, 127–30

Backelin, T., 152, 211
Bagge, G., 38
Balance of payments
  development of, 20, 59–63
  problems of, 29–30
Barometer data, 64–7
Bellman, R., 95
Bentzel, R., 27, 170–2, 189, 196, 219
Bergström, V., 22, 220
Beveridge, W., 31–2, 38–9
Browaldh, E., 75, 127
Brown, C., 89
Budget balance, 83–7
Business cycles
  early development, 10–19
  model of, 50–63
  phases of cycles, 53–4
  postwar development, 19–21
  53–61

Cash reserve requirements, 124–5
  secondary requirements, 125–7
Commission for Postwar Economic
  Planning, 25, 27, 38–9, 74, 226

Consumption
  private, 57–9, 175
  public, 173–8
Consumption function, 88–9
Co-operatives, 8
Credit rationing, 111–13
  criticism of, 121–4
Credit supply, distr. of, 216–19

Dahmén, E., 5, 128–9, 147, 149,
  185, 193
Davidson's norm, 27–8
Devaluation, 22–3
Dickson, H., 189
Direct controls, 26
  criticism of, 31–6
Duesenberry, J., 96

Econometric model building, 68,
  81, 89–90
Economic system
  early development, 5–7
  postwar development, 7–10, 24,
  245–8
Edenhammar, H., 98
Edgren, G., 158
EFO-model, 157–61
Eliasson, G., 98, 120, 128, 137
Environmental Policy, 193–4
Ex ante - ex post analysis, 30–1
Exports, 3–5, 50–1, 54–5, 176

Faxén, K.-O. 158
Fluctuations, *see* Business cycles
Forecasting
  methods of, 64–70
  record, 68–70
Full employment, 37–49, 151–7

Galbraith, J. K., 163, 235
Gårdlund, T., 30
Glauber, R., 128
Gold standard, 22
Goodwin, R., 97
Grassman, S., 63
Growth
    explanations of, 2–7
    export led growth, 3–4
    policy of, 166–73, 179–83
    record, 1–2, 10, 174–8
Gulbrandsen, O., 191

Haavelmo, T., 96
Hammarskjöld, D., 27, 71, 82–3,
    86, 110
Hansen, B., 31, 37, 41–9, 63, 71,
    85-90, 110, 121–4, 129, 145,
    160, 226, 235, 242
Heckscher, E., 189
Hellström, M., 201
Henderson, H., 82
Hjelm, L., 191
Holm, P., 185, 190
Holmberg, P., 144
Höök, E., 165
Hoover, E., 96
Housing policy, 186–90
Hultcrantz, G., 62, 70

Income distribution
    general, 195–6
    personal, 196–207
    public versus private, 207–14
Income taxes, 76–7, 200–7
Incomes policy, 45–7, 144–51
Indexation, 163–4
Indirect taxes, 75–6
Inflation
    cost side, 140–50
    demand side, 142–3, 151–61,
        163–4
    early development, 10–11
    postwar development, 13–14, 20
Interest rate policy, 108–13
    effects of, 119–20
International factor mobility, 4

International interdependence,
    161–2
Investment
    distr. on sectors, 54, 58, 80–1
    housebuilding, 56, 103–4
    inventory, 54–5
    private, 79–81
    public, 56, 79, 102
    theory of, 94–6
    total, 56–7
Investment funds, 98–102
Investment taxes, 97
    effects of, 119–21, 130–8

Jacobsson, L., 68, 120
Johansson, A., 82, 188, 190
Johansson, S.-E. 98
Johansson, Ö., 11
Jörberg, L., 1, 80
Jungenfelt, K., 5

Kaldor, N., 41
Karlsson, E., 130
Keynes, J., 31, 82, 95, 97, 127
Klein, L., 96
Kock, K., 25, 108
Koopmans, C., 179
Korean War inflation, 32, 70, 71–4,
    149, 152
Kragh, B., 31, 64, 122, 130, 166
Kristensson, F., 185
Kuh, E., 96
Kuznetz, S., 1–2

Labour Costs, 222
Lablu mobility policy, 104–7
Labour unions, 26, 28
Labour movement's Postwar
    Programme, 25
Lags in policy, 102–3
Landgren, K.-G., 82
Liberal party, 28
Lindahl, E., 27, 31, 75, 82, 87,
    129
Lindberger, L., 33, 74, 96, 140
Long-term reports, 165–9
    future prospects, 182–3
Lorenz curves, 197–200

Low-Income Committee, 183, 199–201
Lundberg, E., 1, 27, 30–5, 37, 41–4, 49, 58, 62, 64, 74–5, 82, 86, 95–6, 111, 121–4, 127, 149, 160, 163, 191, 226, 231, 235–6

Maddison, A., 2
Marschak, J., 96
Matthiessen, L., 19, 29, 88, 91, 98, 104
Meidner, R., 32–3, 37, 40
Mergers, 221–5
Metelius, B., 73
Meyer, J., 96, 128
Miller, M., 96
Modigliani, F., 96
Money supply, 113–19, 244–5
Montgomery, A., 75
Mundell, R., 87, 115
Musgrave, R., 89–90
Myrdal, G., 25–6, 28, 31, 37–8, 82–3, 86, 95, 191

Nationalisation, 7–10, 26–7
Nycander, S., 145

Odhner, C.-E., 158, 191
Ohlin, B., 28, 31–3, 37–9, 44, 75, 82, 129, 185
Ohlsson, I., 31
Ohlsson, L., 3
Östlind, A., 49, 145
Ownership, 7–10, 214–19

Palander, T., 31, 82, 95, 163–4, 185
Pension System, 9, 75–6
Phillips curve, 41–2, 151–7, 240
Pigou, A., 193
Policy cycle, 255
Price control, 26, 31
Profits, 40, 219–21, 245
Progressive taxation, 204–7
Public sector, 7–10, 172–82
Public works, 104–7
Puu, T., 86

Regional policy, 184–6
Rehn, G., 25, 32–3, 37–45, 49, 79, 104, 157, 225–6, 231, 236
Rehn model, 39–41
criticism of, 41–6
Renck, O., 123
Repressed inflqtion, 31–6, 38–9
Roosa, R., 129
Rydenfelt, S., 188

Samuelson, P. A., 85
Savasnick, K. M., 182
Savings
general, 211–14
optimum saving ratio, 169–72
private, 213–14
public, 9–10
Scitovsky, T., 41
Selander, P., 197
Senneby, B., 121–4
Silenstam, P., 12
Smithies, A., 47
Socialism, 26–7, 245–8
Södersten, B., 190
Södersten, J., 220
Söderström, L., 203
Spånt, R., 197
Ståhl, I., 189
Steiger, O., 82
Sterner, R., 25, 74
Stockholm School, 31, 95, 129
Structural change, 221–7
Svennilson, I., 25, 31, 82, 95, 145–7 165–7, 170, 182, 191

Targets of policy
conflicts of, 37–8, 42–3, 151–6
co-ordination of, 87–8
early development, 22
postwar development, 23–4
shifts in emphasis, 228–33, 236–8
Terms of Trade, 63
Thalberg, B., 96–7
Theil, H., 203
Theory of economic policy, 82–7, 238–43
Thunholm, L.-E., 75, 127
Tinbergen, J., 85, 86

Törnqvist, G., 185

Unemployment, 11–20, 151–7

Virin, O., 65

Wage multiplier, 148–50
Wage policy, 40, 44–5

Wallenberg, J., 75, 127–8
Welinder, C., 83–4, 86
Werin, L., 179
Wibble, A., 236
Wickman, K., 97, 119, 120, 137
Wicksell, K., 27, 47–8, 82, 129
Wigforss, E., 25, 82